AUSTRALIAN
LIVES

AUSTRALIAN LIVES

Stories of twentieth century Australians

Robin Hughes

📖 Angus&Robertson
An imprint of HarperCollins*Publishers*

FRONT COVER (l-r clockwise)
Dame Joan Hammond in *Tosca*. Courtesy ACP Publishing Pty Ltd. © Edward Mandinian
Neville Bonner. Courtesy ACP Publishing Pty Ltd
Nancy Bird Walton. Courtesy Nancy Bird Walton, private collection
Donald Horne. Courtesy Donald Horne, private collection
Sir Mark Oliphant. Courtesy ACP Publishing Pty Ltd and Camera Press/Austral.
© Camera Press/Austral

BACK COVER
Dr HC 'Nugget' Coombs. Courtesy Film Australia. © Film Australia
Jack Hazlitt. Courtesy Film Australia. © Film Australia

INTERNAL PHOTOGRAPHS
Courtesy Film Australia. © Film Australia

Angus&Robertson
An imprint of HarperCollins*Publishers*

First published in Australia in 1996
by HarperCollins*Publishers* Pty Limited
ACN 009 913 517
A member of the HarperCollins*Publishers* (Australia) Pty Limited Group

Copyright © Film Australia and Robin Hughes, 1996

HarperCollins*Publishers*
25 Ryde Road, Pymble, Sydney, NSW 2073, Australia
31 View Road, Glenfield, Auckland 10, New Zealand
77–85 Fulham Palace Road, London W6 8JB, United Kingdom
Hazelton Lanes, 55 Avenue Road, Suite 2900, Toronto, Ontario M5R 3L2
and 1995 Markham Road, Scarborough, Ontario M1B 5M8, Canada
10 East 53rd Street, New York NY 10032, USA

National Library of Australia Cataloguing-in-Publication data:

Hughes, Robin.
    Australian lives: stories of twentieth century Australians.

    ISBN 0 207 19125 5.

    1. Interviews — Australia. 2. Australians — Interviews. 3. Australia — Biography.
    I. Film Australia. II. Title.

920.094

Set in Goudy 10.5/12.5
Printed in Australia by Griffin Paperbacks, Adelaide on 79gsm Bulky Paperback

9 8 7 6 5 4 3 2 1
99 98 97 96

Contents

Preface

𝒯he seven interviews in this volume of **Australian Lives** were originally recorded for Film Australia's *Australian Biography* project. Australian Biography is one of a number of long-term and large-scale projects designed by Film Australia to mark the end of the twentieth century and the approaching centenary of Australia's Federation. The project is intended to continue into 2001 and, hopefully, beyond.

Since 1991, more than 30 prominent Australians have been interviewed. Their stories form the core collection of a growing audio-visual portrait gallery which contains hours of interview produced under Film Australia's National Interest Program. This raw material has already been edited for television into a series of half-hour profiles screened by the Special Broadcasting Service.

Spanning the greater part of our century and our continent, these stories are told by some of our most distinguished elders. Their lives have shaped history. And history has shaped their lives. Robin Hughes's intelligent, rigorous and sensitive interviews have elicited so much of value from her *Australian Biography* interviewees. Now the first seven interviews have been edited by Robin Hughes to form this book, **Australian Lives**, a welcome extension to the project.

Many people have helped to make *Australian Biography* happen. Bruce Moir, Film Australia's Managing Director, and Ron Saunders, former Film Australia Executive Producer, launched the project in 1991. The involvement of Frank

Heimans, producer, director and editor until 1996, ensured its success. Thanks are due to all those interviewed for the *Australian Biography* project, especially the seven whose stories appear in the following pages. Thanks also to their helpful friends and relations.

SHARON CONNOLLY
EXECUTIVE PRODUCER
FILM AUSTRALIA

FILM AUSTRALIA
NATIONAL INTEREST PROGRAM

Asking Questions

When I was a schoolgirl I often got into trouble for asking questions. It seems strange that from time to time throughout my life I have found myself earning my living from the very thing my teachers discouraged. Looking back I'm not surprised that my persistent curiosity irked them. But it is fortunate for this book, and for the television series that gave rise to it, that the people I interviewed seemed to welcome the opportunity my questions afforded them to share their stories and insights with others.

We all depend on the remembrance of things past to understand ourselves and our place in history. What follows is an illuminating collection of memories drawn from lives lived in twentieth century Australia. Emerson asserted that the only true history is biography and he believed that 'the real source of all biography is the confession of the man himself to somebody'. The memories in this book were recounted to me because I asked certain questions. The act of thinking about what to ask, and how to ask it, itself raises yet another set of questions about the value of this method of chronicling the past and how it differs from other historical records.

All history begins with reported memory, but we depend for a true understanding of the past on the way in which that memory is shaped, on what the remembering mind notices, and on whether the witness is asked to interpret or elaborate their account. In other words, history stems from enquiry and depends greatly on what questions are asked and on who is asking them. This seems to be particularly true in the case of biography.

A human life can be seen from many different angles and can be interpreted and judged in a variety of ways. So if questions are the implicit vehicle for determining the story, for guiding the process of remembering, we might ask: 'What is the role of the question in biography?' Good autobiography, for instance, demands an imaginative self-questioning, a self-directed introspection in which the author/subject sets their own agenda. On the other hand, the questions in the mind of a third-person biographer seek answers from many sources and the evidence of one source will be set against that of another in an effort to cancel from the final work the notoriously distorting tricks of subjective human memory. A third and different form of record, with its own particular characteristics, is the biographical interview of the sort presented here. In this form the questions are overt. The subject must respond or, sometimes perhaps even more revealingly, avoid response. The questioner presents possibilities and highlights aspects of the story that may otherwise have escaped notice.

From time to time the people I interviewed commented that they had 'often asked themselves that same question'. But much more frequently they said they had never thought to ask themselves about some of the matters I raised with them. This illustrates a unique characteristic of the face-to-face interview and helps place it in relation to other forms of biography. An autobiography reveals one perspective; a biography usually synthesises many. The interviews in this book have one dominant view, but that view is shaped and framed by the questions and articulated in response to them.

For me the art of the interview, whatever its purpose, is to ask questions in a way that allows the person interviewed to say what they really mean. The questions are there to provoke the true story or to evoke the real thought or emotion. They are not there to confront, to accuse, to trick or to bamboozle. Above all, they are not meant to draw attention away from the subject to the interviewer. It seems to me that in encounters such as these the interviewer's job is to listen well and to follow her curiosity. Her voice is the voice of the audience or of the reader.

People have asked me how I go about conducting these sorts of interview. I like to read widely about the person I am about to talk to, to think deeply about them and to make a kind of mental map of the ground I wish to cover. I never use a clipboard or prepare specific questions. I find this distracts me from what I think of as my cardinal obligation: to listen as intelligently as I can.

In the course of each interview some of my questions simply ask for narrative details, some are directed at probing motivation or eliciting reflection and sometimes I put my own interpretive propositions inviting agreement, elaboration or rejection. I try to conduct a 'contributive' interview, where part of my role is to take from the storyteller some of the burden of signposting the story, thus freeing them to concentrate on the more subjective impressions of whatever they are relating. Because these questions inevitably affect the nature of the response, they are included in the text of this book, so that the reader can know the context in which each story was told.

The long archival interview, from which the television half hour was excerpted and on which each chapter of this book is based, was spread over two or three days. After the first day, memory often stirred and long-forgotten events were brought to mind. These recollections had a freshness about them that the much-repeated tales that so often make up autobiography can lack. But although I was anxious to stimulate memory, I wanted to avoid clouding or contaminating what was remembered with my own expectations or attitudes. Of course, with such independent, strongminded individuals as these, this routine professional precaution was hardly necessary. Whereas I could always prompt them to turn their thoughts to new territory, there was little chance that their opinions would be affected by anything that I said.

All the people included in the *Australian Biography* film project have reached a stage where they can look back and reflect on the way they have lived their lives, see patterns in the choices and decisions they have made and ponder, with hindsight, their own motivation. These are very personal stories, but between them they provide a fascinating account of twentieth century life in Australia.

Cumulatively, they also provide an interesting insight into the Australian character. I was struck by certain shared characteristics in this very disparate group of people. They all display a certain optimism: a belief that action will be effective, that an ingenious way can usually be found around obstacles, and that effort will ultimately be rewarded. Even Nugget Coombs, who says he is a pessimist, has always acted hopefully. These old Australians see the absurdity of pretension and the value of humour in adversity. They share a great capacity for enduring what must be endured and an active dislike of whingeing in all its forms.

ROBIN HUGHES
SYDNEY 1996

Nugget Coombs

The Establishment Radical

*N*ugget Coombs has spent his life as an accepted member of several of Australia's most powerful Establishments. He has held the top positions in his country's economic, public service, academic and arts sectors. For many years he was a central banker. The experience and status offered by such respected positions often engender in those that hold them a conservative spirit. And yet Nugget Coombs is a radical.

He was probably the most influential public servant Australia has yet seen. He was Head of Post-War Reconstruction after the Second World War, Governor of the Reserve Bank, Adviser to seven Prime Ministers, the founding Chairman of the Elizabethan Theatre Trust and the Australian Council for the Arts (later the Australia Council), the founding Chairman

of the Council for Aboriginal Affairs, and Chancellor of the
Australian National University, which he helped to establish.
And yet he nominates as his life's greatest achievement his
fathering of four children who are all good citizens.

He has spent a great deal of his life in the company of the rich,
the powerful and the famous, and yet now in his old age he
prefers the company of old friends, his family and Aborigines.
He has presided over the wealth of the nation, but for years has
lived very simply, dividing his time between a hut in the
Northern Territory and a simple home unit near the ANU
campus in Canberra.

At the heart of the apparent paradoxes of his life is a strong
concept of what constitutes a civilised society. His favouring
of Keynesian economics is based on its underlying assumptions
about what an economic system is for. His objection to much
that is done in the name of economics today stems from his
rejection of the kind of society that many contemporary leaders
wish to foster.

This interview explores not only the way in which Nugget
Coombs has used the extraordinary opportunities presented by
the times in which he has lived, but also the vision and values
that have always underpinned his actions.

Herbert Cole Coombs, known as Nugget Coombs, was born in Kalamunda, Western Australia in 1906. His father was a country stationmaster and every time he was promoted the family moved. This itinerant life exposed Nugget to a number of different influences which helped shape his distinctive view of the world.

NC Although I was born in Kalamunda, which was a tiny little village in the hills just east of Perth, within a few weeks we moved off somewhere or other. Later in my life when my father was getting a bit old it used to be a kind of family joke, because he remembered the place and the people very clearly and he used to say to me, 'You remember old Hummerston?', and my mother would laugh, 'How could he remember old Hummerston, he left Kalamunda when he was about three weeks old'.

RH *So you got the idea at a fairly early age that the world could be different.*

Oh yes. Until I came to live in Sydney the longest time I had ever been in one town or location was five years. I remember Kalabaran and Bridgetown and Karacatta — a suburb of Perth, a funny place. It had the lunatic asylum and the cemetery and the relics of an old military camp and that was all — plus the railway station, you see, which was why we were there.

All the essential human institutions. Where were your parents born?

My father was born in England. He was the son of a marine engineer. I don't know what kind of a marine engineer my grandfather was but he did have some kind of technical qualifications. He was drowned in a river in India and as a result my father was educated at a school that was a kind of charity school. It was established for the sons of officers of the Merchant Marine, so he got a fairly good education. He came to Australia when he was about 19, I think, just when the railways were being established, to work on them.

My mother was Irish, the daughter of a very well-educated man. He was a scholar of Trinity College, Dublin, and he came to Australia. The gossip was that he got into trouble at the university in Dublin and, so to speak, was sent off to the colonies. He became the Town Clerk of York — a country town in Western Australia where my mother grew up. As a result, although she had a fairly normal Australian country education, she had the benefit of growing up in the company of her father who was very well educated. He was a great reader, with a cultivated mind, and she acquired a great deal of what you might call quality, from which I also benefited. So it was a household where books were part of life, where conversation about intellectual and cultural things was normal. I think that had an influence on the way I grew up.

Why are you called Nugget?

Yes. Well, in Western Australia, in the country, Nugget was a kind of generic name for a creature, a person or a dog or a horse, which was short in the legs with a stocky build. And associated with that image of shortness and stockiness was a certain character — things that were supposed to go with being nuggetty. You know, they used to say every bullock team needs a nugget. They're a bit stupid but they work hard. Nuggets are reputed to be energetic, vigorous, not necessarily terribly clever, I think. So that right from when I was about this high I was always short in the legs and stocky and active, and the name followed me. I didn't have to tell people that I was called Nugget. They just had one look at me — he's a Nugget! I discovered that Aborigines in Central Australia have a similar word for people who are built that way — they call it Toonkoo. Toonkoo is the Pitjantjatjara word for Nugget. I had a very interesting experience of being introduced to two Pitjantjatjara people called Nugget. Both of them were like black versions of me — short and stocky. So in Pitjantjantjara land I'm a Toonkoo. So really it has nothing to do with gold or the bank. But I like being called Nugget.

How many children were there in your family?

There were five altogether. I had an elder brother who died when he was about six, and I had four sisters all younger than me, so that for most of my life I was the eldest in the family.

And the only son.

And the only son. But being the eldest I had fairly considerable domestic responsibilities. I looked after the girls and nursed the babies and I learned to be a good cook. At the age of about 11, I think it was, my mother had to go to hospital for an operation, the nature of which I don't think I've ever known, and she was in hospital for some weeks. So I kept house and did all the cooking, cleaned the house, did the washing and all those things because my father was — he was a kindly man, but he thought that a husband was performing properly if he stayed out of the kitchen. 'I never interfere in the kitchen', he used to say. So I interfered in the kitchen.

Not many men of your generation had that experience of being involved domestically.

I suppose not, but I think it was much more common in the country. I don't remember feeling that it was unusual. I think in the country all children, if they were on a farm, had regular routine jobs to do: they did the milking, or they brought the cows in. I think every boy or girl that I knew at school did things like that — that was normal, and part of growing up.

What were your parents' aspirations for you?

I don't know whether they really had any. The fact that I went on to secondary school was not so much pressure from the family as pressure from one of the headmasters at the school. He was a very good teacher and he was very ambitious. There were 50 scholarships set up by the government for students to get into secondary school and he was very anxious that the school should get some. He picked me out and made me miss a year of one class and move up one so that I could sit for this examination. And he bullied me and incited me and stimulated me so that I got the 49th of the 50 scholarships. I just made it! So you see I had good reason to be grateful to that particular headmaster who decided that I was going to confer credit on his school. Most of the scholarships used to go to the children from Perth, from the big private schools and from the bigger state schools.

Had you done well at school? Did he pick you for that reason?

Well, he thought I had potential. I was never very interested in school, even right through to when I was at Perth Modern School. I was more interested in cricket and games. The first time I became interested in the education that was being provided was when I went to Teachers College, where they were running the training course rather like a university college. The subject matter we did was — oh, logic, psychology, philosophy, educational theory, and also economics. I got interested in those things because the subject matter was interesting.

Until that time you hadn't connected education with ideas?

No, I really only began to connect it with ideas when I got into the Teachers College and then, after that, when I went out teaching. I did my university course part-time by correspondence. But it was that change of subject matter that made a tremendous difference to the quality of my performance. At primary and secondary school I never came top, but once into Teachers College I did come top in a number of things. And at the university, particularly in economics and philosophy, I began to get occasional distinctions and credits and finally I got a first class honours degree. On the basis of that I won the Hackett Scholarship to do postgraduate studies in England. There was nowhere in Australia where you could do postgraduate work in economics in those days.

What kind of children were in the schools that you attended?

Many of them were the children of people who ran farms in the area. The majority were like us — people who had functions in the town. Their fathers worked in the post office, railway or the shire council. And there was the butcher, the baker, the policeman and that sort of thing.

Aborigines?

There were a few in Bridgetown, not very many. The main thing I remember about them was that they were very good at football. But I didn't become aware of them in school, really, until I became a teacher myself. The first real experience was in two places, Katanning and Pinjulee. There was quite a significant proportion of the children who were Aboriginal and I was horrified by the experience they were subjected to. They didn't get any attention. They were usually thrust up at the back of the class and ignored. But they always passed at the end of the year because every teacher was determined to move them on and out of their area of concern. So I became concerned about that. And it was during that time that I taught for a while on an emergency basis in a one-teacher school out of Katanning, where nearly half the children in that school of about 30 were from two Aboriginal families. And that was a very interesting experience. One girl I remember was really very able. She was a very good student and she mothered her brothers and bullied them into doing things. But I was very much aware of the kind of educational handicaps that Aboriginal children were suffering under. And I also became aware of the really bad racial antagonism towards them in some of the country towns.

Why do you think you had a different approach to these Aboriginal pupils? What was it in your background that made you different from the others?

Well, neither of my parents knew much about Aborigines but they certainly would have been kindly and tolerant towards them. That

kind of almost intuitive antagonism which seemed to be characteristic of country people wasn't characteristic of them, anyway. And
certainly religion was important to my mother — we were a
churchgoing family.

What kind of church?

It was an Anglican Church — although my father had been brought
up a nonconformist. But under my mother's influence, I think, by
the time I came around we were going to the Church of England and
I was in the choir and I went to Sunday School, all those things. But
I suppose our mother was a kind of Christian Socialist. I mean, she
believed that Christianity meant what it said about sharing and
having care for other people, and that certainly influenced my ways
of thinking and was perhaps the reason why I was shocked by what
seemed to me to be indifference and antagonism.

*Did you feel there was anything you as an individual could really do
about it?*

No, I didn't think of it, really, in that way. One of the things that
puzzled me was that people, particularly women, in this town, who
were really very generous kindly people in my relationships with
them, still shared this hostility, this antagonism. And I asked one
woman why. She was a much older woman with whom I'd become
friendly. I knew her children and so on. And I'll always remember
how she looked at me and said: 'Well, I'll tell you if you were a
woman and you went down the street on shopping night, and you
saw children who you knew were your husband's children, how
would *you* feel?' I can remember thinking — but I don't think I said
it — 'I might hate my husband but I wouldn't hate the kids'. But
that was a real factor in the little community. So that was part of the
background to that hostility.

One of the things that has always struck me about that country
life was the degree to which certain antagonisms were normal or
expected. At that time, for instance, in Bridgetown — the country
town that I may have spent most of my formative years of
childhood in — the religious antagonisms were very very strong. It
was proper to hate Catholics. They went to a different school, they
went to a different church, and you didn't talk to them, or at least if
you did you felt a bit guilty about it. There were stories that would
go around about the terrible things they did, so that you grew up
with an almost instinctive antagonism towards Catholics.

These prejudiced feelings were not shared by Nugget Coombs because they were quite alien to the ethics and principles of his upbringing. The books his mother gave him to read, the conversations that took place at the dinner table at home, the opinions that were expressed by his parents, all ran counter to prejudiced attitudes. His mother's liberal humanism was based on Christian principles and, remarkably for that time, she was an Irish Protestant who didn't hate Catholics. Whenever Nugget referred to his mother during our conversations his eyes would brim with tears and he would be forced to pause in order to recover. It was clear that the memory of her filled him with strong emotion.

When you were growing up in those towns in Western Australia, what contact did you have with the arts, with the world of culture generally?

Well, we were certainly a literate family. Books were part of life, and important. My mother saw that I had books and we talked about them. But apart from that a major source of what you might call artistic or cultural influence was the church. I went to church regularly. I went to Sunday School, I sang in the choir. I was very influenced by the language of the King James version of the *Bible* and the *Book of Common Prayer* — the bits I had to memorise for the Sunday School, you know, all that. But also, it introduced me to music. I wasn't musical. Although I should say that one of the things which was characteristic of the time was that I was not allowed to learn music because my sisters had to learn music. They had to have some privileges, you see. One of my sisters proved to be a very good pianist and played the organ at church. Consequently that kind of music — church music — was part of the family life. I think poetry was very badly taught in schools but those sources — the religious sources, the Anglican liturgy and the readings from the *Bible* — were a kind of introduction to poetry. And that interest in words and their arrangement has been a factor in my life all through. So those were things which I acquired without ever being consciously taught about them.

When did you first encounter the theatre?

I acted in some plays at Teachers College — Bernard Shaw and James Barry — and I went to concerts. I heard Madame Melba sing one of her farewells. But I didn't really become interested in the theatre until — well until I became involved in the Elizabethan Theatre Trust, I suppose.

And when you went to London, did you encounter theatre and galleries and so on as a student?

I did all of that. I liked it, but I think it was, as it were, part of my 'program'. I didn't know whether I'd ever get back to Europe and while I was there I felt that I had to experience all aspects of European life, as part of the purpose of being there. We went regularly to the Old Vic, to all the Shakespearian plays and the contemporary plays, and to the ballet and to the opera. But it was quite a long time before I could take an interest in the opera. In fact I don't think I ever got any real pleasure out of it until I became involved in the formation of the opera company in Australia.

Why do you think that was?

Well, my response to it was that it was so artificial. It took actually a long time to realise that that doesn't matter, that the idea that you would make love to a girl by standing about like this and beefing it out . . .

It wasn't the way you did it?

It wasn't the way I did it or the way I *thought* about doing it. But I took to ballet very very quickly. I can remember getting very great pleasure. I saw Pavlova dance the Dying Swan in the theatre in Perth, but that was like football, it was movement and I got the thrill of watching bodies in motion, which — well, it's a very natural kind of thing to get pleasure from, I think.

Nugget Coombs began his autobiography Trial Balance *(published in 1981) with the words, 'The publication in 1936 of John Maynard Keynes'* General Theory of Employment, Interest and Money *was for me and many of my generation the most seminal intellectual event of our time'. Nugget had first encountered the ideas of the Cambridge School, and particularly of Keynes, while he was studying economics at the university in Perth. When he won the scholarship that took him to the London School of Economics in 1931 he was looking forward to strengthening his understanding of the theories that, for him, were beginning at last to make real sense of the way in which economic systems worked.*

In a way I was very disappointed. I went there passionately concerned about economics. It was the time of the Great Depression and this affected the things that were brooded about when I was at the university in Perth and that were the motivation for my doing economics. But I found when I got to the London School of Economics that the teachers of economics were very conservative. They were very much influenced by monetary theory based upon the teachings of Austrian economists, with which I didn't feel much sympathy. But the main task of the PhD degree was the preparation of a thesis and I already had an idea of what I wanted to do. When it came to attending lectures and participating in seminars the system was very flexible. You could really plan your own course. So I attended lectures to fill in what I felt to be gaps in my training and my experience. And I went to listen to people that I thought were interesting. Two parts of the university, the economists and political scientists, were really at daggers drawn. The political scientists were headed by Professor Laski, who was Professor of Law really, but he was a Marxist. And so the university was a kind of hotbed of dispute between the conservative economists and the Marxist political scientists. And they used to run quite separate seminars. But Laski, who was a very interesting man, used to have a seminar which you only got into by invitation. He invited people who he thought were good students from both economics and political science to meet in his room and to argue and debate. He used to lie back on a sofa and just throw in a word when the argument seemed to be flagging. It was great fun. He invited me to go to one and from then on I went regularly. It was a very intellectually stimulating thing because they read very widely. And I was interested in politics. You can't be an economist if you're not.

But at the same time I found the whole thing really quite a burden. You see, I got married the day we left Perth to go to London. Our first baby was born nine months later. I had the thesis to do, I had to work for money and I had quite a lot to do in the household, with my wife pregnant and the rest of it. We also wanted to go to theatre and to travel a bit here and there. So that, while it was stimulating and I got great benefit from it, I can't say that I enjoyed it. I found it a burden.

Nevertheless, you managed to write your PhD thesis in only a couple of years — the shortest period that you could do it in.
Yes.

And what was the subject?
It was an examination of the policies adopted during the Depression by the governments and central banks of the British Dominions, as we called them then — you know, Canada, South Africa, New

Zealand and Australia. I was looking at the theoretical basis of the decisions that they made and how this could mitigate the effects of the Depression.

I wonder if you could tell me a little bit about the Depression as you experienced it personally in Western Australia and in London.

Personally I was one of the very lucky ones, in that the Depression in Western Australia imposed no personal hardship on me. I was by that time in the process of becoming a teacher. I had a job. And while I earned, I think, £78 a year as a pupil teacher and I contributed one pound a week of that to maintaining the household and so on, it was surprisingly adequate. Although there was some degree of hardship in the family, it wasn't really serious. But I was aware of its affecting other people. However, London was different.

The impact of the Depression in England was much more obvious to me than the effects in Western Australia had been. One of the things I had to do while I was in London was to register myself at the London County Council as a qualified teacher, which meant that they could offer me a short-term employment. They'd ring me up saying there was someone away from Hammersmith High, or someone from Shoreditch Primary, and would I be interested in a week's work? Well, it was against the rules of the university to do that in term time, so I began by accepting it only during vacation times. But after a while, as money became scarcer, I began doing it in term time too. I taught the social middle class in Highgate and Kensington — but I also taught in the slums, so that I saw a cross-section of London life. And it was not a very pleasant experience, because the slum kids suffered very badly in the Depression. They were short of food, rickets were common, and they were pasty-faced and skinny and miserable-looking. It must have been much much worse in Wales and Yorkshire and the places where unemployment had really hit the factories. London was not quite so badly off. But it was enough at any rate to intensify my concern about the economic system and my conviction that it wasn't operating — certainly not operating fairly, but not even operating efficiently. It intensified my anxiety to understand it.

When Nugget Coombs came back to Australia with a PhD and a young family his aspirations were somewhat different from those of a young man in a similar position today. His thoughts were not of entering the private sector and making his fortune. Before leaving

Australia he had become interested in the way in which central
financial management might help mitigate the effects of the
Depression. While he was at the LSE, Leslie Melville, the man who
was at that time the only economist at the Commonwealth Bank,
came to London for a conference. He suggested that Nugget might
join the Bank on his return to Australia.

I was about 18 months in Perth, I think, after I came back, then I
got the offer to join the Commonwealth Bank. There was apparently
some quite high level discussion about whether the Commonwealth
Bank should have more than one economist.

They were wondering what economics had to do with banking?
[Chuckling] Yes.

When you arrived at the Commonwealth Bank what were the main issues
that confronted you?
Very shortly after I got there, when it became evident that we were
heading for trouble in Europe, the government in Canberra set up
two committees to prepare for the war. One was to look at
economic and financial policy for wartime activities. The other was
to examine our international trade and identify what problems
could occur if lines of communication were interrupted by war and
we found difficulty in selling our exports. Melville and I worked on
these problems together. I was also anxious to continue contact
with the university and a friend asked me to take his class on
History of Economic Thought, while he went on study leave. I said:
'But I don't know anything about it. I have never really studied the
history of economic thought'. 'Oh', he said, 'you could read it up
you know' — and I accepted. It really was a very enlightening
experience because it was my real introduction to the economic
classics — Adam Smith, John Stuart Mill, Marx and all the really
great men of the origins of economics. And since I had to teach it, I
really had to read it.

So you read them in the original — a tremendous number of people have
only ever read them from secondary sources.
That's right. My own acquaintance with them up to that time had
been entirely from textbooks. I had read bits about them, I could
quote from them, but the quotes were all second-hand. I gained a
tremendous amount from reading those original writings. They have
influenced me profoundly in my thinking ever since.

Were you able to apply any of the new ideas you'd been developing and acquiring to the actual practical problems that confronted you?

Those things only really came alive when I went to work in Canberra, which I did just after the outbreak of war. I was lent by the Bank to act as Economist to the Treasury. I was the only economist on the Treasury staff at that time — now they've got hundreds of them. When you had to find resources out of the total pool to put into the war effort — where did they come from? What was the effect on the civilian population of taking those out? These were now urgent questions. The Keynesian theory, the whole structure on which his work was based, became bread and butter in the working out of economic and financial policy, once we were involved in the war.

Was this very exciting to you?

Oh it was. It was tremendously exciting, yes. And also I was a pacifist and the question of whether I should enlist was an issue. The idea of working on how to manage the war so that its adverse effect on people was minimised gave me a kind of intellectual escape from the dilemma. When I was put in charge of rationing, what I was doing was protecting the civilian population's share of the resources — seeing that they got a fair crack of the whip and that individual people got a fair deal and so on. But it seemed to me at the time, and has seemed to me ever since, that the conduct of the war in Australia, more than anywhere else, was an exercise in Keynesian economics. 'How do you manage this in terms of Keynesian theory?' was the question asked. That was partly because I was involved, but also because people from Sydney University, who came into the bureaucracy to manage different aspects of the war, shared this intellectual approach. We were all Keynesians.

So when the theory was put into practice it actually worked?

Certainly it made trying to understand the problems very much easier. I still believe that, as a kind of framework for thinking about economic policies, the Keynesian model is still one of the best tools.

What do you think it was that led to its becoming unfashionable?

Ah, well. You see, it assumed that the purpose of economic management was to use all the resources, including human resources, in a more equitable way. Keynesian theory was a theory which was sympathetic to what you might call small 'l' liberal thinking. It didn't say: we must destroy the existing system. But it said we must manage it so that there are jobs for everybody and the things that are produced are the things that people need. In contrast, there are people whose concern is much more in quantitative terms — in measuring the total output and the prosperity of industry and commerce — and this goal has now begun to drive policy, rather than equity doing so. The big change was when the Keynesian stuff was pushed on one side and followed by monetarism and the view that the most important thing is the money supply. This led to a different kind of model, of interest to different kinds of people, who thought in different kinds of ways.

Do you think it would have been possible for some of the new ideas — about money supply being the prime factor in managing the economy — to be adapted into a Keynesian model?

Oh, certainly. The period when I was at the Commonwealth Bank and later the Reserve Bank was a continuation of the wartime policy of using the Keynesian model as the instrument for analysis and exposition of monetary policy. I wrote a lot about it. Most of the stuff that was written at that time was, of course, internal. But I did a series of lectures which were published subsequently under the title, *Other People's Money*. That's what I thought we were doing, managing other people's money. That was Keynesian, there's no doubt about that. Until I left the Bank the intellectual thinking there was conducted in essentially Keynesian terms.

During the war you were in charge of rationing. Could you describe how you went about that?

The main Keynesian aspect of it was that you looked at the total resources available and argued that a certain amount of those resources had to be reserved for the maintenance of economic activity in the civil sector. If you put it all into the war you'd lose the war, because your population would starve and you wouldn't even be able to feed and clothe your armies. So it was fairly simple economic theory. The rationing part of it was simply a distributional exercise. It was establishing a system by which there was equality of access to the goods available. What was available was a question of how much you could produce with that section of the resources reserved for the civilian population, less what you wanted to send overseas to Britain and so on.

Did you run into any problems in implementing the rationing? I mean, were any of your ideas challenged about what should be rationed and how it should be done?

In the period leading up to the actual start of rationing there was a period where shops selling clothing and so on used to open at nine o'clock and close at five past, because there was just not enough production to satisfy possible demand. And once people realised that things were getting scarce they grabbed everything they could get. So there was that period of about six weeks, while we worked out a system of rationing, when there was absolute chaos. And if it hadn't been for that chaos I suppose it might have been much more difficult to introduce rationing. But people realised straightaway that dresses and socks could disappear from the shelves and there had to be some way in which you got your fair share. And that was the motto. We had this all around the country — fair shares. Fair shares, fair shares — heading every press statement, every advertisement, everything coming from the Rationing Commission. It was an introduction of a second form of currency which allocated the goods not merely to the people who could pay for them, but to all the people a quantitative fair share.

Now of course, calculating fair shares is pretty arbitrary and therefore people were dissatisfied. Some felt that they should get more than they were getting and when restraints were put upon the degree to which they could borrow somebody else's rations there was resentment about that. And there was resentment about things that were rationed in ways other than by coupons. Resentment from people who couldn't buy beer and cigarettes because we rationed them by cutting the supply to retailers. Well, believe me, the antagonisms that were generated by the people who didn't want to crawl to the tobacconist to get a packet of cigarettes were pretty bitter! Believe me! So it was a very interesting exercise. We had a complaints department and I can remember on one occasion we had a letter from the Archbishop of Melbourne complaining that he didn't have enough tea to entertain visiting clergy. He wanted a special allowance. In the fashion of archbishops in those days he signed himself John (or whatever his Christian name was) Melbourne. And so the girl who was doing the work on this, who was very efficient and, you know, blunt, wrote back: 'Dear Mr Melbourne, you can't have any more tea and if you have guests coming you'd better ask them to bring their own coupons'. As a consequence, another complaint came from the Archbishop that one of my staff had been rude to him.

Another one of the things we had to do at the time was to persuade people to use less material where things were pretty scarce, and this was particularly important for uniforms. I had some bother with the Nurses Association because they were really in those times very extravagant in the use of material, including great veils, and dresses that came right down low. I went to consult with the head of the nursing service about this and, boy, she was most dismissive. She just wasn't prepared to contemplate any change at all. So I went on with my usual spiel about how important it was. I said: 'You know, you don't really need veils that come right down below the waist; you don't really need to have skirts that cover their ankles.' She said: 'Dr Coombs, I will not have my male patients disturbed by the sight of naked female flesh!' And I said: 'I think you underestimate your patients' imagination!' So I didn't get anywhere. Actually they did make some changes finally, but it was a very reluctant exercise. Oh, there were quite a lot of things like that that caused some entertainment. We had an interesting group. I recruited people from universities, some of them teachers, some doing postgraduate work. They were young and lively and intelligent, and on the whole they came to it because many of them were opposed to wars generally. And they saw this as a way of satisfying the social demand that they be involved.

Your work during the war years also introduced you to the process of international negotiation, and you attended the conference in Hot Springs in the United States that founded the international Food and Agriculture Organisation. What was that like?

It was in an odd sort of way an Australian initiative. Lord Bruce, who was our High Commissioner in London, knew a chap who'd worked in Australia. He had been a soldier settler on the land after the First World War. He generated this idea that the solution to the problems of the Depression was that agriculture should be planned so that, instead of growing things simply for profit, it should develop the kind of products that would enable people to be fed better. Bruce became interested in the idea. And it was the basis of the British food policy during the war and it meant that British children were for the first time, at least since the Industrial Revolution, decently fed.

That first conference on post-war agriculture, designed to promote international planning for the world's food supply, was the last conference the Russians attended as our noble allies. You know, even before the war was over they became the focus of the Cold War. I got to know some of the Russian delegates really quite well. In fact it was at this conference that I had both my first introduction to international negotiations and my first introduction to vodka. I had an idea that there was a basis for establishing shipping between Vladivostock and Sydney. That we could bring in paper, timber and agricultural products that were plentiful in the eastern provinces of Russia, and send them wheat. I happened to meet the head of the Russian delegation and he said: 'That's a wonderful idea. You and your delegates must come to our party and we'll talk about this thing.' So we all went and I started to talk about it. But fairly early in the conversation a chap appeared with a tray of drinks — it was vodka in what looked to me to be claret glasses. So I said: 'Look, I've never drunk vodka — what's the drill, what do you do?' And he said: 'Well, there's some caviar there — you grab a handful of caviar and you put that into your mouth and then you toss the vodka down on top, you see, in one fell swallow.' It was a bit of a jolt but I did that and we went on talking about this great idea of mine.

We were making really good progress but after a while the chap came around with the drinks again. So I repeated this drill, grabbing the caviar and downing the vodka. But within about, oh, 30 seconds I suppose, I realised I was not merely drunk but I was absolutely blotto! It was as much as I could do to excuse myself and get out before I collapsed on the floor. Fortunately this particular party was being held in the hotel where we were all living, so I just had to get out the door and down the passage. I collapsed onto the bed and the bed began to sway like this, you know, up and down and up and down and I felt as if I was a bit like Mohammad's coffin — sort of suspended halfway between heaven and hell. Anyway, that was pretty nearly the end of that whole idea. By the time we got home the honeymoon between the allies and Russia was over and everybody here was hostile to the idea of having anything to do with a Russian.

With an international weapon like vodka, you wonder why they ever wanted to develop the bomb.

Well it certainly was absolutely explosive as far as I was concerned.

All his life Nugget Coombs has had a great capacity to enjoy himself. He is a lover of life and the good things it offers. He has always had an appreciation of good food, fine wine (especially the great Australian reds) and exciting and original artwork of all kinds. He also has a distinctive sense of humour and throughout this interview his characteristic chuckle would often break out as he recounted with relish an anecdote or recalled some amusing event.

Some of your international travelling at this time was done with Dr H.V. Evatt. What was he like?

Well, finally we got on pretty well, but we started off rather badly because right through his life he was inclined to be a bit paranoid. He was very suspicious of anything he hadn't initiated. This was a bit of a problem for me, because Chifley had sent me overseas for other negotiations relating to the establishment of the Monetary Fund and things like that, so I had an agenda which was quite separate from Dr Evatt's. I used to tell him what I was doing, but on the day we arrived in Washington he went off to talk to the head of the State Department, and people from the United States Treasury rang me up and said, 'Why don't you come around straightaway and we'll have a preliminary chat'. So I went off and while I was away Evatt came back and said: 'Where's Nugget?' And I was in big trouble! However, we survived that and on the whole we became quite good friends. He was accompanied by his wife, Mary Alice, who was amongst other things quite a good painter. And also he had, as a kind of offsider, another painter — Sam Atyeo. He was the traditional court jester who told stories and entertained Evatt. It was very handy because, when the Doc got upset, Sam could always go and slap him on the back and say 'you poor old bastard'. He managed him really quite well.

Mary Alice and Sam Atyeo and I visited every place of artistic importance in every town we went to. It was really great fun, because although Sam was a bit of a licensed fool he was a very very good judge of a painting. And it was about the only thing where you could take anything that he said seriously, because it was the only thing that mattered as far as he was concerned. It was a great opportunity, because I find that on the whole going to museums and art galleries is a bit of a bore after a while — your feet get tired and so on. But in going around with them I was listening to two of the best informed people about contemporary art that I'd ever be likely to meet. And certainly I profited very greatly from it later when I was at the Bank and we were buying a few pictures. I was very much influenced by the kind of judgement that I acquired during that time and also I began to know from them who were the important Australian painters. I think the collection of contemporary paintings that the Reserve Bank still holds, as a result of that, is probably the best financial investment that the Bank has ever made.

So there you were, dealing with very important matters of state, but you found time to pursue your interest in the arts and to have some fun and relaxation. Is this something you've always been able to do in your public life?

I think I have managed fairly successfully. It was one aspect of travelling with Doc Evatt which was interesting, and also when we were in Europe — he and his wife both had some background of classical knowledge.

What did you admire most about Dr Evatt?

I think I liked him best when he was not being official. We lived in the Embassy in Washington, Burton and I and the Evatts. Our Ambassador at that time, very cunningly I thought, decided that when Dr Evatt was going to be in Washington he ought to vacate the Embassy — because Evatt was a difficult man and you could find yourself in quite difficult circumstances sometimes. But on the other hand he had a gift of relaxing very completely. He used to go off to meetings in the evening and he would come back — Burton and I would perhaps be having a last drink before we went to bed — and we would sit and talk. And he really had an incredible range of knowledge. I think he had one of those photographic memories. You couldn't begin a quotation without his providing the rest of it. He was a very interesting conversationalist and in that kind of atmosphere, when he was relaxed, he was very good fun.

Was he a good negotiator?

He was really very successful in the negotiations for the setting up of the United Nations. And he was of course the first President of the United Nations, which was — well, he wangled that. The only place where I personally saw him in action in negotiations was in Japan at the time of the occupation, when he negotiated with General Macarthur. My own feeling was that he gave in to Macarthur far too much. But that was perhaps an expression of my prejudices rather than a reflection on his capacities as a negotiator.

Your feelings about Ben Chifley, whom you also had a lot to do with during the war, were different, weren't they?

Quite different, quite different. I had a tremendous respect for Chifley but also a very great affection. He was Treasurer when I was at the Treasury. John Curtin was Prime Minister. Curtin appointed me as a member of the Bank board, which was an astonishing thing to do. Here I was, a relatively junior officer of the Bank, on loan to the Treasury, and they appointed me to the board of the Bank which is — well everybody's eyebrows went up. Some of the senior people in the Bank were quite appalled by this. Here was I, only 29 or 30 . . .

How did you feel? It was a terrific vote of confidence in you, wasn't it.

Well, yes, but it was a time when the board of the Bank was still very conservative, and when Chifley came he understood that. He'd read some of my material; we had things in common. It was he and Curtin who appointed me to run rationing when I'd never done a major piece of administration before in my life. When I look back on it now I feel I ought to have been terrified.

And weren't you?

Well, at times I was. But this group that we gathered together, partly by accident, it was such a lively group that I don't remember feeling oppressed by it.

You weren't the only person who worked with Ben Chifley who had a great admiration for his approach to leadership. Can you say what it was about the way that he went about his work that drew so much admiration?

I think it was partly that he always worked *with* people, they never simply worked *for* him. He was a remarkably tolerant man. He led the Labor Party at a time when the divisions within the party were staggering. But he always used to talk about why they thought like this or like that. He was a practising Catholic, but when he talked about the DLP, you know, he talked like somebody who understood where their prejudices were leading them and was sad about it, and sad about the divisions. But his relationships with people were always pleasant. Sometimes he could be quite blunt. He was very blunt with Evatt from time to time because he thought that Evatt was arrogant and, you know, often caused problems with other people unnecessarily. I can remember when Doc asked him what impression he had of Doc's performance at the United Nations, and he said: 'Doc, it was excellent, but they tell me that you were the rudest bugger there!'

So Chifley said what he thought. But not with animosity.

Exactly. And he always read what you wrote. Your work was never dismissed as not what he wanted. And he welcomed disagreement. Also he was true to what he believed in. I remember once when we were visiting London, he had to go to Buckingham Palace to meet the King. Now, normally he was never without his blue shirt, which was very much in those days a sign that you were a worker. He wondered if he should wear a more formal white shirt as a sign of respect for the King. And he said: 'Well, I wouldn't want to be discourteous to the King, but I wouldn't want to let the boys down either.' He went to meet the King in his blue shirt.

You said that Chifley worked with you, it wasn't as if you were working for him. What do you mean by that?

I think it's a thing that's changed quite a lot in the relationship between ministers and their senior officials. At that time the relationship was one of discussion.

You were his adviser, but did he ever offer you any advice?

Yes. We did have quite an extensive discussion about the role of the central bank as one of the government's main advisers on financial and economic policy but also having a considerable degree of autonomy. And I felt that that autonomy was important. I said we ought to provide in the Act for a way of resolving the issue if a disagreement emerged. I said: 'There could conceivably be situations where the Governor of the Bank would feel that a very important principle was threatened by what the government wanted to do, and then the only thing open to him would be to say, "Well, Prime Minister, if you're going to do that I must resign".' Chifley broke in and said: 'Never, never resign.' I said: 'Are you sure? What about the question of principle?' He said: 'Well, if you have that situation, if you resign, you're finished! They do what they like. If you stay in you lose the battle, but there will be other governments, other ministers, other opportunities to be effective — but once you resign you are finished.'

When you became Head of Post-War Reconstruction, what did you identify as the main task that you really had to get right in that period?

It was a progressive thing. The department was originally set up to prepare for the transition from war to peace and that meant demobilisation, to get people out of the Army and the Navy and the Air Force, and out of munitions factories. That meant that we had to have jobs, we had to have houses where they could live. So you can see the way in which the responsibility of post-war reconstruction spread to become the department which planned the economic programs for that post-war period. We attempted to anticipate what kind of skills would be required and to set up training programs to enable people in the armed forces to go out prepared for doing the jobs that we could reasonably anticipate would exist. So there was almost no part of government that wasn't involved. We drew staff from almost all departments and we also brought in people from universities who had never been in the bureaucracy. But we had to promise all those departments — I had to give my personal guarantee — that the Department of Post-War Reconstruction would be abolished in due course.

You were instrumental in setting up the Australian National University — how did that come about?

It was a dream that was shared to varying degrees by quite a lot of people, and in a way post-war reconstruction brought together a series of disparate ideas which created the basis for a university of a particular kind. I suppose the real beginnings are associated in my mind with Howard Florey who came back to Australia during the war at Curtin's request to advise the government about medical problems in the armed forces, particularly in New Guinea. It was not long after the development of penicillin with which he was associated, and its use became widely practised because of his involvement. He talked to Curtin about the way the penicillin discoveries came out of fundamental research work which was being conducted at Cambridge and Oxford. So Curtin said, 'Is there any reason why we couldn't do that kind of research in Australia?', and then as an afterthought, since he was a bit of an advocate of Canberra: 'And in particular is there any reason why we couldn't do that kind of work in Canberra?' Florey said: 'It would make a fine foundation for a function for Canberra.' At the same time there were ideas being tossed around in other places. In Post-War Reconstruction itself, we were very interested in the way in which the social sciences — economics and other studies of the way society functions — had provided us with answers to problems in the war, and we realised that we had to have more research if we wanted our society to be properly run. Another contribution came in relation to Mt Stromlow, which was the observatory. Here was something Australia could do better than anywhere else in the world because of our physical location.

All these things were initially being looked at separately, but the work that Post-War Reconstruction was doing meant that they could be grouped and combined into an institution which provided real opportunities. At that time we had distinguished scholars in the classics, in physics, in medicine all working overseas. They had left Australia because opportunity wasn't here for them. And the idea was that in this new post-war-reconstructed world they would come back.

We had done great things during the war, now we could do them in peace. And they would want to come back to take a part in it. We talked about Oliphant coming ... Florey coming ... Hancock coming. It could be one way in which we could end this braindrain — the loss of our best people to other places. We would offer a chance for them to share, we thought, in this creation of the new Jerusalem.

The idea of the clever country is not new!

No, no, certainly not.

During the war and continuing into the immediate post-war period Nugget Coombs was involved in the international effort to develop trade agreements designed to free up world trade. There were two parts to the international talks. One related to bilateral trade agreements between specific trading nations. The most significant of these from Australia's point of view was the one with the United States which was successfully negotiated by Coombs during nine months intensive work in Geneva.

At the same time a parallel proposal was being negotiated. It was to establish a charter and an international trade organisation which would regulate the General Agreement on Tariffs and Trade (GATT) and provide some protection and a court of appeal for the weaker trading partners against the stronger. This plan was particularly dear to Coombs's egalitarian heart, not because he was proposed as the possible first head of the organisation but because the charter was designed to take care of the interests of developing nations. At the heart of it was an obligation on industrialised nations to adopt policies conducive to full employment for their people. Coombs saw this as essential to prevent the freer trading arrangements disadvantaging developing countries. It was also important to the interests of small agricultural nations like Australia. Details of the charter were finally agreed on by the international negotiating teams, but at the eleventh hour the plan was scuttled by US self-interest.

Finally, after three years of negotiation, we reached a kind of agreement on the content of that charter, and it was right at the end in Havana where we were going to have a great celebration. And the Americans came into the meeting and said that they wanted the two parts of this deal separated. They wanted GATT to be dealt with first, separately from the charter. We had quite a violent discussion. I felt

that the negotiations on tariffs had been made on the understanding
that the charter would also be adopted. The leader of the American
delegation was outraged that I should suggest that America would
ever go back on this commitment. But in fact President Truman, after
GATT was signed, just announced unilaterally that he was not going
to put the charter before Congress.

Now, I believe that the present international economic situation
with its problems has to be seen in the context of the United States
having one of the highest levels of unemployment in history. If all
those people had incomes to spend, they would want the things which
we have to sell, and which the developing nations have to sell. That's
what we wanted to achieve and we had entered into the negotiations
believing that we were getting a commitment not only from the
United States, the biggest, but also from other big industrialised
nations that they would perform their part of the function.

*Do you feel that when the chips are down the big powers will always act in
their own interests?*

Yes, I do. I think it is characteristic. We will never get countries of
that kind to go back on what they feel to be interests which are
critical to their economic advantage.

*After all the work that you'd put into this, the enormous amount of effort
and energy and thought, how did you feel when that happened?*

Oh, it was hard! I just felt utterly and completely disillusioned. And
that disillusionment in a sense continues to this day, because I
believe there was an opportunity to establish a pattern of
international trade where the participants were conscious that they
had to make concessions — particularly to the needs of the poorer
and developing countries. And that is what is missing in the world
at the present time. We still can sometimes negotiate about tariffs
and the other mechanical things which are seen to be mutually
beneficial. But we lost an opportunity to establish a much better
system with agreed principles, and with a regulatory body that you
could go to and explain your problem if for some reason you needed
an exemption from the agreed rules. For example, you could go to
them and ask for a temporary increase in tariffs for an industry that
was just starting up, or you could say: 'We want to put on an
exchange control for a while to deal with our immediate balance of
payment difficulties.' Well, you can't do that now.

*After the Post-War Reconstruction you went to the Commonwealth Bank
and later the Reserve Bank, and there began a period of quite astonishing*

stability. *We had general prosperity, and really no major economic crises despite some very difficult things happening internationally. This period lasted until about the time you left the Bank in 1968. Why do you think that was? How did you achieve it?*

Well, I think it would be arrogant to suggest that it happened because of what we did, although I think that was a significant part of it. But it happened because the influences in operation in the economy were compatible with the kind of arrangements we made. And the constraints which we found it necessary to impose were by and large accepted by the financial system, not as perfect but as acceptable. There were times when they got sick of us, when they felt they lost opportunities, but on the whole I don't look back on those debates with the private banks and the people who ran finance companies as periods of intense hostility. On the whole there was — a kind of consensus.

For most of the time you were at the Commonwealth Bank and then at the Reserve Bank you had the one Prime Minister — Menzies — and so all this has often been described as the stability of the Menzies era. What role do you think he played in that? And what did you think of him?

When he came to office, he and Arthur Fadden were promising to sack me — they were promising a lifting of controls. Not merely to get rid of rationing, not merely to have petrol freely available, but to get rid of controls altogether.

Deregulation?

Exactly! Deregulation. To have the whole financial system released from the central bank controls. Now, they started to do that but it happened to coincide with the period leading up to and including the Korean War and, in the second or the third year of the Menzies period, we had inflation at the rate of 20 per cent per annum for one year. That terrified them. And so they looked with much less hostile eyes on ideas for constraint. After that no one was suggesting that controls should be completely abolished, and the period of stability began.

So you had been appointed by a Labor Government and then, when Menzies arrived on the scene with a philosophy that was going to be a little different from what you stood for, there were meetings I understand all over the country of Country Party groups and so on calling for your resignation. Why didn't Menzies listen to them? Why did he keep you?

Oh I think he listened to them, but he explained to me afterwards why he didn't accept that advice. He asked Ben Chifley what he thought of me and Chifley said he didn't believe that I had ever given him politically motivated advice. Well, I thought that was stretching it a bit! Still, it was welcome in that it influenced Menzies. It was interesting — they had quite a friendly relationship. Once when he commented that he'd talked to Chifley about an issue of policy I expressed some surprise, and he said: 'Well, you may be surprised, but let me tell you that I never make a major decision, particularly of an international kind, without talking to Ben.' Then he said: 'My party doesn't know this!'

And this was just because he respected the man.

Yes, they had quite a degree of respect for one another. I think the relationship was pretty badly damaged by Menzies's involvement with the anti-communist campaign. But nonetheless, right through, there was certainly a relationship where they accepted mutual responsibilities.

What did you think of Menzies yourself?

He was a very interesting man. He was the first real professional politician I'd ever worked with. Politics to him was a career. He wanted to be Prime Minister, and that was really what it was about. He didn't come in with a program. Although he once said, when I was talking to him about universities: 'I'm not a Prime Minister who wants to leave monuments to my prime ministership. But if I'm to be remembered I would like to be remembered as the Prime Minister who gave opportunities to Australian universities.' As he did, of course. I like to remind some of his successors of that one. But in general his whole approach to politics was pragmatic. He didn't have an ideological point of view. I mean, he was a conservative, but he used to say that when he was preparing for the next election he had a careful look at the Labor Party's program. And he would say in some of his speeches: 'Now I know you want this, but wouldn't it be better to get it from us rather than from the Labor Party?' He had that pragmatic, professional kind of quality in his approach. And he was lazy. He didn't want to run the whole business. Provided the ministers didn't get into trouble he was happy to leave them alone. But he was ruthless in getting rid of them, if he thought they were unduly ambitious or not doing a reasonably good job.

He was good to deal with because he didn't resent you saying things which weren't in accordance with what he was doing.

I expect that meant that you had a great capacity to influence him — because he was willing to listen and didn't have a rigid ideological agenda.

That gave you quite a lot of power didn't it?

I don't mind the word 'influence' but I have never thought of the work that I did as an exercise of power. I might have been wrong about that, but I don't think so. I think I'm a competent persuader. And I like persuading.

But you didn't experience that as power. What did you experience it as — what did it feel like to you? A lot of responsibility?

Yes, but it was a pleasurable thing. And I was lucky. All the key people that I worked with, from Curtin through to Whitlam — they all had something. Australia has been really very lucky.

Nugget Coombs's own personal demeanour has certainly never given any indication of a love of power or the trappings of power for their own sake. He has always been modest and self-effacing in manner, as he is today, absorbed with the task at hand and seemingly undistracted by personal ambition.

After Menzies departed the political scene, Coombs served a number of different Prime Ministers in fairly rapid succession. The first of these was Harold Holt, and it was while Holt was Prime Minister that Coombs finally retired from his position as Governor of the Reserve Bank. During this same period his involvement in the cause of Australian Aborigines began, leading to a passionate concern which has dominated the rest of his life.

What was your relationship with Harold Holt?

Well, before he became Prime Minister he'd been Treasurer for quite a while. I had been dealing with him in relation to the Bank and economic matters for quite some time, and I liked him. He was a very kindly, rather gentle sort of person, and eminently decent. I don't think he was a great man, but he was reasonably intelligent and so he was quite a good Treasurer to work with. He was very surprised by the referendum about the power of the Commonwealth in relation to Aboriginal affairs. He was not only surprised, in fact he was astonished. So were a lot of people. But he was puzzled. He couldn't see what it meant for the Commonwealth, what they should do. He felt it was an indicator that some substantial change in Commonwealth attitudes should take place, but he didn't know what to do.

Holt came to see me at the Bank and we talked about the referendum and what it meant for government. I said: 'Look, I don't know enough about the problems but if I were you I would pick out two or three people, one of whom at least should be an anthropologist, one who knows about government organisations, and someone who's had some experience at dealing with racial problems. Give them a year to go around the country to talk to people, to listen to Aborigines, and tell you what they feel.' He said: 'That's a good idea.' And when he met me next time he said he was going to set up this Council for Aboriginal Affairs and that he wanted me to be the Chairman. He reminded me that I had said many times that I had been Governor of the Bank too long, and that I wanted another job. And he knew that Menzies had offered me various ambassadorial-type jobs but I'd said no, I wanted a job that was a challenge [he chuckles]. So Holt said, 'Well what's wrong with this, it's a challenge!'.

Did you have any idea what a challenge it really was at that stage?

No. I certainly didn't know the magnitude or the difficulties of it. I really saw it as an opportunity to do some things for Aborigines. I'd never forgotten my horror at the way in which Aboriginal people were being treated when I was a young teacher, and as an Australian I was ashamed of it. I felt I would respect myself less if I didn't accept it. And I did feel that perhaps I could do something about it.

And was that feeling vindicated — did you feel that during the time you were on the Council real progress was made?

Not very much while we were on the Council, because within a month or two of its establishment, and before it had been given any terms of reference, Holt drowned. And so I found myself working for John Gorton who certainly wasn't very interested in Aborigines, and who wouldn't give the Council any terms of reference. He said: 'Oh well, you go ahead and do what you think best and we'll work out some terms of reference later on.' Nevertheless, he is one of the Prime Ministers who I think is very underrated. Very! He's very interesting if you go back and think about the things that he did and the views that he expressed when he was Prime Minister. He did, in a way, anticipate quite a lot of the Whitlam attitudes. He was the first conservative Prime Minister who had any sense of autonomy in relation to the British or the Americans. He had a sense of Australian identity. Also, of course, he established the Film and Television School, and he really backed the development of film in Australia. He was capable of enthusiasm — picking up ideas — and very good at getting action taken.

After Gorton, you had a period dealing with Bill McMahon, and with Peter Howson as the Minister for Aboriginal Affairs and the Arts. That represented a fairly big change from Gorton, didn't it?

Oh yes, it was a very considerable drop down. Gorton was a very characteristic Australian and he didn't have any hostility to Aborigines. He said: 'They're Australians and they should have all the opportunities that other Australians have.' Anything which opened the white doors to Aborigines he was in favour of. He put up the money to educate their children — that was his initiative. He set up a fund to enable them to establish their own enterprises such as cattle stations. That was fine. But he didn't see any reason why they should be helped to be different. He would help them, generously, to be the same. Although he didn't object to their being different, he saw no reason why that should be a matter of policy. I think he was wrong ... but still.

Now McMahon was a much more limited man. Indeed, when I said that all our Prime Ministers had something — really, in essence, Billy had very little. He was thought to be a reasonably competent Treasurer — well, some people thought he was. But I think he became Prime Minister because the business people thought he'd been a successful Treasurer and, you know, favourable to them. But he never was strong enough. He was never sufficiently in charge of his Cabinet to be able to do things. When I agreed to work with him, it was on the probably improper understanding that he would change things for Aborigines. And he made some quite good statements promising these things. I can remember a conference in Cairns where he made a very good statement which was, in a sense, to accept differences and to abandon the assimilation objective. But on the following day the Minister for the Interior made statements to the effect that in the Northern Territory it was not going to be like that at all. And it wasn't. Ah, Billy was a weak man.

What was he like to deal with personally?

Well, except for the fact that he had a very unpleasant habit of ringing me up at all hours of the night to ask me what I thought about something or other, he was all right.

But you feel that on the whole Australia has been served reasonably well by its Prime Ministers?

Certainly as far down as Whitlam, but even — well even Fraser. I didn't like Fraser. I disapproved of a lot of things he said. But over recent years I have begun to feel that perhaps he was better than I judged him to be at the time. You know, he did introduce the land rights legislation, carried it through the Parliament; he did protect the Barrier Reef; he did carry on the movement towards independence for Papua New Guinea; and his attitude on South Africa has been, I think, good. It was the way that he achieved the elimination of the Whitlam Government that made the Dismissal such a stressful event and, to me, something which made it impossible for me to continue to work for the government. That was when I resigned from government. Not because a conservative government had taken over, but because it was done in a way which seemed to me to be not only unconstitutional but also immoral.

Going back one stage, what were your feelings when Whitlam came to power?

Like many people I felt that this could be the beginning of something really exceptional. His entry into the political scene had been marked by the involvement of people who were interested in a better quality of life. These were creative people, the intelligentsia, the artists, the poets, the people from all those little groups in town and in the country where people were beginning to get together to talk about how life could be better. He came in with a wave behind him, so to speak, sympathetic to change of that kind. And he was an orator. He was an impressive person and I really did feel that for the first time since Ben Chifley we would have a Prime Minister who had a vision of Australia as a place in which you could be proud to live. So when Whitlam asked me whether I would act as I had before for McMahon, in an economic capacity, I agreed. But I could see difficulties in it. And they were very real difficulties.

One of the conditions I made was that, if I were going to advise on economic matters, it had to be with the knowledge and consent of the Secretary to the Treasury and my successor at the Bank. They both agreed. But the agreement of the Secretary to the Treasury didn't stand up, because he was not prepared to accept a situation in which I would give advice incompatible with the Treasury view. And at one stage we had a real row about this. And so I went to Whitlam and told him that the Treasury was not happy about my acting as his adviser and that therefore I couldn't continue. And he said: 'Well, last week I asked you whether you would be Chairman of the Royal Commission on Australian Government Administration and you declined. Would you be prepared to do that now?' So that's how I came to be Chairman of the Royal Commission on Australian Government Administration. A mighty job, which unfortunately wasn't finished when Whitlam was dismissed — at which point I resigned from all government offices except that one. I didn't regard it as a government thing because it was set up independently.

This leads us to your whole role as a public servant, some would say the consummate public servant. How do you see the role of the public servant?

Well, I do think the circumstances are different now. I cannot remember any time when I was in the Public Service when I felt futile — when I felt that I was wasting my time. The people who were in Post-War Reconstruction and in the Treasury — I think we all felt that we were part of the team, that we all had the right not simply to say what we thought but to argue and to say to ministers: 'Look, you're wrong about that.'

I do myself believe that many public servants today feel that they are in a futile occupation. That they are not creative members of a policy team. That they're there to tell the minister what they think he wants to hear. Now, I think that's a tragedy. And I think it's one of the reasons why the bureaucracy is so cynical, why when they meet together they very rarely talk about policy. They talk about salaries and working conditions, particularly comparing themselves to people in the private sector. Many public servants used to work for less money because public service was something you wanted to do, where what you did really mattered. In more recent times I've heard public servants say: 'What's the good if all I'm allowed to do is give the minister reasons for doing what he wants to do?'

Was your style one of manipulation, or one of direct argument?

I daresay there was some degree of manipulation. You always used arguments which you thought would appeal to this or that minister. You used your character assessment as an instrument to achieve your agenda to some degree. And I suppose you do acquire some skills in assessing what will work. You don't put forward proposals to nationalise an industry to a very conservative government. But it doesn't stop you putting forward proposals which would have some of the same effects. I always felt that there were things which they could be persuaded to do which would be beneficial, and in accordance with things which I valued, and which I thought they might value.

Nugget Coombs dedicated himself wholeheartedly to trying to find solutions to the problems of Aborigines during the time of his chairmanship of the Council for Aboriginal Affairs. But it was a period in which he now feels that he learned more than he contributed, and in which many of his previous assumptions about the way forward for Aborigines were shaken, challenged and changed. Since that time he has thought deeply about Aboriginal issues and has developed his views about what the rest of Australia needs to do if reconciliation and justice are to be brought about.

Do you feel you achieved anything at all that was useful during your time at the Council for Aboriginal Affairs?

I think there have been changes which reflect activities that I and others on the Council were associated with, and some of them were good. But I think that what has happened since that time is that attitudes have become polarised. I think there are very many more people now in Australia who are aware of Aborigines and aware of their problems and are concerned about our treatment of them. But at the other extreme are the people who are hostile, who fear Aborigines, or distrust them, or hate them. And I believe that their attitudes are now more intense and actually their numbers may very well be greater too. In other words, when we began the people who hadn't even thought about it were probably the great majority. I think we greatly expanded the group who are concerned, who are beginning to understand, and who would like something to be done. On the other hand, the people who make money out of economic development, the people who want access to Aboriginal land, who see Aborigines as a barrier to their profitability, are devoting more resources to expressing fear and hostility than they were before. So you've got a polarisation, which has produced a position in which no government really has the guts to put forward a constructive policy, because they see more danger in the loss of support from those people who are hostile than benefit from those who would welcome change favourable to Aborigines. Now that's as I see it at the moment.

What changes do you want to see?

There are so many things. But my own feeling is that what we have tried to do from the beginning is to offer Aborigines a role in our society which they are unwilling to accept. What we want them to be is an unpaid or a poorly paid proletariat working for our enterprises. They have never been willing to accept that. They will starve rather than do that. So that if we want anything to come out of this what we have to do is to accept the fact that Aborigines are different. They do have a different way of seeing the world and understanding it. They have a different vision of what the place should be like. A fundamental thing in Aboriginal life is what Judge Blackburn described as a society which is run by laws, not by men or women. And I think that's important. No Aboriginal has the right to tell any other Aboriginal what he or she must do. Autonomy is fundamental to their way of thinking. We have been prepared to spend money on them, we're prepared to offer them this and that and to educate them. What we won't do is allow them to be different. I know I've been involved to some degree in making the wrong choice in these things. When I was involved in the Council for Aboriginal Affairs I put a high priority on spending money to offer them some of the benefits of our society: facilities for education, money for enterprises — not access to land.

But you have since dedicated yourself to trying to get a treaty.

Yes.

You're a practical man. You're someone who's tried to find solutions. In what way is a treaty a solution?

It depends on what's in the treaty. A treaty embodies a relationship. And what we need is a relationship which says for Aborigines: 'Yes, you are here. You're part of Australia, but you're different from us and we guarantee your right to be different. And we will give you access to a fair share of the resources of the continent, so that you can make your differences effective there.'

What's your vision of how they might live if all of this came to pass? I mean, some people fear a sort of apartheid arising if there is a separation. What kind of a pattern of living can you see emerging?

It would be lots of different patterns of living. At the minimal level they would have their own land and the right to use the resources of that land. They would get some share of the common resources to enable them to conduct their own services for education, for health and so on. They should have their own institutions, their own organisations for those. I think the homeland movement is a clear demonstration of what they want. They want the right to be on land which they believe is theirs, and to be able to conduct their society in accordance with their ways of thinking, educate their children in relation to that, and conduct their own ceremonies.

This is not incompatible with their also having access to our education and training — which doesn't mean that they must wholly accept what we do — but they learn how to live in our society, and still continue to think of themselves and act as Aborigines. There will be pop bands, ballet companies, theatre companies, painters and sculptors, and they can express the separateness of their view of the world in those ways. Those things are happening on a far greater scale than white people are aware of. And you'll find them turning up as lawyers and in due course they'll even be turning up as doctors, despite the hostility of doctors to such an idea. But their medical programs will be different. We are talking about the virtue of diversity.

I am impressed by the things that happen in Aboriginal society wherever they are in a position to make decisions for themselves. What was wrong with apartheid in South Africa was that it was compulsory. There's nothing wrong with people becoming like us if that's what they want to do, and that option should always be open.

Have you got any other ideas or schemes for the ways in which Aborigines might be able to find a place in Australia that's suitable and they're happy with?

One idea that I've got arises from the fact that even now Aborigines who live in Melbourne will tell you, 'I'm a Worageree'. They think of themselves not as Aborigines but as Yonyu or Worageree or Murrays or whatever. They have tribal groups, language groups, with which they still identify even though they may have lost the language. Now suppose we had, for every one of those tribal language groups, at least one area which we set aside as an Aboriginal national park. The people would manage it as a national park while using it for traditional tribal things. They could have arrangements for their children to spend school holidays there from Melbourne or Sydney or wherever and learn about the plants and the animals of the country that their ancestors knew. They could be told the stories of the way in which the land came to be as it is. This wouldn't prevent those national parks serving *our* purposes as well. Indeed, it would add very greatly to their effectiveness from that point of view. In a study carried out at Uluru (Ayers Rock) — asking tourists why they came there — a very large proportion of the people said they came because they knew that it was Aboriginal country and they wanted to have some experience of Aboriginal people and Aboriginal ways of living. And if these parks were consciously being used for the maintenance and the preservation of language, the practice of traditional dances, the bark and rock paintings and engravings, that would add very greatly to the interest of those national parks. And it could become a very interesting aspect of Australian life.

It sounds like a very good idea. How could this idea actually happen — what do you think is needed for it to happen?

Well, you see, I think that what is important is not that they get this offered by us — to be really effective it's something which should be part of *their* political program. They should *ask* for it, perhaps on a regional basis. Every tribal group should have in its demands — We want our national park!

At about the same time that Nugget Coombs's official interest in Aboriginal policy began, an opportunity to expand his interest in the arts presented itself. He was already Chairman of the Elizabethan Theatre Trust, which was founded in 1953 to support activity in the performing arts. But it was Harold Holt who approved a broader vision of government involvement in support for the arts. In 1967 the Australian Council for the Arts (later to be reconstituted as the Australia Council), was set up under Coombs's chairmanship.

In a sense that happened because, in talking with Holt about whether I would take the Aboriginal job, I mentioned my involvement in the Elizabethan Theatre Trust and said, 'I think that's important, that arts work'. And of course Holt was interested in the arts himself. It was then he had this idea that, instead of supporting a semi-autonomous body like the Elizabethan Theatre Trust, they should set up a government-sponsored body to advise them and to administer their patronage.

So that was actually Harold Holt's idea?

Yes, it was.

What did you see as your real purpose at the Council for the Arts?

Somebody once asked me what I thought was the function of a bureaucrat in relation to the arts, and I said: 'A good bureaucrat makes other people's dreams come true.'

And in what way did the Council help to make people's dreams come true?

I think it was an organisational thing. You see, these things were already happening. Dedicated people had been fighting over the years to make things happen. The Council acted as an intermediary between them and the government. People who understand the problems of the government but also are sympathetic with the arts — that was my image of the role of the Council. And it was like that with film. There had been people who'd been trying to get film things started, but the fact that there was the Council enabled us to set up a Committee consisting of Phillip Adams, Barry Jones and Peter Coleman. And we could feed ideas to the Prime Minister, keep him interested. So that role of an intermediary is a very important one and it's one which in a way has been destroyed, you know, by the bureaucracy. Somebody who is not a public servant is regarded with suspicion. Now, a very good example of that was when I was Chairman of the Council. I set up, through the Elizabethan Theatre Trust, an arrangement with the companies that ran the opera and the ballet and the drama so that, when they had a success, they would deposit a substantial share of the profits with the Trust on the understanding that, if they had a failure, we would carry the financial risk . . .

A 'rainy day' fund.

A 'rainy day' fund. Now, it went very well. Fortunately, most of the losses were fairly moderate and we had some quite big successes, so there was a fund built up. But the day I left, the Treasury set to work and they abolished that fund, not because it wasn't a good idea but because it was money out there that they thought was government money. You can't keep money if you're not part of the bureaucracy!

Despite his age, Nugget Coombs has kept on working hard for the causes he believes in. He is someone who has always looked ahead and been deeply aware of the potential effects of today's decisions on tomorrow's reality. His views on how he sees the future evolving, and the question of whether the vision and values that have sustained him all his life will be seen as relevant in the world of the twenty-first century, are a cause of some anxiety to him.

You're still working hard for change and improvement in the world. Do you feel optimistic or pessimistic about the future generally?

I think I feel fundamentally pessimistic, because I think we are not dealing with the fundamental problems of our society. I suppose the difficulties are expressed best if you look at the population issue.

You see, the population is continuing to increase at a fantastic rate, and it is just going to be impossible for the population, as forecast, to be fed, clothed and all the rest of it. It's impossible even if we transform all the ways in which our society is run so that we too accept a lower rate of consumption of resources, so that the rest of the world can come closer to the kind of lifestyle that we live. I think Malthus, 180 or 200 years ago or whatever it was, said that unless we learn to control the growth of population it will be imposed on us by famine, pestilence and war. Now, we have famine in very many countries. There's food, but they can't afford it. They are starving except for some internationally organised charity. Pestilence — well AIDS is a pretty good form of pestilence. And we have wars all over the world.

But even so, despite those things, the population continues to rise. And I just don't see any way in which catastrophe can be avoided. At one time when I was particularly interested in this population thing, I went to a friend of mine who was a biologist and I said: 'Is there any other species on the earth which has this rapidly rising population?' 'Oh', he said, 'yes, there are quite a lot of them, particularly insects, but others too.' And I said: 'Well what happens? They can't go on rising forever.' He said: 'No, it rises slowly and then it becomes exponential and goes up fast.' I said: 'Well what happens when it gets up here — to the top of the graph?' He said: 'Well, it collapses. It doesn't flatten out, it doesn't drift down, it collapses. Sometimes it collapses into extinction, but most frequently it *almost* disappears — there are a few left and in due course the rise starts again.' Now, I don't see any reason to believe that human beings are going to be any different. I think our population will go on exploding and there will be a point where it will collapse for some reason, perhaps the one that Malthus identified, but there are probably plenty of others.

But you can't be entirely without hope for the future because you keep on working hard at the causes that you care about.

Well, you know, work is a habit! [He laughs.] What would I do if I stopped? You see, I've learned to live with the conviction that a lot of your efforts are going to be unsuccessful, but that that's not a good reason for not trying. My wife said that I can't leave things alone if I think they should be different. Lots of people think the world should be different, but she said about me that I'm just conceited enough to think that I can do something about it.

And despite the frustrations that you sometimes encounter you have been able to do something about many things. Looking back over your long life and all the different things you've been involved in, what would you say was your greatest achievement? Something that you feel really proud of?

Well, I have four children: they all have interesting jobs; none of them seriously takes drugs other than alcohol; and they all still talk to me. They don't approve of me, but they still talk to me! Now I think in a personal sense that's not a bad achievement.

So in looking at achievement you look at it in human terms rather than in terms of any of the jobs you've done?

Oh, well, those things — I think about them, and I get pleasure from some recollections of them, and I have disappointments and bitterness about others of them. But I think I've been very very lucky to go through life and always have interesting things to do and to be paid to do them. It's miraculous, isn't it? I've never been out of work. After the application I made to join the Education Department of Western Australia when I was 17 I've never actually applied for a job. There's always been one waiting.

Why do you think that was? What is it about you that has made you someone whose advice was sought by Prime Ministers and who has always been offered jobs — what distinguished you that made people see those possibilities in you?

Well, it's partly luck. And maybe my wife's remark is not without some relevance: that I'm conceited enough to think I can do things.

But you persuaded others to think that too.

But you see, people look for advice from someone who thinks he knows the answers. I like trying to understand situations and I enjoy the process of trying to produce change that is humane and moving in the right direction. I think those are qualities which encourage people to ask you for advice.

Was there often a lot of stress in your life?

Oh, yes, there've been some exceedingly stressful times, exceedingly.

Do you remember any particular time that you found really hard to get through?

I found the Cold War period — a period of division inside Australian society where fundamental political and religious attitudes brought people into conflict — very hard. I personally was affected and my relationship with other people was made more difficult.

This was during the ALP/DLP split?

Well, that was part of it. These issues became most dominant for me in relation to my private life.

Your wife was a Catholic, wasn't she?

Yes, she was.

And did you have political differences?

My wife's attitude to political matters is quite different from mine.

Did you feel that your work ever took you too much away from your family?

Oh Lord yes! Well, I mean, it posed problems. The critical time I suppose was when the war came, and I was lent to the Commonwealth to act as Economist to the Treasury. I moved to Canberra. Now that had a very profound effect because it imposed on my wife a transformation of the lifestyle which she was building for herself in Sydney. She was very interested in music and she had enrolled at the Conservatorium. She played the violin and belonged to a chamber music group and was interested in musical composition. We came to Canberra. It was 1939, and you have absolutely no idea what an appalling place Canberra was from the point of view of a woman who was interested in things other than bringing up children and playing cards. And that continued. And then I went to Melbourne to run rationing and then back to Canberra for the Post-War Reconstruction job, with work commitments taking me away all the time. So when we came back to Canberra my wife said: 'Look, you're away such a lot. Why can't I live somewhere where I like living? Where it's not a cultural desert.' It seemed a very reasonable proposition and we bought a house in Sydney, a house that has been the base for the family ever since. And that was where the children came into existence and grew up. It wasn't a separation, my wife and I didn't divorce or anything of that kind, but we did establish a pattern of life which accepted the fact that her pattern was not the same as mine.

Looking back over your life, what has been your biggest disappointment?

I should say that certainly my biggest disappointment is that we have just not been prepared to accept the right of Aborigines to be different — to be part of our society and welcome in it, but to preserve differences which are important to them. I remember Whitlam saying: 'Until we accept Aboriginal rights, and act on that, we are all demeaned.' And I feel that that's a truth, that the thing which demeans Australia and Australians more than anything ... is their failure ... to act on that issue ...

This moment in my interview with Nugget was quite extraordinary.
The strength of his feeling caused a tremor to pass through his whole
body. There could be no doubt that he meant every word that he
said. Silence descended on the room and he wept quietly for a full
minute. Then he wiped his eyes and the interview continued.

Did you, through the course of your life as public servant, banker,
intellectual, adviser — did you have any guiding principles that were
consistently there to help you to know how to respond to situations and to
make decisions?

My mother was very serious in her belief in the golden rule that a
neighbour's welfare is not merely a nice idea but something we
should act upon. And I continued to believe in that. I've always
been guided by Ben Chifley's statement — you know, the Light on
the Hill — that the government and the society have an obligation
to help people who are in difficulties, to ease their problems. You
have standards by which you protect the weak and the damaged. In
other words, I believe that society has a responsibility for its
members, particularly for those members who are unlucky, weak or
helpless in some way. I think that very general kind of philosophy is
the reason why I've been an interventionist, why I've felt that
governments should do things to help.

In a way my concern about the economic system was that I felt
the economic system was society's attempt to provide some greater
security and greater basis for a decent lifestyle for people generally.
That is why I feel out of sympathy with contemporary economics,
which doesn't concern itself with individuals or their needs but
simply with a system which operates like a machine, where you're
not concerned with the purposes of the machine or the results it
has achieved but only with whether the wheels continue to turn.
That's why I don't like economic rationalism. It is not a way in
which people are enabled to live better, to be happier, to be more
civilised. It's a way of enabling production to be maximised, for
wealth to be maximised, for property to be maximised. Well, I'm
not interested in an economic system or in an economic theory
which is geared solely to those kinds of purposes. It's possible to
have a capitalist economic system which is subject to discipline,
which is subject to some degree of responsibility to the society, and
I think we had the beginnings of it here in Australia. But we can't
do it on the basis of economic rationalism.

What are the values that you would like to see embodied in our society's institutions?

I think the purpose of all institutions in our society is essentially to fulfil a function in the service of that society. I think that this also applies to the commercial sector of our community. It is possible to have a commercial sector which is not entirely motivated by greed. It's one of the reasons why I regretted the passing of Keynesian economics. That was an economic system based upon the belief that the economic system is society's institution for the process of giving people access to a livelihood — to enable them to feed themselves and their children, to clothe themselves and to find the material basis for a civilised, dignified human existence. That in my view is what the economic system is for. It is not for the purpose of enabling individuals to become wealthy, nor is it for the purpose of persuading people that happiness comes from possessions and from access to this or that service. On the contrary, I think that from a fundamental point of view of civilised human life those things are largely irrelevant. Some of the happiest people, some of the morally best societies in the world, are ones which value poverty, which value doing without; particularly those which value using whatever they have to assist — pinching Ben Chifley's words — those who are unlucky, those who are ill-informed, or in other ways handicapped. Those are the motivations which appeal to me. And they were the kind of things which, to the extent that I had a choice, motivated the way I wanted myself and the institutions for which I was responsible to go.

In late 1995 Nugget had a stroke while living in his hut in the Northern Territory. At the time, I was working on this text, preparing it for publication. I went to see him in Concord Hospital, in the public ward assigned to the rehabilitation of elderly male stroke victims. At that stage of his recovery his speech was still seriously impaired and he was paralysed down one side of his body. But his eyes were bright and full of intelligence and his grin broke out in recognition as I approached his bed. It was clear that I was going to have to do all the talking, so I began by reminding him of some of the more amusing stories he had told me in the interview. He laughed with pleasure at these memories but was frustrated at his inability to command the words he needed in order to respond. I explained to him that I was at that very time working on this book. I said to him:

'I have been living with you over the past few days on the screen of my computer. Your words made me feel that I was with you. Now I can see you in the flesh. But there are many different ways of existing.' This phrase greatly appealed to him. To my astonishment he repeated it with perfect enunciation. When I left he looked at me with his direct clear gaze and said again: 'There are many different ways of existing.'

Since that time Nugget has made excellent progress, speaking quite well and walking with the aid of a frame. He is now into his nineties. His understanding and intelligence remain undiminished.

Nancy Bird Walton

Flying Free

*N*ancy Bird's family name was prophetic. But apart from that pointer to the skies there was little about this tiny person to suggest that she would make her name as one of the pioneers of aviation in Australia.

She left school at 13 in order to keep house for her father and throughout her life has maintained a strong and conservative concept of femininity. She learned to fly at a time when rich women did it as a hobby, but for her it was always a financial struggle. And she undertook the pursuit of this passion against a background of consistent discouragement from most people and only intermittent support from a few.

The discouragement arose entirely from the fact that she was a woman. Flying was considered dangerous and difficult and *therefore unsuitable for a woman. But it is significant that, at a time when so many of the young male aviators were crashing their planes, against all predictions Nancy never had an accident.*

Nancy's story is the story of the way an obsession can override obstacles. Her practicality and striking energy were the obvious qualities she brought to the task of making her dream of flying come true. But in the end, as was expected of women at that time, she opted to place the demands of husband and family above her love of flying.

The question is what it was that made Nancy Bird succeed in participating in the pioneering days of aviation in Australia, against all odds. And having achieved this goal why did she, in the end, make the life choices that she did?

Nancy Bird Walton was born in 1915 in the little town of Kew in northern New South Wales, where her father had bought a country store. She was the second child in a family of what later became six children. Within a year or two of her birth they moved to a small township a mile away, where she spent her preschool years.

NBW Kew is about 30 miles north of Taree but nobody knows it's there. In fact if you didn't put the brakes on you'd shoot through it on the way to Brisbane without noticing it existed. I was born with the aid of a midwife. There were no doctors. It was 30 miles away and a long drive in the sulky for the doctor. I was nearly lost, but this wonderful woman Mrs Ritchie was a person that went through storm and tempest, flooded rivers, flooded creeks to help the women in that district to deliver their children. She saved my life!

RH *So you are here as a result of a woman who was prepared to face hardship in order to help others. That seems like a kind of foreshadowing of what your own life was to bring in the far west.*

I hadn't thought of that, but yes, that's true. The women were completely dependent upon her to deliver their children. And so I was born in my mother's bed in a little tiny house. Soon we moved to Kendall, named for the poet, and that's where I spent the first four or five years of my life. It's a beautiful part of Australia. That's all that I remember of my early childhood — that lovely country town. When I was about five or six we moved to Collaroy where I went to a little school called the Collaroy Private School run by two old maids who taught us how to be little ladies. We had a house which now is in the midst of Collaroy but it was in the back streets then. Later we built another house on the hill, looking over Long Reef and out to the Pacific Ocean. It was there that I remember getting that feeling of the distant view. And the most vivid memory of my childhood is of an aeroplane making a forced landing on Dee Why beach. Even today I can see that aeroplane on Dee Why beach! It was an old First World War aeroplane and it seemed to have a magnetic attraction for me.

How old were you when you saw that plane land?

I'd say about eight.

Did you think then that you'd like to fly one?

I don't think I thought about flying then but there was a magnetic attraction in that aeroplane. It seemed as if there were a straight line between me and it. And I remember another time when I went to school in Manly, to Brighton College, one day an aeroplane was doing sky writing above the school. Again it was like a magnetic line between me and the aeroplane. That, too, is a most vivid memory. I was going into a sewing lesson, the bell went, everybody else went in — I stood watching that aeroplane. I got into trouble because I was late getting into school to continue with the dirty pillowslip I was making.

What do you think it was that really attracted you to flying? When were your first dreams of flying?

My first dreams of flying were as a tiny child. I don't think I would have ever revealed it, if General Valerie André, the only woman general in the world, a Frenchwoman, hadn't said in her autobiography: 'As a small child I used to dream I could fly.' *I* used to dream I could fly. I used to dream I could lift myself up over the telegraph poles when the lions and tigers were chasing me in my childish nightmares. But I would have thought it was a silly thing to say if General Valerie André hadn't said it. I don't know what it was, but mother said that I was jumping off a fence at the age of four with outstretched arms, calling myself an eppyplane. Now that was 1919, so it must have been the conversation of the adults about the England/Australia air race that was won by Ross and Keith Smith that inspired me to be an aeroplane, to climb the fence and jump off just like an aeroplane.

When people asked you then what you were going to be when you grew up, what would you say?

I didn't know you could fly for a living. I once thought I might be a nurse and wrapped a teatowel around my head and sat studying a book on all the things a nurse should know. You see I left school really early. The Depression hit Australia and my father bought a country store. I was taken out of school early to manage the household for my father; to be the bookkeeper and to look after my father and my uncle. My mother stayed in the city for the education of my brothers and sisters and so, aged 14, I was standing on my own two feet quite firmly in the country. I left school just before I was 14.

Why were you the one chosen to go with your father, rather than your elder sister?

My elder sister was the student — she liked school and was a good student. I was the practical one who liked to help in the house and do all the things to help mother, and I didn't like school very much either. So I often stayed away because mother needed help. We couldn't afford hired help and mother really just needed an extra pair of hands with five little children. It was quite understandable.

Was it hard to go off at 13 to be housekeeper and general help to your father?

No, we didn't think so at the time. I was used to doing things. At the age of eight, I had given a fete outside the fence for the Collaroy Children's Hospital. I was a very practical sort of person. No, I didn't mind. It wasn't hard at all though it was very primitive. We had no electricity. We had oil lamps that had to be cleaned every morning. We had a fuel stove. We had a great big bathtub that was put in front of the fire every Saturday night to have a bath. We carried water in four-gallon kerosene tins to the laundry. I did the laundry. I did have an old black lady to come in to help scrub the kitchen floor sometimes, but I wasn't above doing it myself. I just did everything that was expected of me. In fact I like to be able to say: 'I have served potatoes at my father's country store and I have been a guest at Buckingham Palace.' So if you can do those things and not lose your head — it's a jolly good idea. Keeps your feet on the ground!

Was there ever any suggestion made that it was a lot to ask of a child, or in those days was it quite the natural thing to do?

Children helped their parents in those days. They pulled their weight in the family. All the dairy farmers around that area had children who helped. They started in the dairy at five and six in the morning before they went to school. And in the Depression people didn't ask whether they were trained to do a job or not. They just did it. They had to! People lived on the river bank and their children walked to school and helped in every possible way. Children left school early. You'd see a bullock team driving along the road and probably the 12-year-old son walking behind his father, looking after the rear part of the team. This was up in the Manning River district. By that time my father had moved there.

Was his store a success?

Yes it was. He was very enterprising. He would ride a horse way up into the mountains to Cooplacaraba station and collect orders, and then he would send his horse team — four horses — right up into the mountains to buy gold and rabbit skins. People had streamed out of the city during the Depression to search for gold, to live on rabbits and golden syrup up in the mountains, trying to scratch a living out of the soil. In those days of course there was no way of crossing the rivers except by horse team. There were no cars up there. You could count on one hand the number of cars in the entire district. That was a great luxury, to own a car. We had a cream truck. My father sent the cream truck up to collect the cream for the Wingham butter factory. And incidentally that horse team was driven by a First World War pilot who had been grounded because he had buzzed a sulky somewhere and there had been an accident. And in the Depression he had taken this job with my dad. He used to terrify the locals. He would race down the mountains with the brakes off and swim the flooded rivers with the horses. But he was the man who taught Ulm to fly. And after Kingsford Smith flew the Pacific in 1928 they must have given him a present because he bought an aeroplane and went back into flying, barnstorming around the country like so many of the First World War pilots did. But he was killed in a motor car.

And his story seemed glamorous to you?

Oh yes, Bill Wilson's story was a glamorous one. He inspired quite a few people, I think, in those early days of aviation.

What was life like for you there?

Mt George was a beautiful country town with the Manning River running through it and orange trees growing along the river. We swam in the river, swinging ourselves out on the weeping willows and jumping in. It was a good life but we worked hard. We got up early in the morning. My father was a workaholic and expected everybody else to be. You started at six or seven o'clock in the morning with a cold wash from the tank. You'd tap the tank to see how much water was in it; that was very important. At the end of the day, when I got the dinner, it was too late to get out in that beautiful sunshine and I think in my heart — when I was doing the books and I'd look out that little window — this is probably when I felt that with flying I could get out in the open air. And when I was 13 I went into Wingham on the cream truck, rattling cans behind me, and went to an air pageant.

That's where I first found out what it meant to fly in an aeroplane. I went up for a flight — a ten-shilling flight — and then I gave a whole week's wages — £1 — and asked the pilot if he'd do some aerobatics with me, and he did! And so began the ruling passion of my life. I then bought a book on flying and studied it.

Everybody laughed at me, of course. My father said that he wouldn't mind if I learned to fly, but of course it was about three years before I actually did start learning and by then he felt differently about it.

How differently?

Well, first of all he said he couldn't afford to keep a crippled daughter. Then, it would kill my mother if anything happened to me. And of course aeroplanes did crash a bit in those days. And also I'd become a bit indispensable to him as a bookkeeper and a housekeeper.

So how did you get around him?

I just told him that I had finally saved up the £200 I needed. Kingsford Smith had come barnstorming around the country too, and I met him at Wingham giving flights. Kingsford Smith told me he was opening a flying school and I said that I would come down to the city and become one of his pupils. I think that I was one of his very first pupils, if not his first, when he opened that flying school in August 1933 at Mascot. And Dad wasn't at all pleased that I was leaving him. But my elder sister and my younger sister also later went up there and 'did time' at Mt George.

Was there any suggestion that it wasn't right for a girl to learn to fly?

No, because it was just coming out of the Depression and the flying schools had had such a bad time that they would willingly teach anybody to fly who had enough money to pay for lessons. Women did fly but they flew as a sport. But everybody who flew, with the exception of one woman engineer pilot, May Bradford, and myself, was of independent means and flew for the pleasure of it.

On a wage of £1 a week how could you manage to save up £200?

Well, I got some insurance too, when I was 16. My father had bought insurance policies for all of us and that helped considerably too. And I went without everything that young girls like, you know. I'd throw material on the floor and cut out a pattern myself, even though I knew very little about sewing. And I was economical. We were very economical in those days. I'd do without things.

So you knew that you really wanted to do this and you got the £200 together and you simply told your father you were going?

That's true. I said I was coming down to live with mother and to go out to Mascot to learn to fly. After all, I'd told Kingsford Smith I would be joining him, so I had to keep my word, didn't I!

But what did your mother think of it?
She accepted it. I think that's one of the advantages of being in a big family. You can do things a little independently that you can't do if you're an only child, and too precious. I'd made up my mind and my parents didn't try to stop me. That's why I'm grateful to them — very grateful. Because I know many people who would have liked to learn to fly in 1933 but their parents wouldn't allow them to.

Looking back on your whole childhood, what were the things that you learned then that have really stood you in good stead for the rest of your life?
I think I learned that if there is a job to do, get in and do it. Don't say 'it isn't my job'. Don't avoid doing things that have to be done. If the potatoes have got to be peeled then get in and peel them. If the napkins have to go out on the line go and put them out. If there is something to do, do it. Don't just hang around waiting for somebody else to do it. I think I learned that because I was one of a family.

How did you get on when you went to the Kingsford Smith school?
I just rang up and made the appointment with Charles Kingsford Smith. I took the tram out to Mascot, walked from the station, about a mile to the aerodrome, and had my first lesson with Charles Kingsford Smith on the 11th of August, 1933.

What was the set-up at the school? Were there other people on the staff there?
Well, there was his engineer, Tommy Petherbridge, who died with Charles Kingsford Smith. Bruce Cowan was just a little boy, an apprentice who used to sweep the hangars. There was Charles Kingsford Smith's secretary, Marg McGrath, and John Stanage, his manager, who was married to Kingsford Smith's niece. That's all.

How many other pupils were there?
They just came and went. There weren't any other pupils at that time. Jack Kingsford Smith was learning to fly, I think as the guest of his uncle. I don't think he was a paying pupil. Another woman came out but she couldn't learn to fly — they just couldn't teach her. She was a nurse. Then others: some civilian airforce pilots, people that belonged to the Civil Airforce; a boy by the name of Peter Bjelke-Petersen; and Bill Perton, a delightful young man that I later fell in love with. Then there was Harold Durant who had flown in the First World War, and there were people like that who would just come out to do an hour or so's flying. There was Jim Broadbent, a famous pilot who kept his aeroplane there and often asked me to fly with him.

Nancy Bird started flying simply because she wanted to fly. She had no idea of where it might take her or how it might relate to earning a living. She was so small and slight she had to sit on a pile of cushions to reach the controls. There was little formal instruction provided and she learned from experience and from what she could glean from other pilots. She enjoyed the atmosphere of friendly camaraderie at Mascot and the feeling of being part of a small pioneering band who were discovering together the joys and dangers of flying.

We used to sit in the grass at Mascot and watch other people fly. You learned from other people's experiences. The hangar talk — people laughed about it and said flying people get together and all they do is talk aviation. That's perfectly true. Even watching other people fly, you say: 'Now pull back a bit, get the nose up a bit, get it down.' You literally fly them on to the ground! And then you hear of what experienced pilots came through — near misses and all sorts of things. And that was the only textbook we had.

How long did it take you to qualify as a pilot?

I started on the 11th of August, 1933 and I had my 'A' licence on the 28th of September.

That was quick.

Well, I flew in the mornings and I flew in the afternoons. When you get to Mascot from Manly you might as well stay there for the day. Sometimes Charles Kingsford Smith would pick me up from the Manly Wharf when he was in Sydney. He had this beautiful silver Armstrong Siddeley and of course all of the people who came on the boat would look and say, 'Charles Kingsford Smith!'. After all, he'd already flown the Pacific, circumnavigated the world, crossed the Tasman and he was famous. Very famous! In fact sometimes when we drove in from Mascot and we drove alongside the tram, people and the tram guard would turn around and shake hands with him. And people in the tram would all stand up and look out at Charles Kingsford Smith in his open-topped Armstrong Siddeley. That was quite a sensation, so I felt very important then in such company. But when I drove with John Stanage in his third-hand Chev jalopy, nobody took any notice at all.

I used to stay there as much as possible trying to learn what I could about aviation. There was no syllabus in those days. For the 'A' licence test all we did was go up to 1500 feet, cut the motor of the aircraft and come down in a series of gliding turns. You had no brakes so you had to come over the fence as low as you possibly could to get in and sit down on the paddock that was called Mascot. There were no runways or anything like that and no radio. We did a series of figure eights over the windsock and the building that housed the aeroclub and that was part of the test too. People say it must have been hard then. I think it was a lot easier than it is now. Now there is a lot of air regulations to learn and a lot of study to do.

What kind of plane?

It was a Gipsy Moth. That's the grandmother of the Tiger Moth. Everybody knows about the Tiger Moth but it was the Gipsy Moth in those days, prior to the development of the Tiger Moth.

During the period that you were doing this initial learning did you ever doubt that you'd done the right thing or was it all as exciting as you had hoped?

Well, it was an ambition and it was a dedication to aviation. We were all very defensive about aviation in those days. People who flew were seen as daredevils or people who took risks and aviation hadn't been accepted as a means of transport in Australia then. Kingsford Smith was trying desperately to introduce flying as a means of transport. He'd started his airline in 1929 and they went broke when the Southern Cloud disappeared and wasn't found for 29 years. And then other companies started up, but they all went broke. People weren't ready to fly and we were very defensive about aviation. Whenever there was an accident it was always the pilot's fault, never the aeroplane's. We were just so dedicated to aviation!

Had you in a sense fallen in love with flying?

No, I didn't feel it was love, but you know we were just so determined to continue, to make it a success, to fly and to keep flying. I know that when we arrived at Mascot every morning we'd look around the perimeter of the aerodrome to see who'd spun in on the 'S' turns. Often there was somebody on the edge of the airfield in the Chinese Gardens with the tail in the air. One day there was Sergeant Brown, who built a beautiful Moth to fly in the England–Australia 1934 air race. He'd had engine failure on take-off and gone straight into Cooks River. He was killed, of course, instantly. One day it was Dr Lee Brown in the first Tiger Moth to come into Australia. You know, you could feel it as you got near the airport there'd been an accident. We all rushed down to Kiama where he'd crashed the Tiger Moth and I remember seeing the blood all over the cockpit. They'd rushed him off to hospital and, of course, he didn't survive either. But he and his wife Ainslee Brown had been the first people I'd ever gone out to Mascot with.

This didn't make you feel like taking your goggles and cap and going home?

No, no. It never had that effect on us at all. And when the press wanted to take pictures of crashed aeroplanes we all ganged up on them. But the very same people, you know, wanted the support of the press when they wanted to do any long-distance flying. People like Charles Kingsford Smith or Jean Batten who did those long-distance flights needed the help of the press and the oil companies who were the real pioneers of aviation in Australia. They were the people who supported Charles Kingsford Smith and the others.

I suppose the oil companies saw potential profits in the future of aviation.

They were more farsighted than any government, I can assure you. The Vacuum and Shell oil companies and Castrol by way of Lord Wakefield, you know, sponsored many flights. They were the people who pioneered aviation.

What I'm wanting to understand is what it was about aviation that got this dedication and loyalty rather than a sense that it really was very dangerous. What was it about it that was so attractive?

I just don't know, I just don't know. I can't put my finger on it. My teenage was through the 1920s when aviation was developing. The pilots of the First World War came back. And even before that we had a history in aviation going back to Hargreaves lifting himself off the cliffs of Stanwell Park before the turn of the century. So we were trying to fly. And I suppose we just believed in aviation. But perhaps Amy Johnson's flight in Australia in 1930 — I can remember being a bit jealous of her, in fact I was very envious of her flying from England to Australia. Then she was followed by the German aviatrix, Elly Beinhorn. I had already had my first trial instructional flight when I went to hear her speak in 1932 and saw her little aeroplane that she'd flown all the way from Germany in, and I just thought she was the most marvellous person I'd ever seen. My ambition was to be like Elly, to be as attractive, as feminine. Now she's one of my best friends! So it's really rather wonderful how the wheel turns. And then Jean Batten, of course. I was already flying when Jean Batten flew to Australia and she, I think, was the greatest aviatrix of the early pioneer days because she did everything in a single-engine low-horsepower aeroplane — a 90-horsepower Gipsy Moth. Twice she started out from England and crashed. And when she achieved it the whole of Australia was thrilled to pieces. Then she got a 200-horsepower Percival Gull, flew the Atlantic, and flew from England to New Zealand and that record stood for 44 years!

Nancy Bird was enormously excited and inspired by the great women aviators who set records by pioneering long-distance flights. But by this time all the important records seemed to have been broken and sponsorship for long-distance flights was going to be hard to get. Nancy faced the reality that, in her economic circumstances, if she were going to continue flying she would have to think more commercially. One thing she clearly needed was a commercial flying licence. She studied hard for the examination at the Kingsford Smith School. She went to the aeroclub and had free lessons in blindflying from George Littlejohn, the man who later perished with Ulm crossing the Pacific. But there was another problem. She also needed instruction in navigation and she could not afford the lessons.

One day at the aeroclub I asked P. G. Taylor if he would teach me something about navigation to help me out. Of course I couldn't have picked a better person. He was the greatest aerial navigator of the time — absolutely wonderful! It was P. G. Taylor who navigated Charles Kingsford Smith across the Tasman to New Zealand on the second and third trips. It was P. G. Taylor who climbed out on the strut and took oil from one dead engine, and transferred it to the other engine, which literally saved the life of Charles Kingsford Smith. The Southern Cross limped back to Mascot while he did that six times — not once but six times — behind the slipstream of that great motor. It was the most courageous thing that had ever been done. And then he pioneered the Indian Ocean just after the war and it was he who pioneered the South Pacific Ocean — Australia to Chile in the flyingboat. So he was a very very great man. Next to Charles Kingsford Smith I think he was the greatest aviator we had. So I really couldn't have had a better teacher. But of course in those days we mostly flew on road maps. You just drew a line between A and B measured off every 20 or 40 miles and made checkpoints of towns or railways or mountains or whatever it might be. But of course west of Bourke there were so few roads I just had the little map they gave you at the garage.

And did you get your commercial licence without any trouble?

Oh yes, yes. I received my commercial licence in — I think it was April, 1935. I was congratulated by the Department of Civil Aviation. They thought my examination was better than my flying! But then there was the problem of how I could earn my living. So I decided to go barnstorming in my Gipsy Moth, which my father and my great-aunt had put up the money for me to buy. And that was the first time a woman had thought of barnstorming. The men from the First World War and the boys who had learned to fly in the Depression said there was nothing in it. But I was prepared to give it a shot because what else could I do? I had nothing to lose once I had an aeroplane. At least I could try flying from town to town following the shows and the race meetings and gaining experience and making enough to fly on to the next place. I went to the Shell Company. We got out a map of New South Wales, I got a list from the *Country Life* newspaper of all the shows and race meetings and where they were — Tamworth, Inverell, Moree — and planned that I would land in the nearest paddock and hope that I would get some paying passengers at ten shillings a flight.

Now, I had to have a co-pilot because you can't stop the engine of a Gipsy Moth every time you've got a passenger to put in. So I looked around to see if any other woman would come with me. And I found a wonderful co-pilot in Peggy McKillop — she'd been flying for two years longer than I had but she was doing the same commercial licence exam. I asked her, and of course Peggy would fly with anyone to get some free flying, so she was delighted. I told her I'd give her ten per cent of the takings and she said: 'You don't have to worry about that, I just like to fly for free.' She was very wealthy, she had a private income of £5 a month, but she had another great advantage that I didn't realise at the time. She'd gone to Rose Bay Convent from the age of six and she knew all.the country Catholic aristocrats, who provided us with wonderful hospitality when we travelled. This meant that we could avoid staying at the two-bob country hotels which our male counterparts had to do. Believe me, in those days those hotels were pretty basic!

And how did you do financially?

Well, not too badly. We were paid enough to keep the aeroplane in repair, to pay for our petrol and oil, and to pay for our accommodation. But I probably ended up with no more than my original £400 — that was the price of the aeroplane. Then I went into debt and bought another aeroplane, which was the one that I finally went out west in.

It was a big change of heart for your father to buy you the aeroplane.

It was. It was wonderful of him. Because £200 — that was his share of it — was a lot of money in those days. My great-aunt had been going to leave me £200 in her will and she said she would match his amount. I think they were a bit proud of the fact that I had got my licence and had become a little bit newsworthy because of my flying.

What sort of an aeroplane did you upgrade to?

A Leopard Moth — which was the aristocrat of the light aeroplanes, a beautiful aeroplane made by de Havilland. It was a cabin aeroplane. Two people sat behind and one in front. It was heaven! It had leather seats, a beautiful smell of real leather, and a shiny finish to it. It cost £1800 and I went into debt to buy it and every hour I ever flew the jolly thing I was paying it off.

And so how did you do that, did you continue with the barnstorming?

No. It was while I was barnstorming that I met Stanley Drummond of the Far West Children's Health Scheme who asked me to go to Bourke to fly his baby clinic service. It went way out beyond the railhead of Bourke, out to those little homes where boundary riders lived with their little families, often in corrugated iron places. These people were bringing up their children there on what Stanley Drummond said was black tea and salt mutton.

So you were taking a baby health sister out there to see them.

Yes, and also providing an air ambulance service. The first sister I took was Sister Webb who was an army nurse in the First World War and she hated flying. But even in that temperature of 40 degrees she'd wear leather gloves and the old-fashioned nurse's uniform out into that back country. She was terrified but very brave.

Did you feel that this work was really important, that it really made a difference?

Well, it just meant that women who lived 120 miles from Bourke could have a doctor in an hour instead of being on the road for six hours, that if people were in doubt about the health of a child or if there had been an accident the aeroplane was there. I think I was too young to realise the true significance of it to people. But Stanley Drummond knew, the Rev. Stanley Drummond, who like John Flynn had God-given vision. He knew what he was doing when he stationed me at Bourke to provide an air ambulance service and a baby clinic service.

Did you ever fly in circumstances where it really was a matter of life and death?

Oh, yes. One was a pneumonia case when I picked up a man off a station who had been marooned for several days. His wife couldn't drive the car to go and get help. They had little children who were too young to drive or ride for help and it was just good fortune that a boundary rider came by on horseback and rode to the nearest telephone and called the air ambulance. I landed in the paddock beside the homestead. I don't think his wife ever expected to see him again. It was a terrible wrench for her to have her husband taken away by a little girl in an aeroplane. But when I had delivered him to Wilcannia I flew back and dipped over the station to show her that he had been delivered safely. He always says I saved his life. In fact he later named a racehorse after me! He called it Miss Bird. But I don't know that I saved his life; maybe I helped.

When you described the early years when you were learning aviation it sounded as if the cameraderie, the feeling of having a group, was one of the very attractive things about it. What was the effect of going from this sense of belonging with a group to a job that took you right out into the far west and into almost complete isolation?

That was when I got the Leopard Moth. I remember I took off for Bourke, for the west, and as I approached the mountains I suddenly felt very very lonely and I looked back and all I could see was the tail of the aeroplane. And of course most people had said, when they heard that a woman was going to be flying outback: 'There's an end to a beautiful aeroplane.' When I got out west there were no other flying people around, so from that point of view I was lonely — there was nobody to discuss things with. But later when I went up to Charleville I would sometimes be lucky enough to be there when the de Havilland 86 came in from Singapore — the first Qantas flights. And then I would see the Captain and the First Officer and talk with them. And that was wonderful! They'll never know how much it meant to me to see those people from the outside world of aviation. And one of the First Officers was rather attractive too and I think I had a little bit of a spot in my heart for him — he could make my day just by saying hello!

Well that seems right for a 20-year-old, or were you 21 by then?

Yes, 21 years old. There would be something wrong with you if you weren't attracted to the opposite sex in those years of your life, wouldn't there. All young people, I think, fall in love.

But when you first went to Bourke what did you do for company?

I used to play tennis a little bit, I made friends with a few of the people about my own age. I was pretty busy looking after my aeroplane — it was probably the cleanest aeroplane ever because it was constantly washed down. I took a great pride in it. I did a lot of writing, I wrote letters to people trying to get the Department of Civil Aviation to select aerodromes and things of that sort. I was a copious writer of letters. But I was reasonably lonely. I suppose I went to bed early. I was living at the hotel with all these nice commercial travellers coming in and talking to me in the writing room and that sort of thing. That was very unusual for a girl in those days and some people wondered whether I was quite respectable. In fact one person was very very nasty. He really doubted my reputation and said so to a group of men — one of whom threatened to knock him down. I heard about it, and do you know what I did? I went straight to the Sergeant of Police and told him what I had heard, what had been said. And he said: 'Little Miss Bird, don't you worry about it, you just leave it to me.' I never heard another word! I can't imagine why I had the sense to do that at 20. You know, instead of being upset, I just went to the Sergeant of Police — a good thing to do, wasn't it.

Yes, I think you were very practical.

I was very practical, yes. He was a nasty man. He was just a big fat bouncy man who had no right to tarnish a little girl's reputation. There were also some little irritating jealousies. Especially from the sort of crème de menthe, cake-eating, bridge-playing women that couldn't get out of Bourke because their husbands were in jobs there. And I had very beautiful hair. I was completely unaware of it — this mop of red hair. It was already the bane of my existence because when I was young I'd be out playing and I had to come in while my mother's friends admired my wretched hair. But this woman in Bourke said: 'You know she goes to Dubbo, 200 miles away, every week to have her hair done.' God, I couldn't have afforded to buy a newspaper, let alone have my hair done — I was paying off an aeroplane! So I did strike some troubles like that, but generally speaking I had good friends. But my aeroplane was my true companion.

During the nine months in which Nancy Bird was stationed at Bourke she had to tackle some extremely difficult flying. Landing and taking off in rough paddocks strewn with stones and dotted with rabbit holes was a testing and hazardous business. The intense heat of the outback meant that the Leopard Moth's framework and even the glue that held it together were sometimes affected. If any engine problems developed on her flights she had to deal with them herself, using the basic maintenance training she had acquired at Mascot. She often felt the lack of more thorough mechanical training. Nevertheless, by a combination of care and skill she managed to survive this period without serious mishap and grew to love still more the unique joy of being alone in the great outback sky. When the government funding on which the Far West Children's Scheme depended to pay her small retainer was withdrawn, it could no longer afford her services. But Nancy knew by then that she did not want to give up the life. She moved to Queensland, supported herself by offering charter flights, and at the same time undertook voluntary flights for the Queensland Bush Children's Health Scheme.

I tried very hard to get the Queensland Government to establish in Charleville but they were not interested. Many years later they had a flying doctor service there and all those facilities. I was before my time.

There were flying doctor services in other parts of the country, weren't there?

Yes, in Darwin Dr Clive Fenton flew a Gipsy Moth and flew into the inland to help people. He was a real flying doctor because he not only flew the aeroplane, he was also the doctor. And the Victorians subsidised a flying doctor service at Wyndham. The Bush Church Aid at Ceduna in South Australia had an aeroplane and gave a medical service too. But there was nothing in that great area of the inland that I was in. In 1937 the Royal Flying Doctor Service was established at Broken Hill, but that was still 300-odd miles away from where I had been. And of course it was doing a different job. It was a medical service to the people in the inland, whereas I was a baby clinic service and an air ambulance in an emergency.

How did the charter side of your business go?

There was no set pattern. It was hard to predict when somebody would need a plane to inspect a mob of sheep or to make an urgent flight to Sydney or Brisbane. And when you're 21 you haven't got much business ability. I didn't have anybody to advise me. But then John Flynn came through — you know, Flynn of the Inland, the great man of the Flying Doctor Service — and he said: 'You've got to leave this, it's killing you! You're a woman, you can't go on doing this, it's too much for you!' P. G. Taylor came through and he said the same sort of thing: 'You can't stick it out here.' And the Qantas pilots used to say: 'How that girl sticks it out there we don't know, we went up to 8000 feet and we couldn't get out of the turbulence!' You see, in the summertime the air is very turbulent and it is very rough flying. It was like riding a bucking horse to fly in that country and I hated that turbulence. Nowadays, of course, people fly up to 10 000 feet or 12 000 feet and get out of it. In those days we didn't and the turbulence used to get me down, particularly in the summertime. And years later I learned that de Havilland Aircraft Company were very concerned about me flying out there because they knew the performance of the aeroplane fell off very much in that heat. But they didn't say so at the time! I didn't have a safety certificate, I didn't have an engineer or anything.

When your friends came through, Flynn and so on, and said to you 'this is too much for you as a girl', do you think they would have made that comment to a boy or do you think he would have got encouragement?

I think they would have encouraged him, actually. What John Flynn said to me was kindly and gentle and old-fashioned. It was mostly because I was a woman.

Now, although all these people were coming through telling you how much they doubted your ability to keep slogging on at this work, did you always maintain your own confidence?

Yes I did, even though everything was so uncertain — the weather, the work, the money. But one day I came to Sydney on a trip from Goodooga. I brought a man in because his wife was very ill. I landed a little bit out of Goodooga, beside the telegraph line on a clay pan, picked up this gentleman and flew him into Sydney. And then several days later I was to take him back. As I set out for the west, the clouds came down on the mountains and I thought, I can't get through. I'm not sure whether I could've got through if I'd gone down the Jamieson Valley and circled my way round. But everything in me revolted about going back. It was like being on a rearing horse — that aeroplane just didn't want to go back! I turned back to Sydney, landed, and burst into tears. And I never wanted to fly again. The pilots said: 'Don't be silly, it's only a fool that pushes through when the clouds are on the mountains, don't be upset by it.' But it really wasn't that. I just couldn't take it any longer. Something had happened. I just couldn't face flying again, and I was so ashamed. Later P. G. Taylor told me it had happened to him. And I've heard of several other people that it happened to. Suddenly they develop a fear or a nervousness and never want to fly again.

Had you ever had a crash?

No, I never had a crash, never damaged an aeroplane and just as well because in those days aeroplanes weren't insured — or at least I certainly couldn't afford to insure mine.

Now, you'd always been a careful pilot, you'd never had a crash and yet you were overcome with this feeling that you couldn't go on flying. Why do you think that was?

Because I think I'd got rusty. Because of the lack of association with other flying people I'd become a very rigid pilot. I was a very safe pilot but I was too safe, I didn't get the best out of an aeroplane. Flying safely all the time, the responsibility of the aircraft, the heat and the weather of the inland, the isolation, the loneliness, I think that that probably caused it. I couldn't afford a holiday, I'd never had a holiday. I was paying off an aircraft every hour I flew and I think that that was probably responsible for it. I was worn out. If I had left my aeroplane in the hands of somebody else, and had a holiday, I'd have probably been running an airline today! I would say I just cracked, you know. And one day I heard somebody say: 'Did you hear about the woman pilot who had a breakdown while she was flying?' I thought, oh how awful, they're talking about me. But I don't think it was a breakdown. I would say it was controlled cracking.

Why did you feel so ashamed?

You see, in those days we didn't go up high, over the clouds, because we didn't have a weather report at the other end and we kept under the clouds. So long as I could see the railway line or the top of the clouds I would try to get through. And whether I'd have made it that day or not I don't know. Since then I've driven over those mountains and I see how the mists come up behind Katoomba. Maybe I wouldn't have got through. I wouldn't have been the first person to crash in those mountains either. A few pilots have met their fate there by doing what I baulked at that day. We had memorials in the aeroclub to the people who hadn't got through — like Neil Stewart and his wife who had been killed in the Jamieson Valley. So of course the pilots supported me. They said I would have been a fool to try to get through. But somehow I felt in my own heart that I might have turned back because I didn't *want* to get through.

Of course, you'd had an extra pressure that the men were spared. You had people persistently telling you that being a pilot out there wasn't a suitable life for a woman. So perhaps a loss of confidence wasn't so surprising, given that it had been put into your head over and over that it was too much for you. Do you think that could have influenced you?

I don't know, I'm not quite sure. I didn't analyse the reason. I just felt awfully ashamed that I hadn't been able to take that man back to the country and ashamed of myself for breaking down and feeling I couldn't fly again. I didn't even want to fly again in a Link Trainer and that never leaves the ground, so it really was a crisis.

How did the man get home, by the way?

Oh, he took the train! He took the train the next day.

And what did you do next?

I had an invitation from the Dutch East Indies Airline to go overseas and I knew that I would never be able to afford to go overseas myself, so that was very attractive. They had been wanting to extend to Australia since 1931 — they were flying to Batavia in the Dutch East Indies (now Indonesia) and they wanted to come on to Australia and the Australian Government wouldn't allow it. And in December, 1934, Imperial Airways and Qantas extended the service to Australia. Well then they allowed the Dutch to come in and they asked various people to make the flights. I wasn't one of the important people, I went away on the third flight. But the head of the Dutch shipping company invited me to make that flight to Batavia and then go on to Amsterdam with KLM, and that to me was the opportunity of a lifetime. So I sold my aircraft, got back the £400 that I started with, and went away overseas with a total of £400. And I was just so well received by the Dutch airlines who introduced me to all the other airlines of Europe. I was able to study civil aviation, and collect an exhibition which I brought back to Australia.

What sort of an exhibition?

An exhibition of all the things that had been done overseas that we knew nothing about. All the airlines like Swiss Air, Air France, Scandinavian Airlines — I flew as a passenger with the Swedes from Moscow to London in a day, via Sweden. They were all marvellous to me! I really went to Sweden to study aerial ambulance work and I flew to the north of Sweden, landed on a frozen lake with a Swedish pilot and saw how they operated their Red Cross medical service in the wintertime.

And this was all part of a sort of PR push for KLM, was it? I mean, what was your actual role?

The only way I could repay KLM was by writing back to Australia letters of what I was doing. And that wonderful woman Connie Robinson, who was the editor of the women's section of the *Sydney Morning Herald*, used to print everything that I wrote. In those days women never got off the women's pages of course, you never appeared anywhere else in the newspaper, but everybody read it anyhow and the Dutch were delighted. They introduced me to Lufthansa and Swiss Air and all the other airlines. In Germany I flew on the maiden flights of some of the big new aeroplanes they were building. I flew into France, to the Paris Aviation Exhibition, which of course is the great thing for all flying people. And that was when they were showing the first of the Heinkels and the Messerschmidts and the Spitfire, but of course I didn't know their significance. I didn't know anything about politics. I had wonderful friends in Germany and they obviously didn't think I was any security risk because I was invited to the Junkers factory and all sorts of places like that.

Elly Beinhorn, the German aviatrix who'd flown here in 1932, introduced me to people too, so I wasn't a tourist there. I was just a person who enjoyed meeting the well-known aviation people of Germany. And, of course, Germany in those days was really doing things with aviation. We all now know why. But I didn't know why then. I just knew they were all enthusiastic about aviation whereas other countries of the world were not. England wasn't. I flew to Berlin from Paris in a Messerschmidt 108 with Elly Beinhorn. It was a lovely aeroplane with a retractable undercarriage and of course it was the forerunner to the 109, which was the fighter. I was invited to the Haus Der Fliegen which was the most beautiful aeroclub, housed in the old Legislative Assembly building. I was invited by the Americans to a big celebration with the German–American Association when Hannah Reich was made the first woman officer in the Luftwaffe. I sat next to the American Consul, Hannah was next and then Louis P. Lockner, the great American writer who was the president of the club. And that's the day I fell in love with an American from the Embassy — another little happiness in my life!

And was that a romance that lasted very long?

Well, for the month I was there. I shed a few tears when I took off for Sweden but it was a very happy occasion.

Were there many signs of what was gathering in Germany around you?

I stood on the side of a street once with an American foreign correspondent and she said: 'You know, Nancy, this means war.' I didn't know anything about politics at all. But you used to see all these marching Nazis and the salute, you know, and their dedication to their country, but it didn't mean war to me. I went to Germany after Munich. I wasn't afraid of it in any way. I didn't understand it sufficiently, obviously. When you're out at Bourke and you can't afford to buy a newspaper you don't know much about what's going on in the world! The radio was in the bar — tuned to the races — and we didn't have transistors in those days.

You were lucky you didn't get caught by the war.

Very fortunate. I was in Russia in May, 1939.

So when did you come back to Australia?

In July of 1939. I came home via America and there I met all the international women pilots in New York. They literally carried me across America. And then I was three weeks on the *Monterey*, coming by ship home to Australia. It was on that voyage that I met my husband. In fact they sat me between the Chief Purser and my husband — to control my exuberance, they said.

So it was a shipboard romance.

It was a shipboard romance that lasted 5½ years! I was very very happy, I had a wonderful trip. We danced every night to American music and we went ashore at New Zealand and it was a very happy, romantic time.

And did you have children during the war?

No, no, my daughter was born in 1945 and my son in 1946.

As soon as Nancy Bird Walton returned to Australia she was asked to join a flying club that had been formed a year earlier. The club was training girls in aviation-related subjects and offering scholarships. When war broke out the club immediately began to recruit and train women to serve in a Women's Auxiliary Air Force (WAAF) should one be formed. As chief of the Women's Air Training Corps, Nancy went to every State overseeing the work. This included recruitment training and general support for the RAAF, particularly in helping with transport which was often a problem for officers in the early days of petrol rationing. The work was provided by the women on a voluntary basis.

Girls who worked in offices all day long came to 221 George Street, where we had a room let to us free, and trained in air subjects. So eventually, when the WAAF was formed, all the senior officers with the exception of myself went into the WAAF and then the government stopped recruiting. They didn't want the women in the war service — they said we were playing at being soldiers! They definitely didn't want it. You see, the unions were dead against women being used in any of the occupations the men were doing in the Air Force because they were frightened they'd stay on after the war and do the men out of jobs. And we were struggling to have the value of what we were doing recognised.

So what was the outcome of this struggle for proper recognition of the women?

Well, they finally started a Women's Auxiliary Air Force, but that wasn't until considerably later. And once they started it, they took in all the senior officers with the exception of myself and they didn't take me in because I was married. By this time, in my voluntary capacity, I'd become the Commandant of the Women's Air Training Corps.

Do you think the women really made a difference during the war?

Oh, the war couldn't have been fought without them! That was proved. And of course the English Air Marshal who came out here realised that. But he had a terrible battle with the government and the Civil Aviation Department and the unions to get them to use the women. In the end they were ready to do anything to release men for active duty. All the ground work, the cipher work, the clerical work — all those things — were finally done by women. They had 25 000 in the WAAF alone. The Army took in women, then the Navy started the WRANS and then Lorna Burns started the Land Army. So the women were vital to the whole effort.

But you yourself didn't fly?

People think women flew here during the war, but there was no flying in Australia for women pilots then, because we always had more pilots than aeroplanes. We had very few aeroplanes at the beginning of the war years. We even put bombs on the wings of Tiger Moths, that's how badly off we were. And we had flyingboats trying to evade the Japanese Zeros. It was just criminal, our lack of defence. So the women didn't fly.

Now during all this time, since that time of crisis when you came back from the mountains, you hadn't flown. When did you start flying again?

I took out my licence again in the 1950s.

Why was that?

Well, I started flying with Maie Casey when her husband was Foreign Minister and, when he was abroad, often I would go to Melbourne and do some flying with her. I'd formed the Australian Women Pilots' Association in 1950 and I was called the Penguin President — the non-flying president — so I decided to start flying again. And I started flying on a student's licence. In 1958 I decided I would fly in the Powder Puff Derby in America. I'd been invited to come over and fly in it. But I didn't have an aeroplane. And we were only allowed a small amount of money to go overseas with in those days — £700 I think it was. I tried to get a job as a co-pilot but couldn't. So I decided to forget everything else, hire an aircraft, get a co-pilot and fly in the race myself. I got a little 172 with the help of my wonderful friends in America and I flew solo in it. I'd never before flown in an aeroplane with radio in it. I'd learned to fly on a joystick and I'd never before flown in an aeroplane with a tricycle undercarriage. It was a completely new world.

What did it feel like to be back in the air again?

Oh, I was quite at home. It was quite a sensation to take off from Lindbergh Field with the great jets. Because you share all the airfields there, you know. The private pilot has as many rights as the astronaut in America. You're not banished to Bankstown! But they can't understand you in America when you talk on the radio. It's, you know, like that line from *My Fair Lady* — 'there were even places where English completely disappears. In America they haven't spoken it for years'.

Did the fear that had overtaken you, when you gave up flying before, did that ever come again?

No. But I don't think I ever regained my full confidence either. I've done a few solos but I prefer to be a co-pilot. Of course it has changed so — with all the avionics and electronics and the radio and things of that sort that I'm not very familiar with. So I feel that I would be a bit of menace in the air unless I did it regularly. And, if I had the time, and lived in the country, I probably would fly regularly. But it's not much fun in the city when you take an hour and a half to get to the airfield to do half an hour's or one hour's flying. And I have so many friends who fly, that if I want to go somewhere it's just a matter of calling up someone and saying: 'Would you like to fly me to Mudgee?'

You described how naive you were about politics when you first went to Europe. But later that changed, didn't it, and you became quite active in political circles for a while.

My husband was very interested in politics and I became interested in politics as a result of my association with people who were often guests in our house. The Liberal Party found that, if they took a woman along to a meeting, often women would come to the meeting too and their husbands would come to be there with them and so they got better meetings. So I took a very great interest in politics and spoke in support of various politicians. Then I got the idea that I'd like to go into the Legislative Council because I wanted to bring women into politics. I wanted to open the doors. Now I don't think I had any brains for the job. But believe me, I would have used everybody else's because there are specialists in all those fields. You don't have to have brains yourself. I think women are humble enough to ask the specialists what are the right things to do. And I used to hear these wonderful talks from these various very clever men.

Anyhow, the first time I had no hope of getting in. I was flying the flag, we didn't have enough votes. The second time they chose a woman from Bankstown who said how awful it was to be a Liberal in Bankstown. And she was chosen! The third time they put in a woman who was Vice-President of the Liberal Party and she went in unopposed. But if I had defeated her in a ballot, I don't think I could have looked at my face in the mirror because she really worked hard for the party and she didn't have children. And frankly my intention was to open the gates to women and get women interested in politics. We formed a women's movement against socialism and we educated women all over the country, rallied women all over the country to be interested in politics and not to vote, blindly, as their husbands told them to. I can tell you I felt very guilty when I first voted differently to my husband.

How did your husband feel about your activities as a pilot, as an organiser and as a politician — or as a would-be politician?

He supported it very much indeed. But my husband was a quiet Englishman and I don't think that he would have liked me coming home at midnight from Parliament. He liked me to be at home when he came home for dinner.

You've kept up a lot of activity, haven't you. Right through your life.

I've always had a finger in some pie. Ever since at the age of eight I organised a fete for Collaroy Children's Hospital and raised £2. I think I've always been organising something. I was involved in the Australian Heart Campaign, I was Patron to the Asthma Campaign and worked to help set up the NSW Air Ambulance Service. Then there's the Fear of Flying Clinics which Qantas run — the Australian Women Pilots' Association encouraged that. There's always plenty to do!

You're in your late seventies and you're still tremendously energetic. What's the secret of keeping that energy alive?

Well, my mother had it, so I think I got it from her. Also I'm interested in everything. I'm interested in politics, I'm interested in international affairs, I'm interested in women pilots, I'm interested in people. And I love living. But it's also true that I have reasonably good health. I think keeping busy is important. Where does my energy come from? I've also got a nasty thing called a driving force. This means you can say you're not going to do a thing, no you won't do it, but you end up doing it! I'm rather like the mother in the play *Dear Octopus*. She could always find a job for everybody. I am terribly like her — I'm ashamed of how like her I am. Always finding jobs for everyone including myself. It's rather fun to see how much you can fit into a day sometimes. It might be a bit exhausting by the end of the day, but you don't feel it until you stop.

Do you ever wake up in the morning and think, 'I really don't want to do everything I've got organised today'?

Sometimes I probably wish I didn't have to do something, but when I get into it I thoroughly enjoy it. I know I laugh at myself because once, when I was to speak at a school, the headmistress told the pupils about how they would all reach their greatest potential and so on, and when I finished my speech I said you'll never reach your greatest potential if you walk past the dishwasher without emptying it or leave your costume on the bathroom floor. It's doing what's in front of you.

Have you ever been bored?

Oh yes, I suppose I have been. I've had dull moments in my life — very dull and dreary moments — but you know there's always something to do if you just look around you, when you're waiting for someone or waiting for something. If you use that time, you don't get bored. Sitting and waiting is when you get bored. But there's always something to do. It might just be to run off a letter of thanks to somebody; it might be while you're on the telephone to somebody, you can have a pen beside you and you can scribble a note or something— it might just be saying 'I'm delighted to hear you're writing a book' or 'Congratulations on selling your house' or whatever it might be. Don't waste minutes. Don't waste time. But then perhaps I'm not a very restful person.

In the course of your lifetime the position of women has changed very dramatically — probably, some people say, the biggest social change of the twentieth century. And you yourself played a part in that by doing things that were difficult and dangerous and not considered suitable for a woman. What do you think of it all, now that you are older and can look back?

Well, first of all, we didn't consider it difficult or dangerous. It was just a job of work; you learned to fly an aeroplane and you were lucky to be able to do a job. In relation to the position of women — I'm so proud of what women have achieved. Executive women, women in every walk of life, in law, in flying, in everything! I think it's marvellous, and I think it has improved the relationship between men and women. They share things now completely. Women were not educated in the old days. Now women are educated and they are able to share with their husbands or their masculine friends their intellectual development and it's wonderful to see. It's all positive, just so long as we don't lose our femininity, our graciousness, and so long as we don't become aggressive. I regarded the word 'feministic' as aggressive at one stage. I don't think it is now. But I feel that it's wonderful to be a woman, to behave like a woman, and for men to treat you as a woman. And I don't see why we can't retain that as well as developing our intellectual capacity. The thing is to be feminine. I've always cut my cake to suit my husband and family. People may not think that but it's true. I've always put my family and my husband first. I'd have done lots more things in my life if I hadn't married or hadn't had a family, but I don't think that they would have been better. I might have been terrible, I might have been a terrible aggressive woman.

If you'd been a man and a pilot, what do you think you'd have been doing now?

Probably flying an airliner or being an executive in Qantas or something of that sort. Gary Richardson, who developed the Victor

Aircraft, once told me I had missed my calling. I should have been an executive woman in aviation. Well, that's what I thought I was going to be when I came back to Australia. But I married instead.

Today, you might have been able to do both.

That's true, I belong to a different period of time.

When you were out there in an aeroplane on your own, flying along and sometimes in danger, did you ever think about death?

Yes, because in the back of one's mind was always the story of Hitchcock and Anderson when they were lost out in Central Australia — and in the country I was flying in, if you crashed an aeroplane or had a forced landing and had no water you could die in 24 hours. Even today, people who are thrown from a horse or get lost or something can perish in 24 hours in inland Australia. So when I first landed on Urosino Station 140 miles west of Bourke the manager said to me, 'Do you carry water?'. I said no. He said, 'Well never land on this station or leave it without carrying water', and he gave me a great big thermos flask to carry water in. From then on I always carried water.

Do you fear death?

No, I don't fear death. Maie Casey said it's just another experience and I feel it *is* perhaps another experience. I would hate to have died out in the bush of thirst, or been injured and not been found. I think I would like to die amongst people, preferably in a nice comfortable bed. But I have no fear of death. It is inevitable.

What kind of experience do you think it will be? Do you think there is an afterlife?

That I don't know. I believe there is, I hope there is. But I think it's by what you do here in this life that you can make a heaven or hell for yourself and other people. I don't think it's worth worrying too much about what's happening hereafter. I think it's important to make the best of your life now. I'm not prepared to sacrifice this life for the next one.

In relation to this life what's the best thing, do you think, that's ever happened to you? Your best experience.

Falling in love and marrying the man I love, probably.

Better than flying?

Yes, much better than flying.

Although she is now past 80, Nancy Bird Walton retains the indefatigable energy that fuelled her early achievements. She still seems to thrive on a schedule of public engagements, including much public speaking and frequent attendance at airshows all over the country, which allows little time for relaxation. In February 1996 she attended the 60th anniversary of the Brisbane to Adelaide Air Race in which, in 1936, she won the Women's Trophy. It was in this same race that Reg Ansett won the £500 that he used to start an airline. She was thrilled, at the 1996 re-enactment, to have the experience of taking over the controls of a Lockheed 10, which she had never flown before. She says she has no intention of stopping any of her activities. The only thing she fears is enforced idleness.

Neville Bonner

Winning Respectability

To be respected by those around him has been a central goal of Neville Bonner's difficult life. As the first and only Aboriginal senator Australia has known in its history to date, he felt himself to be under constant scrutiny. He saw that he was being judged, not just as an individual, but as a representative of his race. He found that how he behaved personally was under closer observation from the white community than how he behaved politically.

Neville Bonner's early life as a fringe-dweller, his limited schooling, his many labouring jobs and his long experience of life on the notorious Palm Island was a background not shared by any other parliamentarian, and his position in Canberra was a lonely one. However, he had won his high public office by attracting personal respect and he believed that it was by a reputation for decency, sobriety and reasonableness that he would be able to maintain his position there.

The question of whom he represented and why he was there in the Senate led him into some significant controversies. As a Queensland senator he saw himself as representing the whole of that State and its interests, as well as attempting to act for the benefit of the nation as a whole. Many Aboriginal groups around Australia saw him as their only representative in parliament and were outraged by his support of policies that they felt to be against Aboriginal interests. This was particularly true in his early days in Canberra and in relation to his support for some of the positions taken by Joh Bjelke-Petersen, who was then Premier of Queensland. Neville Bonner was called an 'Uncle Tom' and a 'tame cat'. Later, when he became more outspoken on Aboriginal issues and took stands against his own party and against Bjelke-Petersen, what he had feared and predicted occurred. He was dropped to an unwinnable position on the Senate ticket.

In the course of this interview, when I put it to him that there was a fine line between being a symbol and being a token, he responded in the most forceful terms that he had never been a token black. The vigour and, at the same time, the defensiveness of his response reflects the qualities he has brought to public life, as well as the strain he has had to endure.

The symbolic importance of his contribution to Aboriginal advancement has secured him a unique place in Australian history, but his path has been a difficult one. For him it is a source of great sadness that no other Aboriginal Australian has followed in the trail he blazed. The work of a pioneer, in any setting, is much easier to criticise than to create. Neville Bonner struggled to pioneer a place for his people in our national parliament, and he would like to see others follow.

Neville Thomas Bonner's birth certificate says that he was born in 1922, the son of an Aboriginal woman, Julia Rebecca Bonner née Bell. Julia was married to an Englishman, Henry Bonner, who together with a fellow seaman called Tommy Beach had jumped ship in Australia. Henry married Neville's mother and Tommy married Neville's aunt. Neville was born in New South Wales on a little island in the mouth of the Tweed River, just south of the Queensland border. Despite the fact that his mother was married to Henry Bonner, his birth certificate is marked 'illegitimate'.

RH *There's a bit of a mystery surrounding your birth, isn't there?*

NB My elder brother was blue-eyed, blond, and very fair. I was born a lot darker. I don't have blue eyes, I have brown eyes and black hair. It was never explained to me whether I was truly Henry's son or the son of another chap in between. And there was also some doubt about the year of my birth. I was always under the impression — I don't know why or where I got it from — that I was born in 1918. But I wasn't, I was born in 1922. I was never sure of how to get my birth certificate because I tried Tweed Heads, and there was no record of it, and I was talking to an elderly lady who knew my mother as a girl, and she knew where I was born and where I was registered. I was registered at Murwillumbah. After I got into the Senate and just before Heather and I got married, we went to Murwillumbah to the Registry Office. The elderly gentleman there asked: 'When were you born?' I said: '1918'. So we started looking through, but it was found that I was born four years later than I first believed. The birth certificate said: 'Born on the 28th of March, 1922.'

Were there other children in the family?

There was my eldest brother Henry and then I came along. I have no memory at all of Henry Bonner senior because he deserted my mother before I can remember and she later picked up with an Aboriginal chap. She had four children to him. There's only myself still living, and my sister.

Did your mother come from the Tweed Heads area?

No, my mother was born at an Aboriginal community just outside of Ipswich called Deeping Creek. That was the first Aboriginal community established by the government in this area, back in eighteen something-or-other. My grandmother was from Beaudesert and she came across here as a young girl, and married my grandfather who was from this area. My grandfather was one of the surviving elders of the Jagara tribe. These were a people who used to extend from the mouth of the Brisbane River to the foot of the Great Dividing Range. My grandfather and his brother Stanley were two of four surviving members of that tribe.

And what sort of circumstances were you born into?

My mother gave birth to me in a gunyah at the foot of a palm tree that is still growing on Ukerabagh Island, in what was termed the blacks' camp. My mother was a crippled woman. When she was very young she fell out of a tree and broke her hip and she walked with a very bad limp. When she was deserted by her first husband we moved to Lismore and she met up with another chap by the name of Frank Randall, and they had another three children between them. Frank was a very lazy person in lots of ways and he depended on my mother to earn the money to pay for the food. Mother worked for a hotel as the washwoman. We used to walk in — about two miles. I'd chop the wood and make the fire under the copper and keep it going for her and mother would wash and boil the clothing and sheets. And she did all the ironing.

Life was very very tough, and grandfather used to go out and do a bit of work for a dairy farm, and he'd bring in a little money. I also helped my grandfather and stepfather when I was old enough, cutting scrub trees down and digging out the lantana bushes and things like that for people who wanted to cultivate the land. So we all had to do some work. Grandma was very thrifty and was able to make that money spin out, plus what mother earned, and Frank got his share of it before any went into food.

What did he spend it on?

Whatever he wanted to. Mostly drink. He drank a lot, and so did grandfather, and one of my jobs was to be on hand when grandfather got paid, so as I could grab his pay and take it home to grandma. If I didn't, it would all go on grog. Alcoholism is not a new thing, it's something that's been with us as Aborigines for a long long time.

There were no welfare cheques?

No welfare cheques in those days. The New South Wales Government did issue some rations to some people but you had to qualify for it, and I was too young to realise what the qualifications were. But we were never in receipt of any of those rations.

Young Neville and his family lived in a shelter which his grandfather built on the banks of the Richmond River. His grandfather used pieces of iron and other scrap collected from rubbish dumps to make a small dwelling in a space cleared out beneath the lantana bushes. They dug drains on each side to make sure that, when it rained, the runoff into the river bypassed their makeshift home. They got sacks and corn bags from the greengrocer and stitched them together to make big hessian rugs, on which they placed blankets to make their bed. Despite these efforts the family was often hungry and cold. From Neville Bonner's description of the difficulties and hardships the family faced at this time, it is clear that he himself took on a level of responsibility way beyond his years. In 1933 his mother became very ill. Neville didn't know what was wrong with her, but he understood that it was serious. He walked the six kilometres to Lismore Hospital to see her every afternoon until she died.

Do you think the circumstances in which she lived there — on the banks of the river, with rather unreliable men in her life, children dependent on her, and the difficulties that she had to cope with every day — led to your mother's death?

Well, that would have been part of it, I think. The cruelty of the man that she lived with played a part in her ill health also.

In what way was he cruel?

He beat her quite consistently. He used to knock her down and kick her with his heavy boots. When Mother died I was only about nine years of age. But I remember her calling out for help and assistance, and Frank continually beating her. I don't know really what the diagnosis was by the medical profession, but my own estimation was that, as you rightly say, the conditions and everything else plus the continual flogging and beating by Frank Randall played a part.

How did you feel about that?

Well, I don't like to say that one hates someone, but there would have been a lot of hate in my feelings towards him because my mother was a very kind and loving person, and worked hard and did her best to raise a family, and the things he did would not have endeared him to anyone. My feeling towards him was very close to hate, if it wasn't really hate.

Do you remember the day she died?

I wasn't with her, actually, when she died, but I was with her the night before and she was still able to talk in a whisper. And when I left she took her wedding ring off her finger and put it in my hand. The next morning we got word that she had passed on. My last memories of her sometimes still haunt me because she was very thin, very frail, and her voice was very very weak.

Did Frank Randall see to it that she was buried properly?
She was buried in a pauper's grave. We had no money, we could not have paid for a funeral.

An unmarked grave?
Absolutely, yes. I've been back to the cemetery a couple of times, but there was no way of finding her.

During these early years in northern New South Wales, did you go to school at all?
I had a very short spell at a small school that was on the bank of the Richmond River, near Lismore. It came about because my stepfather was working as a tracker for the police station, and I used to go in and help him clean out the stables. The Inspector of Police was there one day and asked him why I wasn't at school. Frank explained that we weren't allowed to go to the schools. So the Inspector spoke to the head teacher at the South Lismore School, and he very kindly said: 'Look, we'll give it a go, they can come along.' Well, mother was very handy using cotton and needle. She had some second-hand clothing that she cut down and made nice pairs of trousers and dressed us up to make sure we went off looking decent.

We arrived at school on the Monday morning at about half past eight, and by the time school started we were the only three children left because the white families learned that we black kids were there, and they came and took their children out of the school. Finally the head schoolmaster said: 'I'm sorry children, you'll have to go home.' That ended my first attempt at acquiring an education. Then a lady, a Mrs Hitchcock, talked the New South Wales Government into giving her sufficient finance to start a little school, which she did on the bank of the river at a little dairy — we were in the old cow bails, with a concrete floor. Later we moved out to a place called Tunchester, about three miles out of town. Altogether I had about six months' schooling there.

Neville Bonner's mother was only in her thirties when she died and his grandparents Ida and Roger Bell took over the responsibility of raising him and his younger brother Jim. When he was in his early teens his grandparents decided to return to Queensland. At the age of 14 he enrolled at Beaudesert State School and stayed there until he was 15. In Queensland, unlike New South Wales at that time, Aboriginal children were allowed to attend State schools with white children. Neville was taught three grades in that one year so that he could make the most of the opportunity provided by attendance at a normal school. By the time he left he had been taught to read and write, and had reached third grade level. But more important even than the formal education he received was his grandmother's influence. The period under her care was of crucial significance in preparing him for his future.

I owe a lot to my grandmother. She was a very well-educated lady. She was raised by station owners outside of Beaudesert before she was sent across here to Deeping Creek. She spoke flawless English, and one of the things she assisted us with was teaching us to speak English as English is supposed to be spoken. She had two sayings which she took trouble to impress on us. She always said that courtesy and respect cost nothing but paid great dividend. And she also told us that if you didn't have an academic education, but you were able to speak well, people would not notice whether you were educated or not, and it would get you through life. And I think she proved that quite well. In my case anyway.

While I was with her, being able to go to school where there was other than black kids was quite an experience for me. Although there were a number of Aboriginal children going there it was predominantly a white children's school, and I made some very wonderful friends amongst the white students as well as the Aboriginal students. The teachers were very very kind to all of us and there was no discrimination as we understand it today, there was no difference whether you were black or you were white — you were all children at school.

Your whole childhood and youth had essentially an Aboriginal background and you were part of an Aboriginal family. I presume that brought you into contact with customs and cultural patterns that were clearly Aboriginal?

My grandfather and grandmother taught me quite a lot of our own culture and customs, but because of the racial discrimination and actions of non-Aboriginal people towards us we didn't put our mind, as kids, to learning the language — because if you spoke your language in the streets amongst the white kids or white people you were told, 'Oh, you blacks, if you want to talk your language you're back on the bank of the creek where you belong', and things like that. So we were forced to become ashamed of our own culture, our own language and our own history, and unfortunately we lost a lot of it. I still remember a few words of my grandfather's tongue, and my grandmother's tongue, and I retain a lot of the stories that they passed on to me.

Grandfather taught us how to hunt in the bush for our own natural foods, and we did quite a lot of chasing wallabies and various kinds of animals and getting the various types of fruit that grew in the bush. He also taught us how to track and how to find water and he taught us to make boomerangs. You had to cut the roots of the trees out with an axe, and then out of one root you'd probably only make one boomerang. Today you would take the same root, cut it up with a bandsaw, and get five or six boomerangs out of it. Grandfather taught us how to throw boomerangs also, and how to make them return, and I've retained that all my life.

What about the tribal law — did you learn any of that?
Oh yes! Grandfather taught us all about the tribal customs and laws, and I've retained all that.

And your spiritual life as a child — was that Aboriginal?
My grandmother was a Christian. She was raised by station property owners and embraced the Christian faith, and she taught us of course. But grandfather also taught us our own spiritual beliefs and the Aboriginal spirituality was handed down through grandfather more than grandmother.

How did you make sense of this? These two messages you were getting.
Well, I find that there is no conflict between my Aboriginal spirituality and my Christian faith, for our laws are similar to the Christian laws. We believed in a supreme being, we believed that some supreme body created everything, and we believed that you shouldn't take something that belongs to someone else. So a lot of the laws in Aboriginal culture have little or no conflict, because our laws are based similarly.

Did you see that as a child? Or did you feel that they were different?
The only conflict that I detected was that we were told by the missionaries and the ministers of churches about the God that we worship — a loving, kind, considerate, all-forgiving God, where in his kingdom all people are equal — but it seemed odd that the white

man was much more equal than we blackfellas were. So there was a conflict there, but it didn't conflict with my embracing the Christian faith and still retaining my own Aboriginal spirituality.

Neville Bonner finished his schooling at the age of 15. Just before the end of that year his grandmother died. In the next period of his life he moved back and forth between Queensland and New South Wales, staying with various relatives, taking on a number of different labouring jobs and seeking an elusive sense of stability and belonging. Then his mother's eldest brother appeared in his life. The uncle had come from central Queensland to look for his sister's children. He took Neville back with him to Woorabinda, an Aboriginal settlement on the Dawson River 160 kilometres southwest of Rockhampton. It was Neville's first contact with the ways of a tribal group and he witnessed his first ceremonies. He grew interested in his heritage. At the same time he was given work on a dairy farm and also learned how to be a stockman. Restless, he took off again and roamed about Queensland, jumping trains and working at all kinds of rural jobs. He was working on a sheep station in the central west of Queensland when the Second World War broke out.

In early 1940 I was in my late teens, and one of my mates was coming down to Cherbourg to be married. So we all decided to come down with him. I enlisted in Cherbourg with quite a number of other Aboriginal men. And we were told that we were going to Maryborough for the draft. We were all packed and ready to go, when a telegram came telling us to wait where we were till they notified us. Well they didn't for quite some time, and I decided with another chap to go and try to enlist in Brisbane. We were told that they weren't taking any Aborigines because they were afraid that we would not be able to stand up to the climatic conditions into which they were sending the troops. So we weren't accepted. I gave up my hopes of getting into the Army and went back out into the west, and worked on a cattle station. Later I was called up from the cattle station, but a few months before I'd had a very nasty accident. I'd been riding a buckjumper and I ripped my arm and smashed up my wrist — and of course then I wasn't fit to get into the Army. So I worked on the cattle station all through the war.

I suppose there would have been a big demand for people to work that way, with all the men away.

They told me not to feel bad about it because troops had to be fed, and beef was one of the main diets of the Australians, and so we were doing just as important a job by keeping the cattle industry going as we would have been if we'd gone to war.

Why did you want to go so much?

Well, I felt that I had an obligation as an Australian — our country was at war, we had joined Britain, of course, to fight against the Nazi regime. I had an obligation to be a part of the troops that went over to defend our mother country and our own country.

How did you feel when they told you that they weren't going to take you?

I was terribly, bitterly, disappointed. As a matter of fact, I suppose there'd still be records of it in the Brisbane paper, the old *Truth*. They interviewed us and they gave us quite a write-up about it and demanded that we be given a chance, but of course it never eventuated. We were very very badly disappointed about it. We felt that we were offering our services to our nation and were rejected because we were Aborigines.

When did you marry your first wife?

Mona and I were married on Palm Island in 1943. She had been the first baby born on Palm Island after it was established as a government settlement. She was working on a cattle station and so was I, and when we decided to get married she wanted to go home to Palm Island to be married among her family. After that we worked on various properties and then I decided to strike out and set myself up as a corkwood cutter, cutting wood for bakeries and so on. I was subcontracting to a bloke who had a wood depot, and I'd be camped out in the bush from Monday till Friday afternoons. Mona was living in a house with friends, and she found herself a job as a housemaid with an ambulance bearer's wife. One day she was doing some ironing and she happened to have the iron a bit hot or something and she scorched or burnt one of the hankies that she was ironing. The woman grabbed hold of her hanky and said: 'You stupid black bitch, look what you did!' And of course Mona slapped her. Under the government regulations and rules pertaining to Aboriginal people, that was very very naughty, and so she was picked up by the police, held in the police station, and sent back to Palm Island under escort. That happened early in the week and when I got back to the house on the Friday afternoon there was no one at home. I found my two friends and they told me that Mona had been forcibly sent home to Palm Island. The laws pertaining to Aboriginal people weren't very kind in lots of ways.

What did you do?

Well, there was nothing I could do. I couldn't reverse the decision. It was a decision made by the the Department of Aboriginal Affairs. As soon as I could I took a couple of weeks off and went down to visit Mona at Palm Island. I was down there for a week or so, and when I went back to the station to work Mona got in touch with me by letter and told me she had fallen pregnant. Our oldest son was born on Palm Island, and afterwards Mona was allowed to come back. By this time I'd become head stockman on a cattle station, and so I had the head stockman's quarters. But my son was about six or seven months old, and he contracted an illness, amoebic dysentery, and we very near lost him from dehydration before we got him into town. The roads were bad and by the time we got to Hughendon he'd almost died. So that frightened Mona, and she decided that living on the mainland, living on cattle stations with a baby, wasn't for her. And so we decided to go and live on Palm Island, just outside of Townsville.

But my understanding of Palm Island is that it was in fact a very tough and difficult place to live.

Yes, it was set up as a penal island, where Aborigines from other communities who — according to the Department of Aboriginal Affairs authorities — had misbehaved were sent and would have to remain at the pleasure of the government. Whether they were worthy to go back on the mainland again was determined by the Superintendent and his officers. I went in there voluntarily, to keep the family together, my wife and my son Patrick. And whilst the rules and the laws of the community laid down by the Department were harsh, I managed to survive there, and we had five sons altogether.

By going to Palm Island Neville Bonner had, for the time he remained there, surrendered his freedom. Everything he did was now determined by the Superintendent. But the Superintendent was able to put this hardworking and responsible young man to good use. The island was beset with severe health problems, especially among the children, and it was clear that this was due mainly to poor hygiene. So the Superintendent set up a hygiene gang and put Neville in charge of it. In effect he became the island's Health Officer for the next few years, leading a gang of men who dug pits for rubbish,

*sprayed houses for cockroaches and flies (using DDT) and made
sure that people cleaned up their yards. Neville also helped in a
scheme to make concrete bricks on the island and then supervised a
gang of men engaged in rebuilding projects using the locally-made
bricks. Eventually he became Assistant Settlement Overseer.*

As it was on all of the Aboriginal communities under the
Department of Aboriginal Affairs, a white man always had to be
over the Aborigines, so whilst there was the Superintendent
(white), there was an Assistant Superintendent (black) — they all
had Aboriginal people working under them. And there was a white
Settlement Overseer who came and opened the office in the
morning, and then I didn't see him again till afternoon time when
closing up. I handled all the workforce.

Was he paid?

Yes, the white Settlement Overseer was on about seven or eight
pounds a week, and I was on two pound ten a fortnight. There was a
vast difference between the salaries of Aboriginal workers on the
communities and the white staff.

Tell me about conditions generally on Palm Island.

The rules governing that place were something similar to what
we've all been angry about in South Africa. No Aborigine was
allowed to answer back, argue the point, or disagree with an order
or an instruction from a white officer. It was an apartheid situation
where all the whites lived in one area, all the blacks lived in a
different area. The whites were the authorities. If you were speaking
to a white officer you had to call him Mister and if it was a lady you
called her Mrs. Even if they were only teenage kids they were Miss
or Mister. You were woken by a bell at seven o'clock in the
morning, and when the second bell rang you had to be down where
you were detailed out to work by eight o'clock. Then another bell
rang at ten o'clock, and you ceased work and had a cup of tea. The
next bell rang at a quarter past ten and you started work again. The
next bell rang at twelve o'clock, and you ceased work for lunch.
The next one rang at one o'clock and you started work again. The
next bell rang at four o'clock and the unpaid Aboriginal workers
ceased work; the next bell rang at five o'clock and the paid
Aboriginal workers ceased work; the next bell rang at half past
nine, and you had then to be in your own home. The last bell rang
at ten o'clock. If you were caught outside your home after that bell

you were locked up and put in gaol, and you were put on the punishment sheet by the Superintendent the next day.

So everybody had to work, regardless of whether you were paid or unpaid. If you were unpaid you received your rations — tea, sugar, flour, meat, soap, washing soda, syrup and items like that free for yourself and each member of your family. Some people worked for as low as ten shillings a fortnight. I was the highest-paid Aboriginal on the Settlement after a number of years. When I became the Assistant Settlement Overseer, I got two pounds ten a fortnight — that was the highest!

What opportunity did you have to spend that money?

We had a general store. You could buy food, clothing or whatever you wanted there. You needed to buy extra items of food — you just couldn't live on the basic rations, so if you wanted butter or milk or stuff like that you had to buy it.

Being an Aborigine, did you feel the need to share that with the others? The extra money that you had?

Not in cash, but there was always someone wanting a little bit of help, maybe a cup of sugar or maybe a wee bit of a special tea that you bought out of a shop, or coffee or something like that. You always did share amongst each other. When you were out of something you got it from someone else, and if they were out they came to you, so it was a kind of sharing situation.

How did you cope personally? I mean, you were someone who'd been born free, out there, and here you were voluntarily in what was essentially a penal settlement in order to be with your wife.

When I first went there I was very rebellious, but I soon learned that you catch more flies with honey than you do with vinegar, and I learned to weave between the different white people in authority. I learned to manoeuvre people, I suppose, to get the things done that I wanted to have done for the benefit of myself, my family and other people in the community, and I became quite expert at doing that.

Was this the beginning of the politician?

I suppose it could have been! I was not aware of it in that sense at that time, but I suppose in retrospect it was the beginning of the makings of a politician.

What was the worst kind of punishment that could be meted out to you on the punishment sheet?

If you were an unpaid worker, you could be put to work on Saturdays when no one else would be working, or you could be worked from four o'clock till five every afternoon.

What were the worst things that you saw happen on Palm Island?

Well, they had an Aboriginal police force on the island in those days, and there were some pretty nasty characters who got themselves onto the police force. I suppose one of the worst things I saw happen was two police officers beating an Aborigine up with their waddies, their batons, on the way to taking him down to the cell. While two police were holding the chap, these other two blokes kept hitting him with their batons — and nothing happened to them.

So there was quite a lot of physical violence?

Doesn't happen now, but it did quite often in those early days. Now they have white police on there as well as Aboriginal police, but in those days there were just police working under the instructions of the Superintendent.

So it was pretty much dictatorship by the Superintendent.

It was a total dictatorship, yes. And that was the law of the government.

What about the children, were they well looked after? Your wife had wanted to go there for the children's sake.

We were fortunate in that we had five sons. They were able to stay with us in our home the whole time and go to school, so we were able to take care of them. But if you had daughters, once they reached the age of five they were put into the girls' dormitory under a matron and staff, and they were locked up at night, and they were only allowed out to go to school. As they grew up to be women, they had to stay then in the single women's dormitory.

What was the difference between the boys and the girls — why did the girls have a different rule?

I suppose they were more susceptible to being taken off by men than boys were. There was no homosexuality on the island, so the boys were quite safe living at home with their parents, but the authorities didn't believe the parents were capable of protecting their daughters, so they were put into the dormitories.

While you were on Palm Island, there were the beginnings of some conflict between the Aborigines and the overseers, weren't there? Could you tell me about that?

There was a chap who got into trouble over not attending to his job. This chap wasn't doing his work properly, so he had a set to with the Overseer, and he was then told that he would have to leave the island. And that caused a riot! The whole settlement went on strike, and wouldn't do any work at all. I was the Assistant Overseer, so I sat in my office and I kept working. Actually there was no work to do, but I manned my office.

When trouble broke out on the island, what side were you on, what position did you take?

I took an independent position. I had a job to do, and I was going to continue doing my work. The argument had nothing to do with me. The others went out on strike, supporting this chap because he was going to be put off the island. I said, well, the authorities have the right to put a person off the island if they so wish, so I kept out of it. The authorities sent for the white police from Townsville, who arrived on Palm Island late in the afternoon, just on dark. There was a whole group of Aboriginal people at the end of the jetty as the police officers were coming off, and the only lights were over the top of the jetty. All the Aboriginal people were in the dark. They were yelling and carrying on, and as the police officers were coming off I saw some of the officers loosening their pouches with their guns.

So I walked to the Superintendent, Roy Bartlum, and said: 'Look, Mr Bartlum, there's going to be bad trouble here, can we all go up to the picture theatre and put all the lights on so as everybody can see what's happening?' He said: 'They're your people, *you* go and talk to them.' I went to try and talk to them, and they closed in around me and got me down and they started to sink the boot into me. Two young fellows saved my life — they got themselves over the top of me and then they dragged me out, got me out of the road. The group did finally go up to the open-air picture theatre and they had some talks there, but nothing was settled. I tried to talk to the Aboriginal people to try and get things calmed down a bit, but no one wanted to take any notice of me. The police stayed on the island for two or three days. Then they struck in the early hours of the morning and got all of the so-called leaders, and handcuffed them, and put them on the boat and sent them back to the mainland.

Why do you think it was that when you went to speak to the people in the mob they saw you as an enemy, and attacked you and kicked you?

I suppose the misunderstanding would have come about because I was standing away from the mob when the police arrived. Then when I saw the police officers loosening their revolvers, I spoke first to the Superintendent and the white staff, then went to speak to the Aboriginal people. I think that there was a misunderstanding that I was on the white man's side rather than on their side, and so I was looked upon as a traitor. But I went to the Superintendent because he had the authority to hold the police until everybody had gone up to where the lights were, up at the open-air theatre.

It seems you felt that it was more important to avoid trouble than to fight for the principle that this man had the right to stay on the island.

No, I didn't think that at all. What I saw was a very dangerous situation, where a group of young police officers were coming out of the light into the dark, where there was a whole stack of howling, screaming, yelling, swearing Aborigines. They were armed, the Aborigines weren't. Now any one of those young police officers could have panicked and shot one of them. My idea was to avoid that, and I was prepared to put myself into a situation where I could have been hurt, because I didn't want someone to be shot. As simple as that.

The people who saved your life — the two men who threw themselves over you — what was their motivation?

They were relatives of my wife, very close friends of mine. They wanted to protect me and save me from being killed.

Did the Aboriginal people on the island subsequently accept that you were acting in their interests?

Those who were taken away didn't, but the people who were still on the island got together and we demanded that the head of the Department of Aboriginal Affairs come from Brisbane and talk to us and get the matters all straightened out. Which he did. He brought a couple of other politicians and other important non-Aboriginal people out from the mainland, and we had quite a big meeting and had things sorted out and everybody got back to work again. But the people who were sent away were away for a long, long time.

Did you feel badly about that?

Yes, I did, because they were forcibly taken away from their home. But they had broken the law, and of course the law has to be obeyed. If you break the law then you have to accept the consequences.

Even if it's an unjust law?

Yes. Even if it's an unjust law. The only way you can change an unjust law is get into the system, which I finally did.

Palm Island provided no education past primary school level and Neville Bonner wanted something better for his children. He was generally unhappy with the situation on Palm Island and in 1960, after 16 years there, he and his wife returned with their children to the mainland, where he worked on a dairy farm and then in a meatworks. At the same time his interest in politics was beginning to develop and he became involved with an organisation called the Coloured Welfare Council. It was eventually merged with a larger organisation, OPAL — One People of Australia League. Bonner became one of OPAL's most devoted workers. It was the period in the mid-60s that eventually led to the 1967 referendum on the removal of discriminatory sections from the Australian Constitution. He also joined the Liberal Party and was able to use his Liberal Party connections to assist OPAL's activities.

The name OPAL was taken from the precious gem made up of many colours, and our aim was to weld all people into one as Australians. But most of our work at the time was involved with Aboriginal people because it was Aboriginal people who were down at the bottom rung of the ladder. After I joined the Liberal Party I was elected as the president of the area of Oxley, which gave me a position on the State Executive. There were two federal politicians and two State politicians on the State Executive, which meant that I was meeting with important people on an equal footing, first name terms and all of this type of thing. And I began to think, here's an area where I can do something for my own people, and I achieved quite a lot by bringing problems and the needs of my people to the attention of State politicians and federal politicians. I did a lot for OPAL. We acquired the big Brisbane Motel as a home through Billy Wentworth, who was Minister for Aboriginal Affairs. And through Vic Sullivan, who was the State Minister for Aboriginal Affairs, we got the money to purchase that building for deserted wives and orphaned children. Then we got the headquarters in Ann Street — we bought the big building there with assistance from the government.

Because of my being involved with these people, I started to learn something about politics and how the whole thing worked, the whole system of branches and areas and State Executive, and politicians themselves. Because I was fairly well known as president of OPAL, I had a lot of television coverage and newspaper coverage and I travelled around a bit for OPAL in Queensland. The party used me a lot at election time, at manning polling booths. There was a by-election on the Gold Coast in the seat of Albert, and that evening there was a dinner on the Isle of Capri at the president's residence. I was standing in a group of people when Ruth Lyons, who was there, said to me in a joking manner: 'Nev! When are we going to be doing something like this for you?' So to be in the swim of things I said, just off the top of my head: 'Oh, Ruth, sooner than you think. I'm going to nominate for preselection for the next half Senate election.' I had no intention of doing it — but just to be in the swim of it. The news went around like wildfire, and everybody was coming up and congratulating me and saying they'll support me at preselection. I *was* preselected — that was in 1970 — and campaigned for the election from what was really an unwinnable position on the Liberal–Country Party ticket. I missed it because Vince Gair was coming up and he won the fifth seat. And then in 1971, when the late Dame Annabelle Rankin was appointed High Commissioner to New Zealand, causing a vacancy in the Liberal ranks, I again nominated and won preselection. The rest is history.

Why did you choose the Liberal Party?

A number of things. I was interested in party politics because of a couple of wonderful young people. One became my stepdaughter and the other is her husband. We used to have lots of discussions about politics and I suppose, all my life, being a working man, I felt automatically that I should support the Labor Party because they're supposed to be for the working class. But Robyn and Noel encouraged me to come along to one of their branch meetings. I attended two or three of them. In 1967 the referendum was coming up. One of the questions was about Aboriginal people: would they be counted in the census and should the government make special laws for Aborigines. They invited me to hand out how-to-vote cards at one of the polling booths and I said, 'Oh look, I couldn't hand out Liberal how-to-vote cards', and they said, 'But all parties are in accord with the question on Aborigines'.

So they put me on a school called the Leichhardt School, out at West Dempsey, at about four o'clock in the afternoon — and the member for Oxley stepped out. Bill Hayden walked up to me and said: 'What the hell are you doing handing out those cards? We do more for Aborigines than they do!' Well, there was no Labor person handing out how-to-vote cards there, nor anyone else except me. And I said: 'Well who the hell are you, anyway?' He said: 'I'm Bill Hayden, the member for Oxley.' 'Well look, Mr Hayden, I'd look silly handing out Labor how-to-vote cards when I'm a member of the Liberal Party!' It annoyed me to think that anyone could come up to me and assume that I would be automatically handing out a particular set of how-to-vote cards. No one had that right.

Were you a member of the Liberal Party?

No, not at that time. But I was the next day!

So the Liberal Party owes Bill Hayden . . .

A vote of thanks. For me becoming a member of the Liberal Party. But you know, that's a fact, and Bill Hayden remembers it, and he's mentioned it to me a couple of times over the years.

As Neville Bonner's public life expanded, his personal life was going through some difficulty and change. After the family came back to the mainland his relationship with his first wife deteriorated and eventually they separated. Mona went back to the same kind of job she had been in when she first met Neville, working on a cattle station. She was about 50 years old when she had a heart attack and died. Neville was left as a single parent with one of his sons still at an age at which he needed to be raised. In retrospect, he feels that his marriage to Mona had never really been a happy one.

Why do you think you had problems in your marriage?

It was a number of things. Mona was a girl from a government settlement and I had lived free for so long. I had some advantage, I suppose, because I'd lived for so long in the normal community and I saw things differently to what Mona did. And there was a problem that I'd prefer not to discuss.

And then you finally separated — but you didn't remarry until after she died.

Whilst we had not lived as man and wife for nearly 14 years, we lived separately in the same house, and I kept the family together because I believed that was my responsibility, regardless of our estrangement. I believed that when your mate dies you have an obligation to respect that over a period of time. And so it was almost three years before I decided to remarry.

And you married Heather, who had been your secretary. Tell me about Heather and her place in your life.

We worked together for quite a considerable time, even when Mona was still alive — at first on the Ipswich Coloured Welfare Council, which eventually became part of OPAL. We both became members

of the board of the OPAL organisation. When I became president of
the board, I asked Heather would she take on being my confidential
secretary. And we worked and got to know each other extremely
well. It was a close friendship in the beginning which developed into
something much more than that. Heather was devoted to working to
assist the Aboriginal people. She became mother figure —
grandmother figure — to a whole lot of Aboriginal children, and
confidante to a whole lot of adult Aboriginal people here in Ipswich
and in Brisbane. We enjoyed working together, and I think one of
the greatest blessings that God has ever given me is bringing us
together. I truly believe that.

Has she helped you in a practical way with your political career?

Not in the beginning. Heather was totally opposed to my becoming
involved politically. I became involved politically through her oldest
daughter, who's now my stepdaughter, Robyn, and her husband
Noel. Heather was opposed to it mainly because she grew up in a
political family. Her grandfather was one of the first federal members
for this locality, Hugh Sinclair. He was a member when Parliament
was meeting in Melbourne, before Canberra was established, and so
she wasn't very attracted to the political scene. Secondly, she felt
that getting involved politically would take me away from the work
that I was doing in OPAL, particularly the work that I was doing
amongst my own people. But I continued my political career and,
when I finally became a senator, Heather then took on the mantle of
a senator's wife, and did it extremely well.

You actually met over a political argument didn't you?

Yes, at the Coloured Welfare Council. Heather was expounding her
views about Aboriginal people and what should happen, and she
used a word that always heckles me — she talked about Aboriginal
people becoming assimilated into the broader Australian
community. Well, that's like showing a red rag to a bull, when
someone brings that up to me, because I'm totally opposed to the
Aboriginal race being totally and absolutely absorbed into the
broader white community. I believe in integration — retaining
where desired one's ethnic and cultural identity, and I believe that
for all people regardless of where they come from. If they want to
become assimilated, that's an individual choice, but I don't believe it
should be a policy of government.

Did you manage to convince her that you were right?

Yes, I think I did.

When you were finally elected to the Senate, you were the first Aboriginal senator ever in Australia. What did you feel about that?

The night I was selected by the party — which meant that then I *had* to be endorsed by the State Government — I was on cloud nine. It was an enormous exhilaration; I'd finally achieved what I'd set out to achieve in the political arena. My last job before I went to Canberra was bridge carpentring. I got my last fortnight's pay, which paid all my bills, and then I was going down to Canberra to have a look at Parliament House. Before I left here I had to borrow five dollars to go to Canberra; that's all the money I had. But the day I was sworn in was a very emotional day for me. Sitting in the gallery was my wife, who was my fiancée at that time, and the girl who was to be my stepdaughter, Robyn, and two Aboriginal women. The custom for a new senator coming into Parliament is that two of your colleagues from your side of Parliament are supposed to grab you, one on each side, and drag you up to sign in to be a senator. As they were leading me up I looked around the galleries and I could feel the whole Aboriginal race, all those who had gone before, up there, and I could visualise . . . I could hear voices, and amongst those voices was the voice of my grandfather saying: 'It's all right now, boy, you are finally in the council with the Australian elders. Everything is now going to be all right!'

It was tremendously emotional for me, and I think I became a little scared, because there I was, and with those thoughts in my mind the whole race was on my shoulders — where we were going from there. That's what I felt at that time. And then I signed the register and I was finally fully-fledged, a senator for Queensland, representing the whole of Australia. Everybody was sort of, 'Hey, we've got a blackfella into Parliament at last!' — but I don't think anyone except my wife, my fiancée at that time, realised what I was going through.

It must have been rather overwhelming for the first Aboriginal senator in Australia to go down and face Canberra — with all the white institutions, the bureaucracy, the pomp and the ceremony and all the other things that are part of it. How did you cope with all of that?

The bureaucracy never bothered me unduly. Sure, I had arguments with them, I had my brawls, but I was able to handle it. The trappings and ceremonies are all par for the course when you get into a situation like that — I had no problem with it. I deliberately did not get myself caught up too much in the visiting with embassies and things like that. Most of those things are small talk and drinks. And one of the things I had to be terribly careful of is that there is a general attitude by non-Aboriginal people that Aborigines are all a mob of drunks and can't handle the liquor. So I had to be very careful in the way I handled the drinking situation down there. I got to be known as the 'one-beer senator'. Every time we went down past the bar into the dining room we'd all stop off and have a drink on the way through, and I always got into the chair and had the first shout so as I could leave whenever I wanted. So I'd shout them and then walk off into the dining room.

Did you feel that you were under particular scrutiny because of your race?

My whole political life was under scrutiny. The way I walked, the way I talked, the way I ate, the way I drank, everything I did was being judged, and the whole race was being judged on it. That happens with all Aborigines who start to climb the ladder, whether it's economically, whether it's socially, whether it's employment-wise or whatever. We're always totally under scrutiny.

Did you feel that you were accepted as an absolute equal by all the other senators down there?

In the chamber, yes. On my feet in the chamber I was given no quarter and I asked none. I was treated totally as an equal in any speeches that I made. But I do believe there was a feeling that I was a lesser person than some of the other members of parliament. They didn't quite see me as an equal intellectually, or academically. I was certainly not equal to them academically, but intellectually I think I was as good as anybody there.

What happened to make you feel that they didn't see you as a real equal?

You perhaps would never have experienced what I'm about to say. You know the old Parliament House, with all its hallways? Well, you'd come down the hallways towards the chamber, there'd be a group of your colleagues standing up talking, and you pull up and you join them. Have you ever been in a situation where people were talking to each other and over you, but never *to* you? It's a very eerie feeling, and that has happened to me. It happened to me on a number of occasions. Then you get another situation, where you join a group of your colleagues, sometimes from both sides of the house, and they're talking about Aboriginal Affairs. And one says to the other, 'How much bloody more have we got to do for these bloody boongs?', and I say, 'Hey, hey, hold on a minute! I'm an

Aborigine'. 'But Nev, you're different. You're one of us.' They add insult to injury! That's been said to me in the halls of Parliament. So they say, 'Oh yeah, you're one of us'. But are you? Or are you still one of those 'boongs' that they're talking about? You can never tell. But you get that distinct feeling that you are different, or looked upon as different to the others. Now, I had some very wonderful friends on both sides of the house, from all political parties, but there were some there that I couldn't stand a bar of, and there were some that couldn't stand a bar of me — so what the heck!

In relation to your work as a senator you must have had a lot of speech writing and letter writing to do. Did you feel confident about carrying that out?

I had no problems with that because I had a brilliant young person who was my secretary, Christine. Because of my lack of education my spelling is not really good. I spell most words as they're spoken, but Christine was able to understand that, and I'd do my speeches out in longhand. And Christine would then knock them into grammatical order, and I'd deliver them. Then I had a research assistant working for me, John Hogg, and he was a brilliant man, and the same thing applied there. I'd just sit down and talk to John, and John would make notes and then knock that into a speech. Christine would type it up, I'd go through it two or three times until I got exactly what I wanted, and away I'd go and deliver it.

At a personal level, were there any other adjustments you had to make in your new life as a senator?

Let me say first and foremost that I enjoyed it! I thought it was great. To go from here to the airport all I had to do was have my secretary ring the pool and have the car pick me up here and take me to the airport. Then, when I got to Canberra, there was always a car there to take me up to Parliament House. I thought that was pretty good stuff. My income had just gone from a bridge carpenter's salary of about $40 a week to quite a substantial amount more than that. And this might have brought some problems except for the fact that I had Heather to guide and counsel me about the use of the money. If I hadn't had Heather there, I think I'd have been home with the seat out of my pants. Because being an Aborigine I have an obligation to share the kangaroo, as it were — and this happened to be a financial kangaroo — with those less fortunate than myself in my own community. Heather is a person who understands the ramifications of wasting or giving money away when you have other obligations. I had to dress properly, I had to have drycleaning and laundry done and all that sort of thing, and all this cost money. She was able to help, and when we got married Heather then, at my request, took over the management of our joint finances, and she's made a darn good job of it ever since.

So you think that really had a significant effect on your ability to deal with this overwhelming change in your life?

If I hadn't had Heather with me, even before we got married, it would have been much much more difficult for me to have been able to handle that, because Heather is one of my greatest critics. If she sees a television program that I've been interviewed on, or reads an article about me in the press, she is always able to analyse the whole thing and point out to me where perhaps I could have done better. She's been a wonderful person in helping me in my career.

The new Senator Bonner was highly conscious of the fact that the eyes of the world were upon him. He was also aware that his Aboriginality, though a disadvantage in some respects, could also be used to his advantage. In his campaigns for Senate preselection he had adroitly exploited some of the racism directed against him by certain extremists within his own party by going public about it. And he once used the slogan 'Put a little colour into Canberra'. He was also aware that the novelty of a black parliamentarian could be used to attract media attention to causes dear to his heart.

I tried several times in the Liberal Party to have the boomerang copyrighted exclusively to the indigenous people, because it is an Aboriginal art, it is unique to Australia, it's never been used by any other race of people, and it is being exploited, I believe, by non-Aboriginal people. I had a small boomerang factory at one stage, and I went broke because I could not compete against the imported Japanese boomerangs made out of plastic and various other compositions. So I wanted that to happen, but I was told that because the boomerang had been in common use for so long it could not be copyrighted. I mentioned it during my maiden speech, and I had several letters from non-Aboriginal people who were in the boomerang manufacturing and throwing business criticising and condemning me for for my attitude, saying that Aborigines couldn't make boomerangs come back anyway.

So I was challenged to prove that my boomerangs did come back, and I invited the press to come into the senate gardens. Now, my boomerangs don't just go out and around and straight back; my boomerangs go out, around, right back behind me in a circle, and come back from behind me. Well, I forgot there was a jolly big, bushy tree behind me, and the first boomerang I threw got caught in the tree. Then I repositioned myself so the rest wouldn't get caught. But when I finished throwing them, I asked the young men of the press, would one of the young fellows be kind enough to climb the tree and retrieve my boomerang. Well, they were a little bit smarter than I thought they were because none of them offered to do it. They realised that here was a coup, they could catch this new Aboriginal senator climbing a tree for his blasted boomerang, and they got some darn good shots. It hit headlines quite a lot throughout Australia.

Why didn't you leave the boomerang where it was, in the tree?

No way! I can't leave one of my boomerangs behind.

You were never Minister for Aboriginal Affairs, which surprised some people.

I think if it had been offered to me, I would not have been willing to accept it.

Why not?

Well, two things. First and foremost, my own people would have expected miracles from me which I would not have been able to produce. Secondly, I think the white population would have said: 'Okay, we've got a blackfella there now, he can wear the blame for all of the ills that are besetting the Aboriginal people.' So I think it would have been disastrous for me. I think it would have killed me, because the emotional drain on me would have been enormous. Any other portfolio would have been hard work, but I would have been able to handle it.

You were the first Aboriginal senator . . .

And the only one. Ever! Since I lost my seat in 1983 I've been very very sad about the fact that, whilst the first Australians make up two per cent of the Australian population, there is not an Aboriginal voice in the federal parliament. Rightly or wrongly, I feel that there'll never be another one in my lifetime, because I don't think the mainstream political parties are prepared to give an Aborigine an opportunity where an Aborigine can make it.

Why do you think that is?

It may seem a bit presumptuous of me to think this, but I don't think the mainline political parties want another Neville Bonner down there.

And what did you do to frighten them so badly?

Well, I suppose I was a bit of a rebel. I voted against my own party, in and out of government, on 23 occasions. I didn't toe the party line. I was fiercely, proudly, a member of the party, but I was not blindly a member of the party. I had a conscience, and political parties don't need people with a conscience. They want bottoms on seats — and hands in the air at the right time.

Neville Bonner was a senator from 1971 until 1983. Throughout his career most of the public criticism he attracted came from other Aboriginal people, who attacked him because of his perceived compliance with the party line rather than opposition to it. In his early years he had a fairly consistent record of support for Joh Bjelke-Petersen, who was then Premier of Queensland. This brought particular criticism when Bonner spoke up for States rights in relation to the notorious Queensland Aborigines Act, which the Commonwealth Government wanted to have repealed and which Bjelke-Petersen wished to retain. Bonner outraged black activists again when he publicly attacked them for organising a visit to Australia of black American militants. He referred to the local activists as 'a mob of ratbags'. He was then accused of 'betraying his own race for a seat in the Senate', and he made a public apology for the use of the term. This was a pattern that persisted throughout his public life. He was always a controversial figure and there were many instances where his publicly expressed opinions were in opposition to the objectives of Aboriginal lobby groups.

Why do you think you attracted criticism from your own people?

When I went down to Canberra, I had to consolidate myself within the party and within the parliament. If I'd have gone down there from the beginning, fighting only the Aboriginal cause, I would not have survived in the preselection. I had to present my bona fides as a senator representing all people. As I became more sure of my standing within the party, I then started to speak out on Aboriginal issues. But I believe that my stand on Aboriginal Affairs was the thing that finally brought me down, and it was the reason why the Liberal Party dropped me to an unwinnable position on their ticket.

I suppose inevitably, because you were the first Aboriginal senator, your life in parliament was marked by a number of controversies. They were quite celebrated incidents at the time. I wonder if we could have a look at those with a bit of hindsight. For example, when Gordon Bryant, a minister in the Whitlam Government, went to visit Palm Island and condemned the conditions he found there, once again you supported Bjelke-Petersen — you defended the conditions. You were criticised very severely for that.

You'll recall, if you will, that the Act had changed and Palm Island was not the Palm Island it was when I lived there. It was open and people could leave. They had a form of self-government, they'd already elected their own council on the island, and things had changed considerably to what it was under a Labor Government in the days when I was there. So when Gordon went there, it was after the change. Had he gone there when the Labor Government was in power in Queensland, he would have had a lot more to say about the conditions on Palm Island.

So in defending it you weren't saying it was a good thing, you were just saying it was better than it had been.

That's right. [He leaves a long pause, then laughs.] Okay?

Did you feel that the criticism that came from your own people over that was unfair?

No — it doesn't matter what I think. I believe that everyone has a right to express themselves and someone else can oppose that expression. I made my statement, they opposed it and they criticised me for it — that's their right. I've criticised other people, and that's my right. So whilst I felt that perhaps their criticism was unjust, it doesn't alter the fact that I defend their right to do it.

There was the occasion also of the Springbok tour, when you came in for a lot of criticism because you were seen to side with Joh Bjelke-Petersen on that issue, against a number of black people who were criticising the tour. Could you tell us a little about your thoughts on that now?

I don't think it would have mattered who — whether it was Joh Bjelke-Petersen or whoever. My attitude towards the Springbok tour was that there was a group of sportsmen invited into our country on good faith, by the Australian sporting body, as guests in our country. They should have been treated with respect and courtesy, the same as we would expect if we visited their country. Secondly, I was opposed to people saying that they should have only come if they'd had black Africans with them. Knowing the apartheid situation in South Africa — if that would have happened they'd have come to Australia and then returned to their own country, back to the apartheid situation. I would suggest that would have been a very cruel thing to do to any people. I've always been opposed to the apartheid system as it was practised in South Africa.

Another incident occurred when Billy McMahon was Prime Minister and protesting Aborigines set up what was called a Tent Embassy on the lawns of Parliament House. At first you made a very strong speech in the Senate attacking the whole idea of the Embassy and the young black radicals who were behind it. But later you modified your position.

I didn't believe that the front lawns of Parliament House was the correct place to have that Embassy. I said that. But once it was established, the number of non-Aboriginal people who were visiting there and listening and talking to the organisers made me then think: 'Hey, they have a right to be there, they have a right to put their problems to the people; they're doing it well. Now they should be left alone until they realise that they have achieved what they wanted to achieve and then fold things up and go away.'

There were moves afoot by the government of the day, under the Prime Minister, the late William McMahon, to have the Embassy moved by force. Parliament was closing for the winter session. I had an interview with McMahon and I also said in the Parliament that the Embassy should not be forcibly moved while Parliament was in recess. I was let down by that, because immediately Parliament closed down the police moved in under the instructions of the government. I had very grave concerns about that and felt that I was badly let down by the Prime Minister because he promised that he would not move against the people. Everybody has a right to protest. I don't quite agree that the lawns of Parliament House is the correct place to do it — by setting up a very ragged-looking Tent Embassy. I felt that they overplayed their hand because they shouldn't have gone on as long as they did. I think it became an eyesore, and I think they were turning people off rather than turning people on.

You've been called an 'Uncle Tom', you've been called a 'tame cat', you've been called many names by people who felt that you were in fact 'half on the other side' — that you were in some ways too sympathetic with the white man's view. How does it make you feel when these names are applied to you?

Anyone who is called harsh names like that is hurt by it, and I certainly was hurt by it. But, by the same token, I can understand their frustrations and their annoyances. I wasn't selling them out, but they didn't understand what I was doing and the reasons why I was doing it. I was a new boy in Parliament. I was the first Aborigine ever to go into Parliament. I had to establish myself as a person who was able to make a contribution towards Parliament as a whole, not just on single issues. Having consolidated myself, I was then able to come out on different issues in a more forceful and — if you want to use the term — a little more radical way than I was when I first went there. To have acted unwisely or presumptuously — I could have very well been thrown out of Parliament. That would achieve nothing! So I had to continue to be in that Parliament — to have an Aboriginal voice in that Parliament for as long as was humanly possible, or possible for Neville Bonner to do it. And I had to create an impression on the total Australian population that an Aborigine was capable of doing those things.

Did you feel at any stage of your political career that you were being used as a 'token' Aborigine — as someone who was put on display as window dressing?

That's been said about the Liberal Party. Maybe in 1970, when I first ran in an unwinnable position on the ticket, there may have been some of that in the minds of some of the people then. But no, I don't believe that when I got the 'plum', as it were, in 1971, that the people on preselection really felt that they were using me as a gimmick. You don't win a preselection on the first ballot because you're black. You win it because people have faith in you and believe that you have the capacity to do something. I can't be persuaded otherwise.

There's a very fine line between the concept of a 'token' and the concept of a symbol. The question remains for some people: which were you? Were you a token black? Or were you the symbol of the ability of the Aboriginal people to take their place in the national council?

You, young lady, are in a very safe position — you are an interviewer. If someone else said that to me, they'd find themselves flat on their back on the floor! I am no token! I never was, and I never will be for anyone, in a political party or in any other situation. I am Neville Bonner, proud to be an Aborigine, and proudly a member of this Australian community. I am a token for no person! And if they thought I was, then they were thinking wrong, and let them not ever express that opinion to me. Because — don't let the old grey hairs fool you — I still pack a decent sort of a wallop!

Your particular political philosophy, which was to act as far as possible within the system, often placed you in the position of being 'the man inbetween'. Did you find this position sometimes a bit lonely?

For me, as an Aborigine, being in Parliament was one of the loneliest places I've ever been. You've got to be in that position to understand the feelings that you could have — being the only black in that whole system of parliamentary procedures. It's a lonely place! I've always said that loneliness is something that you can have, no matter if you're in the middle of the busiest city in the world. It's the environment in which you are. The people around you — all sorts of things that happen that make it lonely for you. I had many colleagues that I was friendly with but I had no confidants, as it were.

What helped you?

Having the most wonderful, beautiful human being in the world — having her at the other end of a telephone, and someone to come home to. And also my faith in the parliamentary procedures that we live under. You can make it work for you, with perseverance, quietly and continually hammering at the issues that you feel concerned about. You don't win everything, but you win some things — that gives you the strength. It's like playing golf. You go out there and you'll hit a ball one day and get 250 yards. It makes you come back the next day hoping that you'll do the same. I think Parliament's a bit like that. You win some, you lose some, you win some, you lose some — but the ones that you win make it worthwhile coming back to have a go at the next one.

What do you think was your main achievement while you were in Canberra?

I think the fact that I was there. That an Aborigine was there. I think it gave a lot of the people down there time to have a second look, a second thought, about the whole race, because one of them was their colleague. I could imagine that, before I was present in the party room, when Aboriginal issues came up the kind of things that were being said in the hallways would have been said in the party room. But when there was an Aborigine sitting in the party room, as a fellow colleague, the language was much more subdued. They talked about Aborigines rather than boongs and blacks. So, you know, there was a lot of things that made quite an impact and a difference in the attitudes and thinking of people. If you look at the land rights issue:

strangely enough, in every State it was the conservative governments who gave land rights to Aboriginal people. Strange thing that, isn't it?

The record shows that, as a senator, Neville Bonner became bolder and more outspoken on behalf of Aborigines as time went by. It is easy to underestimate the difficulty he must have had in finding the right way to 'make a difference'. And it was consistent with his whole character and philosophy that he preferred to avoid conflict with authority and to try to find solutions by cooperating with the established order. This attitude persisted despite an early set-back to his efforts to promote a Private Member's Bill, the Admissibility of Confessions Bill. This Bill was an attempt to stop police 'verballing', a practice commonly used to convict Aborigines. Bonner's interest in this particular form of injustice had been given momentum when, in July 1973, his 18-year-old son Peter was picked up by police and charged with begging alms in a public place. The police claimed that he had confessed. Peter denied it. The experience was one that Neville knew to be common among young Aboriginal men. It is a cause of frustration to him still that the Bill did not go through.

What went wrong with the Admissibility of Confessions Bill? It sounds as if it could really have made a difference.

I was fobbed off with that one. It's one of the things I most regret. I had a friend who was a barrister and he was very much involved with an Aboriginal Legal Service. Between us this barrister and I put together the skeleton of a Bill whereby no Aborigine being arrested could be locked up until an independent witness was called by the police to be beside the Aboriginal person, and take down everything that that person or the police officer said — which would be used in evidence. I took the framework of the Bill down to Canberra and it finished up a Bill of about 20 or 30 pages, with all the parliamentary jargon that goes with introducing legislation. I put it up for its first reading, and I waited to put it on for the second reading speech. Then I was told that there was another Bill coming in that would make it much simpler and easier for my Bill to go through — but it never eventuated. I have grave regrets that it never got through. I was fobbed off.

Between 1976 and 1978 you took a strong stand on the dispute at the Aurukun Aboriginal Reserve on Cape York Peninsula. The issue related to granting of leases for bauxite mining in the area. You spoke out against

the Bjelke-Petersen Government on that matter and helped persuade
Malcolm Fraser to intervene on behalf of the Aborigines. What happened?

What happened was that there were apparently some problems
on Aurukun. You must realise that, at that time, the community was
run by a Presbyterian Church — they had Presbyterian people as
manager and in various areas of responsibility. The Queensland
Government decided that the church wasn't doing its job, so they
decided that they would take over the community and — in plain
English — they sacked all of the church leaders. The Aurukun
people did not want that to happen. They wanted the Presbyterian
Church leaders to remain with them; they had a Christian faith,
they were Presbyterians and they wanted their leaders left alone.

I came into it because I believed that they had a right to remain
as a Christian community if they so desired. I didn't believe the
Queensland Government had any right at all to take the action that
they did, and I fought them all the way. A number of the Aboriginal
leaders of the community paid their own fares to come to Canberra
and discuss the whole matter with the Prime Minister. We spent a
lengthy meeting in the Cabinet room with the Prime Minister and
some of his senior ministers. Unfortunately, there were promises
made by the Prime Minister that were never kept: that the
Commonwealth Government would ensure that the State
Government did not take over Aurukun. But they never ever
prevented it from happening. At the time, Prime Minister Fraser
made some statements that I totally disagreed with. You might recall
that I was interviewed on television and I said that, in view of some
of the statements that were made, I would have to consider my
position within the Liberal Party.

In fact the party had begun considering its position on Neville
Bonner. His public brushes with key State politicians and his
increasingly independent stand on Aboriginal issues were making him
less useful to the Coalition Government, which in the early days had
been able to rely on him for public justification of its policies. He had
started crossing the floor on certain social issues in order to prevent
the erosion of some of the rights and privileges of pensioners and
other battlers, and this brought him into public conflict with a
number of leaders on his own side of politics. In 1983 he was
dropped from the position that he previously held on the Coalition's
ticket for the Senate.

Did it come as a shock to you when you were dropped to an unwinnable position on the ticket?

Yes and no. Both Heather and I sensed that something was not quite right. We had attended the Young Liberals convention in Toowoomba early in the year — before the double dissolution was called — and we got a general feeling that things just weren't quite right. We were again alerted when the party decided that it wouldn't be a normal preselection. It was decided that it would be all of the State Executive, plus the chairman of each of the areas in Queensland, which cut the numbers down to about 60. And they met and decided in favour of Cathy Martin taking number one position, Senator McGibbon taking second position and Neville Bonner taking last position, which was an unwinnable one. And that's how it finished up that night at preselection.

How did you feel?

I was in a state of shock, I think, even though the antennas were starting to wiggle a bit, prior to it happening. I returned to my hotel and told Heather what had happened, and I didn't get any sleep that night. I was just so stunned with it all. In the early hours of the morning I think I finally came to the decision that 'a man's got to do what a man's got to do'. And I wasn't prepared to take that insult — because I was the senior senator for the Liberal Party in Queensland at the time, I was the longest serving one, and I believe that I'd served my party well and therefore I was entitled to a better deal than that. So I decided that I would run as an Independent.

I had two telephone calls early next morning, one from Malcolm Fraser who was quite shocked at what had happened and wanted to know what he could do — and I told him it was too late, he couldn't do anything. Then I had a telephone call from Mr Hawke, who was quite confident that he was going to win the election, and he said that if I lost the election his government would ensure that my talents weren't lost to the nation. I made a telephone call to the Secretary of the Labor Party, Peter Beattie, and said that I was making a major statement that day to the press and I was going to announce that I was running as an Independent. Could I count on the Labor Party for preferences? And Beattie said: 'No problems, Nev, you've got 'em!' I knew that without the Labor preferences I didn't have much chance, because it would go to preferences. I finished up 0.05 per cent short of a quota in my own right; but unfortunately Peter Beattie's promise never eventuated, I did not get the Labor preferences. But it was a very close thing and I will always be extremely proud of the support I received from the Queensland people.

Did you feel bitter about the Liberal Party?

I felt very bitter towards the top echelon of the party who organised the preselection, but for the Liberal Party no. The people in the Liberal Party, some of the wonderful friends that I made in the party — had they been on that preselection, I don't believe I would have had the same result.

Under Malcolm Fraser's prime ministership Neville Bonner had been made chairman of a committee set up to examine the adequacy of Northern Territory laws relating to protection of sacred sites and to other matters affecting Aboriginal land. Still a senator, he had also had the opportunity to inform himself better than ever of the broader problems facing the Aboriginal people and some of the possible solutions. Bonner now believes that real equality will not come in his lifetime and that it will take several generations for the Aboriginal people to achieve their rightful place in Australian society. He also believes that nothing will change without continuing positive discrimination designed to make up for the years of ill-treatment and neglect.

I have an all-consuming burning desire to help my own people — the Aboriginal community — to become respected, responsible citizens within the broader Australian community, retaining where desired ethnic and cultural identity but having all of the opportunities that every white Australian takes for granted: education, employment, health, housing and social and economic standing. Those are the things I want for my own people. The deaths in custody, the number of Aboriginal people who are in prison who shouldn't be in prison — all of those things need to be attended to first and foremost before you can say: 'Oh, it's great. We're all now equal! We're all now playing our part in the building of this great nation.'

We've come a long way in the last 20 years, but there's still a long, long way to go. And even though I'm an old man I hope I can still make a contribution somewhere along the line towards helping our people to achieve those things that most Australian white people take as their right. We as Aboriginal people still have to fight to prove that we are straightout plain human beings, the same as everyone else. You know, I was born on a government blanket under a palm tree. I've lived under lantana bushes, I've seen more dinner-times than I've ever seen dinners, I've known discrimination, I've known prejudice, I've known all of those things. Some of that is still with us, even today, and it's got to be changed. It can only be changed when people of non-Aboriginal extraction are prepared to listen, and hear what Aboriginal people are saying, and then help us and work with us to achieve those ends.

Neville Bonner's goal of being seen as reliable, decent and respectable has been quite spectacularly achieved, despite the fact that his early male role models were not ideal for the purpose. He has always lived by a strong code of responsibility, and in the course of our conversations often used the word 'irresponsible' to denounce behaviour of which he disapproved. In public life he has been careful to maintain his reputation for sobriety. Yet his grandfather and his stepfather were both drinkers and he spent his formative years with them.

What did you think about the drinking of the men who were part of your early life?

I was a bit young to really understand what it was all about, when I was only nine or ten in Lismore, except that I knew that we would have a lot more to eat if there was no money spent on drink. Then, as we moved away from there to other places, and I got to about 12 or 14, I started to think, my gosh, when I grow up to be a man I'm not going to spend my money on that sort of thing, I'm going to make better use of my money than that. I think that's stood me in pretty good stead over the years. Mind you, I'm not a teetotaller. I have my few beers the same as any other Aussie does, but I don't spend a lot of money on it.

There must have been a lot of young Aboriginal boys who'd come to exactly the same conclusion but nevertheless fell into the drinking habit?

Not all — but yes, unfortunately far too many did fall into it.

Why do you think that is? Why do you think it is such a problem?

Well, there's a whole lot of things. The kind of lifestyle we live, the discrimination, the prejudice, the denial of an education that would qualify us for good paying jobs are part of it. Then there's the loss of culture, language and all of those things that were important to us as

Aboriginal people. In desperation, looking for a crutch or oblivion, I myself have been intoxicated, so I have an idea what it's like. You are not thinking rationally and you feel that bravado in you from the alcohol. It befuddles your mind. You feel that you're as good as anyone; you can walk down the street and push people off the footpath and say, 'I'm as good as youse — or better'. When you're sober, the realities of what your life is, where your place is in the community, hits you pretty forcefully, and a lot of people want to go back to that oblivion that the accursed grog brings to you, and so they go back to the drink again. So there's a whole lot of reasons why, and basically a lot of Aboriginal people do drink to excess.

Have you got any ideas about solutions to the problem?
It's a big problem, but it is being tackled by Aboriginal people. There are a lot more Aboriginal organisations now working to educate and to help find a solution to these problems, and I think that is the way it should have been going long before this. Far too often and for far too long — I've said this before in many speeches in Parliament and outside of Parliament — all the decisions concerning we the Aboriginal community have been made for us by non-Aboriginal people, looking at the problem through their eyes and coming up with solutions that fit into their particular priorities and values. We are of a different culture, we are a different race; we are a unique race of people. We never had these problems prior to the coming of the white man to the country, and so we fell easy prey to all of these things. But now what we're saying is: 'Let us now start making some of the decisions that affect us. Let's use *our* priorities, *our* values, to find the solution to it.'

Aboriginal culture is said to concentrate particularly on developing spiritual awareness, on bringing a better understanding of what is significant in spiritual terms to human beings. Has this aspect of your background played a part in shaping you?
Whilst the rest of the world was busily involved with the various sciences and technology, we the Aboriginal people lived a lifestyle where we did not feel that we needed to expand or to develop those areas, because we were happy in our life, our relationship with nature and with the land. But what we had developed was the science of the mind. We'd developed that science to such a degree that it is impossible for non-Aboriginal people to comprehend and to accept that we, a so-called primitive people, could have achieved those things — but we did. Certain things happen to me. If one of

my sons or one of my grandchildren has an accident or is ill, or passes on, I *know*. I can tell my wife that I will receive some disturbing news about one of our family within a reasonable time, and I do. So that is part of the development. I haven't developed it; it is part of something that I've inherited from my ancestors. I have an ability to commune. I can go out into the bush and sit quietly in the dusk of the afternoons or the evenings and I can commune with the elders who have gone on before me. I can hear them — they talk to me — and I can commune with them. That's part of this development of the mind.

But we're losing it fast, a lot of our culture has been lost. We've been forced in some way to leave it behind, because we're not accepted in the broader Australian community and people scoff and laugh and ridicule these things that we talk about, and so we don't talk about them any more. A lot of the suburban Aboriginal people have lost so much of it. It's still very strong within the isolated Aboriginal communities, particularly in the Northern Territory and the northwest of South Australia, the Kimberleys of Western Australia, the Cape York Peninsula, some of the isolated communities like Aurukun, Mornington Island, Mitchell River, King Edward River, and places like that. It's still very strong amongst the old people up there, but the young people are losing it because of education, because of the introduction of television and radio, and because they are able to get into the towns and see the bright lights and things that are much easier to handle and to link with.

You were given from your grandfather a certain power and responsibility, weren't you?

Yes, passed down.

In what form did that come to you?

Well, first and foremost I was given the tjuringa [he indicates an object hanging on the wall]. That's come down through my grandfather's family for numbers of generations.

What is the meaning of the tjuringa?

I can't give you all of the meaning, but I'll give you a sort of brief overview of it. It's something that belongs to a family group; it comes down from the elder of each family, in what you might call the family tree. And there are markings on it depicting the life of each of the people in the various generations as it comes down. I have not made any marks on it because I didn't learn how to make

those marks. There are certain marks that tell a whole range of
sentences, with one little mark made in a particular design. But my
life story could well have been told on that, as was the case with the
previous holders of it.

*What is the power and responsibility that comes with it? What does it
enable you to do?*

Well, that again is something that we do not make known to non-
Aboriginal people.

Will it go to your sons?

None of my sons have shown any great interest in the Aboriginal
culture. None of us can speak the language now, but they've become
suburbanites. They don't have any desire to learn or to understand
the things that I'm able to pass on. So the tjuringa now will not be
passed on by me to any of my family. It will go into the grave when
my time comes. I say that with a great deal of sadness.

*This seems to represent quite a loss of faith, a loss of hope for the future of
Aboriginal culture.*

Not in the totality. But as far as my Jagara tribe is concerned, yes.
Fortunately a great deal is still being held in a lot of isolated
communities, but even there some of it is passing, unfortunately.

*What do you think is the future of the Aboriginal people? Do you feel
that, even though the culture is being eroded on the spiritual side, it will
remain in some outward form?*

I don't know. It's very difficult to predict what will happen to
Aboriginal culture. There are a lot of young Aboriginal people now,
urban Aboriginal people, who are trying to relearn and recapture
some of it, and they're going into the isolated communities where it
is still being preserved. Maybe they'll have success in preserving it, I
don't know. I tend to think that the answer to the Aboriginal
question is a total integration into the broader Australian
community, accepting the same responsibilities, having the same
opportunities, as other Australians. I think that is the ultimate
inasfar as we the Aboriginal people are concerned.

*You've lived a long life, travelled widely and seen a lot of the world, and
been involved in debating big issues. What do you feel about the future
generally for the world? Do you feel optimistic or pessimistic?*

I'm optimistic. We've gone through a great deal in my lifetime. I was
born just after the First World War but I recall a lot that was told to
me about it. We went through the Second World War, we went

through Korea, Malaysia, Vietnam, Cambodia. We saw two atomic bombs being exploded and the devastation that caused. I'm optimistic because I believe that God has his hands on everything and there are sufficient people in the world to ensure that those things will not occur again. That may be a simplistic view, but it's mine, and I am optimistic that things will change for the better and mankind will overcome.

When you talk about God, are you talking about your Christian God or . . .

There is only one God.

But do you also have a view of the way in which that understanding applies in the Aboriginal world?

Yes. Look, God is a name. You're talking about God — it's a name. It's an English name. Now, every other nationality has a name for their supreme being, so we have a name for our supreme being too. But when I study the Christian faith and the Ten Commandments that were handed down to Moses, I find that the laws of my people are no different. Maybe in language, of course, it's different, but the meanings are the same. We had our laws which are not exactly the same but similar to the laws that were handed down. So the God that I believe in is the same God as the white Christian believes in. He is the supreme being, the creator, the God all-powerful, all-loving, all-forgiving. The God that I believe in as an Aborigine is the same God as I believe in as a Christian, except that he has a different name.

And after you die, where do you think you'll go? What do you think it means to die?

I can't answer that question because that is in the hands of my God, where I go. I think the only fear that I have is that, when I do pass on, the God I believe in will say: 'Depart from me, I know ye not'. I *hope* that he will say: 'Come into my kingdom my son, my good and faithful servant'. But I don't know. I can only hope that I've lived my life and I've pleased my God, and that there is a place in his kingdom for me. I believe that, and I'll die believing that. As to whether that will happen is in the hands of my God.

Neville Bonner today seems as friendly and energetic as ever. His dignified and courteous manner and his striking appearance — wiry body, strong dark face and shock of white hair — do not entirely conceal the vulnerability and sensitivity that have been a hallmark of his personality throughout life. He serves on the Council of Griffith University and is a Prison Visitor in Queensland. He is on the advisory committee for Old Parliament House in Canberra. With his wife Heather he still lives in Ipswich, in a typical old Queensland weatherboard house set high off the ground and with wide verandahs. His hopes for a better future for Aboriginal Australia remain undiminished; his sober assessment that it will not emerge quickly has not altered.

$\mathcal{S}$ir Mark Oliphant

Ingenuity and Innocence

$\mathcal{S}$ir Mark Oliphant, now well into his nineties, has about him such an air of rosy kindliness and transparent goodwill that it is difficult to connect him with anything but the benign. That his name is associated with the development of the most powerful weapon of destruction the world has ever seen is a source of perpetual surprise, especially to himself. It still causes him pain.

From childhood onwards he showed an outstanding talent for finding ingenious solutions to practical problems. It seems that it was this as much as his academic qualifications that secured him a place in the Cambridge group of physicists who pioneered the exploration of the atom.

Throughout his life he has been confronted with difficult dilemmas; with situations that involved conflict between what *he thought was right and what interested him as an individual. The work that made the development of nuclear weapons possible fascinated and enthralled him even while his awareness of its consequences horrified and repelled him.*

Later in his life his sense of gratitude and obligation to Australia, the country of his birth, took him away from his beloved research into administration, which he loathed. The same desire to serve Australia led him to accept the invitation to be Governor of South Australia. In this position of apparent power he felt himself to be a puppet, the formality of the office depriving him of his personal freedom.

More than most, Sir Mark Oliphant has had cause to ponder the serious choices that human life can present. This interview uncovers his achievements and his regrets and reveals the thoughts and motivations of a man whose profound love and respect for life has brought him through difficult times.

Mark Oliphant was born in 1901 in South Australia. His father was a clerk in the public service and his mother had been a schoolteacher before she married. They had five sons, all born within the space of eight years. The parents were devout Christians, hated cruelty to animals and were vegetarians.

MO I was the eldest of five boys. And I'm now the only one left — which is rather strange. We grew up in South Australia and my primary schooling was in the Adelaide Hills. It was real countryside in those days. I went to a one-teacher school. The master was an Irishman and a marvellous teacher. Despite the fact that he had to deal with all these students, of varying stages of education, he managed them so well that when it came time for me to go to high school, in the city, I had no feeling that I was in any way less well off than those who'd been educated in the State schools in Adelaide itself.

RH *Did you do well at school? Were you a natural scholar?*

No, no. I was never a natural scholar, for two reasons. First of all, I was very nearsighted, and this wasn't realised for some time. I couldn't see the blackboard or the teacher very well. Even when I got glasses it was a bit difficult. I'm also completely deaf in the left ear, and for that reason I also missed much of what was said by the teacher. I was always interested in school and in my lessons, but in the end it was more or less self-education. And my mother, having been a schoolteacher, was a very great help to me.

How old were you when they discovered that you had these two disabilities?

I don't remember when they discovered my shortsightedness, but I do remember the discovery of my deafness. I was at Goodwood School, and it was discovered by the Nursing Sister who visited the school and looked at the students. I remember her making me stand in an open space and then, with my back to her, she walked backwards speaking to me all the time and I had to hold my hand up when I could no longer hear her.

Very precise and scientific.

Yes [he laughs].

And at home — what kind of person was your father?

He was a very dignified, almost Victorian, man. A very cultured, very well-read person, and so was my mother. I got my love of reading largely from them, and their advice as to what I should read. He was a student all his life. Although he was a lowly civil servant he took a great interest in the Workers' Educational Association. In the end he became a lecturer in economics to the WEA classes in South Australia. He was very fond of walking and we went for very long walks — hundreds of miles, carrying our swags and sleeping in the open. He taught me a very great deal about nature, which I've been aware of ever since. For instance, I remember once we were walking along and it was a windy day and the trees were waving very much in the breeze, and I said: 'Isn't there a danger that the trees will break in the wind?' And he said to me: 'Oh no, son, that's the way they take their exercise.'

And what other values were part of the household?

My father was a very religious man, and I grew up to be a choirboy at the church, and then an altar boy, and that continued until I went to the university. We were High Church Anglican and my father was very keen for me to be a clergyman; I think because he rather felt that *he* would have liked to have been one. So he got me tutored at home and at a family friend's place in Latin and Greek, and by the time I went to high school I was quite fluent in both. I've kept my Latin as a result of my experience in Cambridge, where almost everything that could possibly be in Latin was in Latin. I've retained some of my ancient Greek also, but I'm not fluent any longer.

And back in the classroom, did you ever get any better? Were you ever the boy who came top?

Only in Latin and at times in essay writing. I liked writing, and I liked writing essays. But I was never a good student — I was never top of the class or anything of that sort. I was always in the middle range.

So when did the fact that you were going to be remarkable as a scientist begin to emerge? Was it while you were an undergraduate?

I think it was when I was young. I was always fooling about in the shed at the back of the garden, with bits of wire and bits of wood, making what my brothers called my 'raggedy baggedy engines'. And I was always pottering about with my hands. I loved doing things with my hands.

What did the raggedy baggedy engines actually do?

Oh, they just made noises and so on. You pulled wires and things moved. And I developed all sorts of secret ways of locking the door so that my brothers couldn't get in and play around with what I'd been making. You'd have to walk around the back and pull a wire in order to open the front door — things of that sort.

What kind of influence did your mother have on your early years?

My mother had far more influence on me, in reality, than my father did. She was a natural teacher, and she just did it in a natural sort of way. At school we used to have a sort of report book in which your performance in every lesson of the day was marked down by the teacher, and each week you had to have this week's work signed by a parent. And if it was bad it was always to my mother that I took it, rather than to my father.

What made you decide to do science at university?

I was destined originally to be a clergyman but I didn't like that idea in the end, although when I was young I quite enjoyed my religion. I think it was more the ceremony than any sort of belief. It was something that was expected of me and I did it and it wasn't unpleasant — let's put it that way. Anyhow, being a member of what the Americans would call a 'do-gooder' family I decided that I'd be a doctor, so I started out on a medical course. Then I came in contact with Brailsford Robertson, the Professor of Physiology and Biochemistry, who had worked in Toronto with the discoverer of the cure for diabetes, which was one of the first great discoveries of that sort. He was a very tall man and a very nice man, and we got along very well together. Because I was interested in gadgetry, he asked me to help him with an experiment to prove whether or not animals made any direct use of the nitrogen in the atmosphere, or whether it all came through proteins in the food. It was quite a fascinating task for me. In the end I decided that that's what I wanted to do; I didn't want to be a doctor, I wanted to be a scientist.

In this way the boy who was not an outstanding scholar, but who had a curious mind and a way with his hands, settled on science. Because his parents were struggling to find the money to pay the fees at Adelaide University, Mark Oliphant's discovery that he was more interested in becoming a scientist than training to be a doctor opened up the possibility of some financial relief. The Physics Department offered a cadetship which paid ten shillings a week and provided a free course at the university. It was that ten shillings a week that bought for physics the person who was to become one of the world's leading scientists. No other science department offered a similar arrangement. With his father at that stage earning perhaps five pounds a weeks, the cadetship would make a significant difference to the household income. In 1919 the young Oliphant enrolled as an undergraduate student in physics.

Did you have any doubts that you were doing the right thing in shifting from medicine to physics?

What I didn't like about medicine in particular was that a medical course is almost entirely learning-by-rote. I felt that this wasn't for me. When this opportunity came to do some biochemistry I thought it was marvellous to get the opportunity to really think about things, rather than just learn that proteins were molecules with a certain sort of structure and sugars were a different kind of thing and so on.

So at this stage you really had a confidence in your own ability to find a way through things; to be able to take some charge of the way you were going to think about a problem.

I don't think *that* ever occurred to me. The future was something that was the future, and I was quite content to potter around and do things which interested me. I had no great ambitions at that stage. I never did extremely well in my course in physics. I did come top of the second year physics class, but then in third year I didn't do too well. But I did get a first class honours degree, and then pottered about doing a bit of research. Strangely enough, the best lectures that I had on the properties of radioactive materials were given by the Professor of Chemistry rather than the Professor of Physics. He made it very interesting — the changes that took place in this material, radium, as it gradually changed into lead of mass 206, which differentiated it from ordinary lead. I began conducting some experiments myself to try to remake uranium out of uranium X. They led nowhere — but that introduced me to radioactivity and to nuclear physics.

Then in 1925 Ernest Rutherford, who was the head of the Cavendish Laboratory in Cambridge, was travelling by ship to visit his old mother in New Zealand, and when the ship called in at Adelaide he came to the university and gave a lecture about what was going on in the Cavendish Laboratory. He was so generous in giving praise to the people who were his students and who worked with him that I thought to myself that this was the man I wanted to work with. So from then on my efforts were directed towards trying to get a scholarship to go to Cambridge, which I managed to do in 1927.

It's interesting to imagine the impact in 1925 of the visit of a great man. We have them flying in and out all the time now, but it must have meant a lot in Adelaide in those days.

Oh, it did! It was so inspiring to hear a man of that calibre talk, when I'd been taught by ordinary sorts of professors — who were quite good in their way but not presidents of the Royal Society or men who had unravelled the whole story of the way in which uranium changed over time into lead.

And so he became something of a hero to you?

Very much so. And later on he became much more than a hero. He was a man that I grew really to love. He was so inspiring, a man of such incredible personality, that wherever he was he was always the dominant figure. Not in any sort of domineering way, but simply through sheer personality.

How did you manage to get the scholarship to Cambridge?

A lecturer in physics at Adelaide was doing some work on the surface tension of mercury and he asked me to help him. To think of the hours and hours I spent boiling up mercury in flasks and distilling it, blowing all the vapour off the mercury into the subterranean room in which this work was done — and yet I never got mercury poisoning. It's really quite remarkable, because I've handled mercury all my life in experimental work . . .

The Oliphants must be tough.

Either that or the effects of mercury have been grossly overstated! But it was that little bit of work I did, on the surface tension of mercury being affected not by liquids but by gases, and also my attempt to remake uranium out of uranium X, that led me to write some journal articles which were published. These stood me in good stead when I applied for an 1851 Overseas Scholarship, which I was lucky enough to be awarded, along with a free passage by ship to England. So I promptly got married and had to pay my wife's fare to England.

How had you met your wife?

At the university there was a thing called a dancing club — the old-fashioned dancing where one wore a black tie and it was all done in a very proper fashion. My wife's name then was Rosa Wilbraham. She came to the dance and that's where I met her.

What did you like about her?

I don't know, you can't say what attracts you to a person. I think I liked her long hair. She had her hair hanging down her back and that was one thing that I liked.

After you were married, how long did it take you to get to England? You set out on this long voyage to England.

It took seven weeks from Adelaide to Liverpool. It was a Blue Funnel ship which berthed in Liverpool, which in those days was a great port of call. Then we took the boat train to London where my wife had relatives, with whom we stayed for a day or two while we got our bearings. I went down to Cambridge to explore the situation a bit and to enrol myself at Trinity College. I just loved Cambridge from the first moment. It's my spiritual home still. And I became a Fellow of St John's College in the end, although I graduated from Trinity College.

Mark Oliphant had been dreaming and planning and working towards getting to the Cavendish Laboratory for a long time before he arrived. In fact the next few years were to be a golden period of happy and productive scientific discovery, before the pressures of the war years brought the strain of great moral dilemmas into his life. His unusual gift for finding ingenious ways to construct the apparatus needed to test Rutherford's prolific and imaginative ideas was quickly revealed and he became indispensable in the laboratory. But when the young South Australian first arrived at the cold and dusty building that housed the Cavendish he was in for a surprise.

It wasn't at all the sort of place that I'd expected. I'd expected a beautiful laboratory. Instead of that it was a terribly old-fashioned building. It was off an old, cobbled, curved lane, and there was a large door that opened on to what was known as the university museums. All the laboratories in Cambridge in those days were known as museums — I suppose they started as museums and only became experimental after a time. The entrance to the Cavendish was a sort of archway that went through to most of the laboratories. But the Cavendish also had a little foyer, a little place with a wooden staircase going up to the next floor. There were a few portraits hanging on the wall, but the whole of the available floorspace, underneath the staircase and elsewhere, was filled up with bicycles, dozens and dozens of them just jammed together, because everybody in Cambridge in those days rode a bicycle — and still does, I find.

When I got to the top of the staircase, I found myself walking along a passageway with bare, wooden floors and absolutely filthy windows. I got to Rutherford's office and was ushered in.

I could scarcely see Rutherford because the place was so full of smoke. He was a continuous pipe smoker. He smoked a tobacco which had been dried out in front of the fire at home, and it was like a volcano. There were ashes and sparks coming out of it all the time. But I sat down in front of his desk and we chatted away about my ideas and what I'd like to do. Then he said to me: 'Well now you'd better go around and make yourself familiar with the laboratory, go and talk to some of the boys.' I said: 'Which boys?' He said, 'Oh you'll find JJ, he's still working down in the basement, and you'll find Aston next door.' J. J. Thomson was the discoverer of the electron, one of those gods who lived 'up there' for me, and Aston was the man who first measured the masses of isotopes of atoms. Then Rutherford gave me a number of other names of equally distinguished people that I was to go and see, and I was completely awed. But JJ was very kind to me, so was Aston, and so were the other people that I'd been told to talk to, and I felt immediately at home. I didn't feel that I was a stranger.

I *did* feel a stranger, though, at the colloquiums they had each week in the Cavendish, at which some member of the staff or one of the workers in the laboratory gave a talk. Sometimes we were addressed by a distinguished visitor like Niels Bohr or Einstein, or Max Planck or Heisenberg — people of that sort — all of whom were just textbook names to me. The other research students, those who'd taken their first degree at Cambridge or some other British university, just appalled me, because they knew everything, as far as I could see. I felt such an ignoramus. In the end I discovered that this was very much 'put on' — that some people liked to appear very wise, when they really weren't. I then felt able to hold my own with them.

Did it act as a spur to you?

Yes. But the thing that acted mostly as a spur to me was one of Rutherford's assistants, whose name was James Chadwick. He was later to discover the neutron. Chadwick had been a prisoner of war throughout the First World War. He'd been travelling in Germany when war broke out and he was interned there, and this upset his internal mechanism and eating was ever afterwards a bit of a strain for him. He only lived to his early eighties. Chadwick was a rather taciturn sort of person but I liked him at once — because he was so direct and honest — even though my actual personality was rather different from his. He used to go around the laboratory regularly every day to visit every research student and find out how they were getting on. When he came to me he said, 'How are you getting on?' and I said, 'Well I'd rather have a high vac pump because I'm letting gas into the vacuum continuously and it's an awful chore having to turn this handle for half an hour every hour'. He said, 'So you'd like a high vac would you?' and I said, 'Yes'. He said, 'Well you just can't have one!'.

I was a bit disappointed with this and I cycled home to have lunch with my wife, feeling a bit depressed. Then I went back to the Cavendish and there, sitting on my table, was a high vac pump. And so I learned that Chadwick's bark was much worse than his bite. He was about ten years older than me, but we rapidly became close friends and that lasted until his death. I've just been to England to a celebration of the hundredth anniversary of Chadwick's birth.

And what work were you doing?

I was doing some work on the effects produced when positive ions hit a metallic surface. Then, very soon after that, Rutherford asked me whether I'd like to work with him, and of course that was a great honour.

And why do you think he asked you?

He wanted to do some experiments which were like those that were being done by Cockburn and Walton in our laboratory. They had managed to produce the disintegration of an atom by using artificially accelerated particles, and this was the first time that the atom had been split artificially. This of course excited Rutherford and he wanted to do some experiments in that field, and he wanted somebody technically good to help him. He thought that I was the right person, and it was absolute heaven to be working with him. Actually *with* him! It was because he was full of ideas all the time, most of which of course were nonsense. But every now and again there was gold amongst the dirt. We got on famously together, and I had one or two research students working with me also.

We set up equipment in a cellar in the old Cavendish, a room which we had to use because it could be completely blacked out. One detected the products of the formations of the atoms through a very thin mica window. They were fired out like little bullets, struck a zinc sulphide screen and gave a little flash of light. But in order to see this flash you had to sit around while your eyes adapted to the dark and then you looked down through this microscope at the screen and counted the number of flashes of light that you saw. You could only keep doing this for 20 minutes or so until your eyes got tired, and then someone else took over. So it was good fun. You were part of a team; you worked together.

You were sitting in the dark counting particles and you call it good fun?

It was because it was so exciting. You never knew what you were going to see next. You changed the voltage or changed the target and something totally different would happen. In the middle of these experiments, in 1934, there came to the Cavendish a man from Berkeley in California, a very distinguished physical chemist whose name was Gilbert Lewis. He'd brought with him two tiny little samples of heavy water sealed in a glass tube. He handed them to Rutherford, who handed them to me, and straightaway I took the deuterium, as the heavy hydrogen is called, out of the water, and used it in our bombarding experiment. Straightaway a new world was opened to us with a new set of explosions, atomic explosions, which were terrific in their intensity and in the number that took place. It was like entering a new realm of star-watching, looking at these.

One day, in the course of our experiments, we noticed some little doubly-charged particles that we couldn't explain. And we puzzled and puzzled as to what these could mean. Six o'clock came — and Rutherford was insistent on stopping work at six because he said the evenings were times when one should be thinking about what one had been doing experimentally. We dispersed and I went home and thought a bit about this interaction after dinner. I couldn't make head nor tail of it. I went to sleep still puzzled, and at three o'clock in the morning the telephone rang. My wife, who woke up because of the baby, of course, got up. She woke me and said: 'The Professor wants to speak to you.' We always called Rutherford the Professor. So I went to the telephone and sleepily said: 'Good evening'. And he said: 'You know, Mark, I think I know the answer to that problem of ours. Those little particles are particles of helium of mass 3 — not only have we got hydrogen of mass 3, we've found helium of mass 3.' I said: 'But Professor, what on earth are your reasons for thinking that? It just doesn't add up.' 'Reasons, reasons, Oliphant!', he said, 'I feel it in my water!' So the next morning I set to work to do the experiment of passing these particles through crossed electric and magnetic fields, to determine their velocity. And hence, knowing their energy, one could calculate their mass — and their mass was 3. He was absolutely right.

Was Rutherford's 'water' always so bang on?

No. Not always. He had some very funny ideas at times, but he was often right.

Have you ever thought that maybe creativity and imagination are as important in scientific discovery as more conventional reasoning ability?

I think they're more important than anything else. I think that if one's just going to do 'a job' in science then one is never going to get very far. One's got to have imagination. Try first to think how it might be, and then set to work to prove that it is that way — or find out to your consternation that it isn't that way.

Has intuition played an important part in your own work?

Well, I'm not a Rutherford, nor a Bohr nor an Einstein, but I have had glimmers at times of an intuitive approach to things, which have worked out.

Your own star was evolving at this time, and your reputation too, as you were given opportunities. Some young people who get to assist a great man like Rutherford find that their work is not always given due acknowledgement — that the great man encourages the work but takes the credit . . .

But that was one point about Rutherford. The paper describing this work is by Oliphant, Marsdorp and Rutherford. His name was last. He never took any credit for anything that other people had done.

So you were given due credit, and so your reputation was growing.

That's right.

Can you sum up what it was about this work that intrigued and excited you?

Well, one was discovering something about the most minute thing that we could think of in the universe. If you take an ordinary atom, of course you can't see it. You've got to examine it by indirect methods, using X-rays and the sort of light that it emits to give you information about its structure. But that only gives you information about the outside of the atom. The problem was once described by somebody in this way: Suppose you were in a small boat, you were rowing across the sea, and you had nothing but the oars that were in the boat and yourself. You came across a small island, and this island had around it a high wall, and this high wall was smooth and it was too high for you to look over. You had no equipment that allowed you to climb it in any way. How could you discover whether the island was inhabited and what sort of inhabitants there were on the island without ever seeing them?

The answer of course is that you'd pick up some stones off the seashore, and you'd throw them over the wall. If there were intelligent beings there, sooner or later they'd be provoked into throwing the stones back again, and from the energy with which they came you could determine something about the strength of the people who lived on the island. And from the direction in which the stones came, supposing they were thrown directly back along the line that you'd thrown them, you would know that there were reasonably intelligent people on the island. You could elaborate on this to get a pretty good picture of the inhabitants on the island without ever having seen them.

That's what we do with the nucleus of the atom. We fire visitors into the interior of the atom. You've got to fire tens of millions of them, in the hope of one sometimes hitting and penetrating inside the nucleus. And then you look at what happens, what sorts of particles come out, what are the results of the disintegration, the breakdown of the nucleus — or what used to be called the splitting of the atom.

So in order to understand it you had to attack it.

That's right. During these processes of understanding it, it was found that one was creating all the time new sorts of atoms that were unknown on earth. Take something like sodium, for instance, which is the material in common salt — sodium chloride. Sodium is a soft metal, a rather interesting metal, but it is just a normal material and very ubiquitous. But when you hit it with one of these particles, sometimes you knock a bit out of it, and the remaining part is radioactive just like radium. So one can create radioactive species of all the atoms in the universe by hitting them with the right bullets and knocking bits out of them that leave a strange atom that's not a normal constituent of the universe.

In a way you were not only discovering things but were creating things — you were playing God in a way, weren't you?

That's right. That's right to a large extent, yes.

Did your growing reputation start to affect how you felt about your future?

Oh well, I began to feel my oats, as it were, and to feel that I'd love to have a show of my own instead of being a junior in the laboratory. And so when an offer came to me to become Professor of Physics at

Birmingham I went and had a look around and talked to people. But when I went and told Rutherford that I was thinking of going to Birmingham, he was terribly angry. He said: 'Chadwick's gone and let me down, he's gone to Liverpool, now you're leaving me in the lurch and going to Birmingham.' He was really, really nasty to me. The next day I had a letter from him, saying he was sorry that he'd lost his temper and wishing me luck in what I was intending to do. And he said he'd love to talk over with me the sort of program I had in mind and he offered me every assistance. Unfortunately, that was the year he died.

And that was a major loss to you.

Yes, he died at the very young age, really, of 67 — of a messed up simple operation for a strangulated hernia in the umbilicus.

If you had to put into perspective what you got out of your time with him, what would you say? What was the single thing that stood you in good stead for the rest of your life?

Well, I'd got as interested in the internal part of the atom as he was, and I thought I'd like to go on and do this work but do it at higher energies. Now, at Berkeley, in California, Ernest Lawrence had developed a machine that he called the cyclotron. In this you accelerated particles in a magnetic field, where they performed circular paths, and gave them a little flip each time they went past a certain point, so that you increased their energy till they got to the edge. And you could get very high energies in that way. So I went off and spent some time in Berkeley with Lawrence, learning how the cyclotron was made and how it worked, and he was terrifically helpful and became one of my closest friends. I went back to Birmingham and started to build the largest cyclotron in Europe at that time. It was begun in 1937 — and it's still working. But it wasn't finished in '38 when we were dragged, unfortunately, into war work.

It was quite apparent that Hitler was on the rampage, and a lot of us were taken and initiated into the very deadly secrets of radar. They realised that this sort of thing was going to play a big part in any future. Then, when the war broke out — the cyclotron still wasn't finished — I was given the job of trying to produce, for radar purposes, electromagnetic waves of very much shorter wavelength than were available at that time. So we set to work. I got together a small team of people who had no real experience in radio at all. And I didn't know much about it, except that I'd used amplifiers for detecting my particles and for working on the cyclotron. I'd determined to get a group of people who would think fundamentally about the task because, having visited the various establishments that were dealing with radio for the services, I knew that they'd never reach the short wavelengths by the techniques that they were using. So we set to work to try and devise various devices which would do this, thinking in fundamental terms rather than just following radio practice.

Well, two of the boys discovered that they could make a resonator that was like a revolver with holes in a ring and slots that pointed towards a cathode inside. The whole thing was made out of metal, with just a glass fitting to bring the power out, and it worked like magic. This was the magnetron. Of course I'd like to have a dollar for every magnetron that's in the kitchens of the world nowadays — in microwave ovens, you know. And it proved to be extremely good and reliable for radar. Within 18 months or so we'd succeeded. We'd got radar working in the air. We'd got it working at pointing searchlights at aircraft at night. We'd got it working on ships. We'd got it detecting ships at sea. And all in 18 months or two years. And then I thought, bugger it all, this is not really interesting work, this is work for engineers now — so I went back to work on nuclear physics.

There now began in Mark Oliphant's life a series of events that were to lead to some of the most exciting work with some of the most disturbing consequences that could have been imagined. In Oliphant's laboratory at that time were two scientists who were refugees from Hitler's Germany, Otto Frisch and Rudolf Peierls. They weren't allowed to work on radar because they were enemy aliens and excluded from all secret work. In an ironic twist of fate it was their work that demonstrated conclusively that an atomic bomb could be produced. Oliphant found the implications of this finding 'hair-raising' and immediately sent it off to the United States, but got no reply. Because he had to go to America in connection with the magnetron he decided to follow up the matter with the appropriate authorities there.

I went to Washington to see the chairman of the American committee. He was a real stick-in-the-mud and he'd taken our report and stuck it in his safe and hadn't circulated it to the other members of the committee. So I went straightaway to see Bush and Conant, who were the President's scientific and technical advisers. Both of them took the point of view: 'Well this is very interesting, but this is for the next war, not for this war.' So, still dissatisfied, I got on an aeroplane (in those days of course there were DC2s), and took the 18-hour flight to Oakland, next-door to Berkeley in California, and went to see Lawrence. I knew him to be a livewire, and a member of the committee. He was so upset that he got on a plane with me and we went back to Washington. Then, within a few days, the Manhattan Project was formed as a result — that enormous American project was on its way.

That was strange, wasn't it! It all happened as a result of Frisch and Peierls, who were not allowed to be associated with secret work, setting out to do calculations about the possibility of chain reactions with uranium.

And had you not gone across there, and stirred the whole thing up, the project — the Manhattan Project that finally led to the atomic bomb — might never have happened.

It *might* never have happened, but I can't imagine that somebody wouldn't have woken up to the facts of the matter. They had a lot of very experienced people in America.

Why were you so anxious that this should get moving?

Because we had information from the secret service that the Germans were trying to produce a nuclear weapon, and that the man in charge was a very famous scientist. But unfortunately, or fortunately perhaps for us, they took the wrong path. They went for the nuclear reactor, not the separation of the isotopes of uranium.

What was your own part in the Manhattan Project?

There were negotiations with the Americans about our role and finally the Americans relented and the whole of the British team moved to America *en masse*, because there they had the production facilities that in Britain were used entirely for making aeroplanes. British industry was flat out, whereas there was spare industry still in America.

And your contribution to it?

Well, mine was a very minor one. Chadwick was the leader of our team and I was his deputy. So while I was officially attached to a group that was run by Lawrence, separating the isotopes of uranium, in fact I was Chadwick's deputy. I took part in all the discussions and every month or so I went to England to report to Sir John Anderson, who at that time was responsible for all the technical and scientific things connected with the war effort. I flew back and forth across the

Atlantic in bombers on nine occasions. The reason it wasn't ten was because I once went across in the *Queen Mary*, which was fast enough to avoid the submarines!

In the course of your work, leading up to and through the war years, you'd developed a great interest in what was happening in the atom. Did it never, during that time, occur to you where it might all be leading?

I'm not quite sure that I understand what you mean. You see, my work in nuclear physics began in the 1930s, long before war broke out, and it wasn't until the war that we thought for the first time of the possibility of nuclear weapons. And that was the change, a rather horrifying thought, but still one that we had to think about because we knew that the Hitler regime was attempting to develop nuclear weapons. The fission process made the chain reaction process practicable.

So until the war was under way it had never occurred to you that atomic power might be used destructively?

No. In 1916 Rutherford gave a lecture in London — in the middle of the First World War — and pointed out to his audience that there were big energies associated with this radioactive process that he was investigating. And he said in the course of this lecture that some of his colleagues thought that it would be a good idea to find a way of producing radioactivity of this sort artificially, so that one would then have enormous sources of power. And he ended by saying: 'I hope it never happens in my lifetime or some bloody fool might blow the world to bits.' He was just as aware, even then in 1916, of the energy that was locked up inside the nucleus. People have accused him of being not in favour of nuclear power and nuclear energy. Well, he always expressed disquiet about it and was fearful of the consequences.

When war broke out, when did you first become aware of the value that nuclear energy would have in the war effort?

We knew that the Germans were on to it — a very famous physicist, Heisenberg, was in charge of the work. A man who was fully capable of thinking through the whole process. Heisenberg is the author of the so-called 'uncertainty principle' which is talked about so much. So he was an adversary of the first class, and one couldn't neglect the fact that Hitler might get nuclear weapons.

Rutherford had many years before expressed a fear that someone might use this new knowledge to blow the world up. When you started looking at the possibility of the use of nuclear energy in the war effort, did you remember his remark? Were you worried about where it might lead?

Oh, yes. Right from the beginning, one had no doubts whatever of the horror of the situation; that here we had the possibility of mass extinction of people. A whole city being blown to pieces with one bomb, instead of with thousands of bombs of a normal kind. It was something that was really quite horrifying, and it was at the back of the minds of most of us who worked on it. Not all of us. There were some people who just revelled purely in the science and didn't worry at all about the ultimate result. But Niels Bohr was the man who really led us in our worries about the ultimate result if we were successful in the production of nuclear weapons.

And do you remember when it was that you found out what was going to happen? That it actually was going to be used for mass destruction. Could you describe that time?

Well, you see, the difficulty is that one didn't know. When it became clear that a bomb was almost certainly a practical possibility, when it was quite clear to us that the thing was going to be successful, the fears of the Bohr group had became so great that Bohr had an interview with President Roosevelt. President Roosevelt was good enough to give Bohr one and a half hours of his time to talk about it. He expressed considerable interest in Bohr's point of view and the view that this bomb, if it could be produced, should be used for peace and not for war. It should be exploded as a demonstration of what could happen to a country — by blowing the top off Mt Fuji or something — making it clear what would happen if they weren't good boys.

And why wasn't that course followed?

Well, Roosevelt asked Bohr for more information and then Bohr wrote a long screed about it, which I helped him to write because his English wasn't all that good, him being a Dane. (His wife said his Danish wasn't much better!) It was quite a business to get a screed together that was concise and at the same time would be understood by the President. This interested Roosevelt still more, but there were some questions that arose from Bohr's earlier letter that he didn't quite understand, and he asked for enlightenment. So Bohr prepared a second screed, which I also helped him with to some extent, and then he sent that off to Roosevelt. But unfortunately, before he read it, Roosevelt died, and Truman took over. And Truman had no scruples whatsoever. So it looked as though Roosevelt was interested in the concept of using the bomb as a weapon for peace rather than war. But of course once the test in the desert took place, in New Mexico, and it was clear that all our fears were justified, it then was no longer the concern of the scientists — it went straight into the hands of the military and the politicians. Scientists had nothing more to do with it.

And so you had actually left the Manhattan Project when the bombs were dropped on Japan?

Yes, I was back in England at that stage. I was there to 'translate' the information that came from America to Sir John Anderson, who was responsible for all these technical things under the Churchill Government, and to explain exactly what was happening when the bomb was used.

How did you feel at the time? What was your initial reaction?

Well, there was a feeling of utter frustration, in that the message hadn't got across. That the bomb had been used, and used against civilian cities, and that all the moral scruples had been thrown aside, by a so-called Christian nation. Not by the Japanese, or by infidels of any kind, but by a Christian nation! Or nations — because England was behind America in all this. And a feeling, at the same time, that perhaps we were wrong — that perhaps this would end the war and save lives. There was that sort of mixture of feelings. But added to that, the hope that means would be found to control this weapon so that it was never used again.

In talking about the war and reflecting on his role in it there is even now in Sir Mark's demeanour a slight air of bewilderment. It seems as if he is still struggling to reconcile in his own mind the two irreconcilable obsessions that motivated him throughout the entire period of the war — his excited dedication to the science of nuclear power and his love and respect for all forms of life. When he talks of the work done by the scientists during this time his eyes light up at the memory of the scientific mysteries solved. When he recalls the ultimate effects of their labours, his distress is equally obvious.

After the war was over, and you thought about your role in the war — you'd worked on radar and you'd worked on the lead-up to the bomb — how did you feel about your contribution to the war?

That's hard to express, or even to understand for oneself. There was this feeling of gratitude that the war was over. Flying over Germany in bombers to see how the radar worked — on the one hand it had been interesting to see these little puffballs appearing in the air from the anti-aircraft guns, and hang on to the general hope that one of them wasn't too close to you. On the other hand it was terrible to look down on the destruction that had been wrought on those German cities. And also to see the terrible things that *they'd* done in other places. To be in London when a V2 came over was really a rather terrifying experience, if one was in the open and walking around.

So one finished the war with a feeling almost of puzzlement as to why mankind had done this to one another. Why people had deliberately destroyed not only the lives of men, women and children indiscriminately, by the bombing of cities, but had destroyed the works of their hands. Some of them the most beautiful buildings in the world. And this seemed such a wrong thing, for man to be deliberately doing. It was these *general* thoughts that went through one's mind, more than any sort of feeling of close association with it. It was a feeling that somehow or other all of this had to be stopped, and one had of course great hopes that the United Nations idea would produce something that worked.

Was there, mixed in with these feelings, any sense of personal guilt?

Yes. But not overly so. It was a curious sort of feeling of guilt — I imagine the same sort of feeling as the soldiers had, or the airmen had who'd dropped the bombs. It was a sort of feeling of action at a distance. In other words, you didn't personally kill the man, he was killed in an indirect way, certainly through your machinations, but not directly, and this did change one's attitude towards it all to some extent.

Your subsequent involvement in the efforts to bring the world together, and to stop this kind of thing happening again, was based on a more general concern about war rather than being an expiation of some feeling of personal guilt?

Oh yes, very much so. All my life I've been very much concerned for this phenomenon of life, of evolution, of man as the pinnacle of evolution, and hence the responsibilities of man towards the whole of the earth. And ever since I could make decisions for myself — I've been, for instance, a vegetarian because I do not want to kill things in order to remain alive. I think it's totally unnecessary, and after all I'm over 90 now, so I think I've proven my point.

More than most, then, you were faced with the massive dilemma the war presented any civilised person.

That's right, and coming to terms with it was not all that easy. It was a sort of hatred of the Hitler regime that really drove me.

How successful were you in facing the dilemma? How did you manage during that time, inside yourself?

Well, I don't know, you've got to develop a double personality, and think one way one moment and then another way the next. You never do reconcile the two. It's like suddenly being angry with one's wife, and then the next moment one's contrite and unhappy about it all. It's a sort of a dual personality that I think is in every person.

So you feel that it's part of the human condition for a person to have seemingly irreconcilable views?

Yes.

After the war was over Mark Oliphant was anxious to do everything he could to prevent the use of nuclear power for mass destruction. He gave public talks urging international controls, first in England and then in various parts of Australia. In 1951, during the McCarthy era in the United States, he wanted to go to a conference in Chicago on high energy physics. He could not get an American visa. The official line at the American Embassy was that his application had not been refused, it had simply arrived too late for him to attend the conference. After persistent correspondence from Oliphant, who was naturally anxious to know if he had been listed in any way that would cause him similar problems in the future, the Americans conceded that there had been a political problem. They explained that it was not that he was accused of communist sympathies or of communist connections, but that it was felt that his public speeches were providing arguments that the Russians could use against the United States.

What other forms did your action against war take?

I joined various organisations and got into trouble over some of them. One of them was the World Federation of Scientific Workers, which I actually wasn't a member of. In 1947 there was a meeting at the Sorbonne in Paris to commemorate Rutherford, ten years after he'd died, and I was asked to speak, as someone who had been very close to Rutherford and had worked with him. I attended this meeting and it turned out afterwards that it was permeated by people who were in sympathy with the Soviet regime. This of course kept coming up — that I'd attended this meeting — but I merely went because it was commemorating Rutherford, whom I loved.

What movements did you join?
The Pugwash movement was one. When the Americans let off their first hydrogen weapon it so horrified Bertrand Russell, the English philosopher, that he, together with Einstein, wrote a manifesto. It was known as the Russell-Einstein manifesto, and it was an appeal to the scientists of the world to get together and eliminate this terrible menace of nuclear weapons. I knew Russell personally and had done broadcasts with him, so I naturally fell in with this proposal. A gathering was called in London of scientists who had these sorts of sympathies, and then an arrangement was come to through the interest of an American multimillionaire. He'd been born at a little fishing village called Pugwash, in Canada — in Nova Scotia on the banks of the St Lawrence River. He invited this group to meet at Pugwash (where he had transformed the old family home into a place for seminars of a serious nature) to consider the human condition.

I was one of about 30 people at the first Pugwash conference. We were from all over the world including, and this was very important, four Russians. Now the whole concept behind these Pugwash meetings was that they were to be private meetings. There were no press or media people present, so that everybody could let their hair down and say what they liked without being reported in the press. This enabled the Russians to come, in the knowledge that they would not be reported. The leader of the Russians was the Physics Secretary of the USSR Academy of Science and so a very influential man. They brought plenty of vodka with them, so that it was an occasion of enjoyment in more ways than one. But we got down to work and it turned out to be very successful. There have now been many meetings of the Pugwash group — in all parts of the world.

What do you think was the main contribution of the group?
One thing we were very successful in was the very full discussion we had about the cessation of test explosions in the air which were spreading radioactivity everywhere. And we discussed scientifically what would happen if you made these explosions underground, and then we advocated very strongly that tests in the future should be carried out underground. All nations respected that except the French.

You were also interested in the broader hopes that were represented by the United Nations, and you involved yourself to some extent in that.

Yes, I was a member of the United Nations Association and have continued to take an interest in it, although I'm afraid I'm rather disabused of any belief in the United Nations' capacity to control the passions of mankind in the world. The Security Council has proved a bit of a washout. I was involved with the first meetings of the Security Council and the Atomic Energy Commission (the AEC was established by the United Nations as one of its first activities). Because the chairmen of these bodies were chosen in alphabetical order of nations, Australia provided the chairman for the first meetings of both. It was Dr Evatt, and I was asked by the Prime Minister at the time whether I would go as Dr Evatt's expert on nuclear matters, and on military matters in general. I flew from England with Dr Evatt and his wife across the Atlantic in one of the very early Constellations. And that was quite an amusing experience. He was very frightened of flying, but he had the guts to fly!

Meetings in those days had no simultaneous translation; it was a terrible business. The first speech was given by the head of the American delegation in English, and he gave the American point of view about the future of nuclear energy in the world. That was followed by its being translated into French, and then into German, and so on. One had to sit for hours while these translations took place, and then the next speaker would come on. Well, the next speaker was Mr Gromyko from Russia, and Mr Gromyko's proposals were very simple. He said: 'Russia demands as number one priority that all existing nuclear weapons be dismantled'. He didn't use the word 'destroyed' because they realised that the explosive materials were also the materials for use in reactors in nuclear power stations. And he said that no nuclear weapons in future should be allowed to be made and that there should be a universal inspection of every country and its industries, under the United Nations, to verify that no nuclear weapons were being produced.

This produced an immediate reaction in Robert Oppenheimer, who was the adviser to the American delegation on nuclear matters, of course, having been the father of the nuclear weapon. He rushed around to me as the adviser to the chairman of the meeting, and said: 'For heaven's sake get your boss to say something in favour of the Russian proposal, because it's wonderful! I think that we should consider it very seriously, and I'll tell my boss that that's what I feel.'

But I said: 'You get *your* boss to do that.' He said: 'I'll give you a bit of classified information. At the present time there are only three nuclear weapons in existence. It would be half an hour's work to dismantle them. If the whole proposal failed, it'd only take us another half hour to put them together again. So, we've got nothing to lose by considering very seriously the Russian proposal.' Well, as soon as I got a moment I went down to the chairman, who was sitting in the middle of the circular audience of representatives of nations, and said to Doc Evatt: 'I've been talking to Robert Oppenheimer and he and I both believe that the Russian proposal should be considered very seriously. Will you please make a statement to that effect, that we should discuss it in detail?' And Evatt turned around to me and said irritably: 'No, no, no, nothing of the sort! We might want to use weapons against them.' That was the response I got. So we never got anywhere.

Extraordinary, given that Evatt was labelled a communist sympathiser.

That's right. Mr Bernard Baruch, an oil millionaire, was the leader of the American delegation — a very tall old man, gracious, a nice old man; I liked him. Well he seemed old to me at that time — I suppose he was in his late sixties. I would act as errand boy between Doc Evatt and the office of Mr Baruch, and several times I had to go across on behalf of the chairman and discuss the next day's business with Mr Baruch. I found him an approachable man, but he refused to have anything whatever to do with the Russian proposal.

So Oppenheimer wasn't any more successful than you were in persuading the boss to be interested.

No. So that was that. But I was very interested in Dr Evatt because he was a strange man, and his wife was his mainstay, you know. She really took care of him wonderfully well, both on an aeroplane during his periods of excitement and terror and on the ground. He was a terrific believer in the importance of Australia, which of course was miniscule compared to that of the United States and the European countries. When we got to New York the man who had been our Foreign Minister and was the first Australian representative on the United Nations wanted a special car to use while he was in Washington — a Cadillac. When we got there it was a *small* Cadillac! Doc Evatt blew the top off his head in complaint about the fact that it was undignified for him to be riding around in something of this sort, whereas the representative of Uganda or somewhere was driving around in a great big limousine.

Was he concerned about that for himself or for Australia?

I think a little of both. I think he was genuinely very concerned for Australia's reputation and standing in the world, and very much aware of the importance of his being chairman of the first meetings of the Security Council and the Atomic Energy Commission.

Apart from the extraordinary lost opportunity that you were witness to, do you feel that, generally speaking, his contribution and his representation of Australia as chairman were valuable?

Yes, I suppose it must have called attention to Australia. He was an easily flattered man. Mr Baruch took him to some prize fight — a man named Joe Louis, I think, was one of the fighters, but I've forgotten who the other one was — and they had ringside seats and this thrilled him, you know, he really felt that this was a great honour.

You obviously don't appreciate the role of sport in Australian life — for you to be surprised at that so much.

Not boxing, no. I'm very glad that the whole of the medical fraternity is now trying to get boxing banned completely as a sport.

After you decided that you should oppose the use of a nuclear bomb, you turned your attention to developing nuclear energy for peaceful purposes. What were your thoughts about its value in that area?

When I came to Australia in 1950 I was still of the opinion that nuclear energy would be useful. But then I very rapidly realised that the nuclear reactor was the source of the plutonium that was used in the nuclear weapon that was dropped on Nagasaki, and that if you had a nuclear reactor you had access to plutonium — if you liked to spend the money on the chemical plant that was involved — and you could make nuclear weapons. So I'm afraid that I reversed my point of view completely and I feel now that under no circumstances should Australia have nuclear power.

Were your feelings about that only in relation to nuclear weapons, or did Chernobyl make you feel concerned about . . .

I take rather an engineering point of view towards Chernobyl. Murphy's Law holds with any bit of equipment — if it can go wrong it *will* go wrong — and sooner or later we were bound to learn by bitter experience that some of the things that we'd done in the design of nuclear reactors were not good. While the engineers and others had thought very carefully about the whole problem, it was quite clear from two bad accidents that didn't receive much publicity, but which took place in Great Britain, and then the accidents in the United States, and finally Chernobyl spreading radioactivity over a great part of Europe, that we didn't know what we were doing and that the question of safety of nuclear reactors was still to some extent an open question. The French have been very successful so far, they've had no bad nuclear problems. They've had problems, but nothing that has released large amounts of nuclear radioactivity into the air. The Russians have had a number of accidents, some of which have released radioactivity, culminating in Chernobyl which spread more over the Earth than any previous accident. The only reason that the worst accident in Britain didn't produce as big an effect as Chernobyl was that England is a very small country.

With these doubts about nuclear power, what do you see as the alternative form of energy for the future? You've also been concerned about the ecological impact of fossil fuel, haven't you?

Well, I feel that in fact nuclear power *is* the final answer. But nuclear power not on Earth but in the sun's interior. That nuclear power becomes apparent as the radiation of light and heat, and where it hits the Earth a huge amount of power is induced. One can easily show that if one collected the solar power, with reasonable efficiency, from the desert areas of South Australia alone, let alone the rest of Australia, one could provide all the energy needed for the whole of the world. One doesn't realise this — that the sun is such a magnificent nuclear reactor. There it is far enough away to do us no harm. And it works by the fusion process rather than the chain process of fission which is used in nuclear reactors. And what's more it will go on producing this power for the next few million years, so we have no problems whatever about the future.

It's the absolutely clean power, and the right way to get over the fact that the sun doesn't shine all the time is to *store* energy. And the right way to do that is to change the electric energy into the energy of burning gas. The gas that one produces would be hydrogen gas, which when it's burnt produces only water, so it's a completely clean fuel. Already in Germany one has BMW and Daimler Benz running motor cars on hydrogen instead of petrol. The Russians have an aeroplane running on hydrogen. It's a beautiful fuel, a fuel which is non-polluting in every sense of the word, but it has problems. Because hydrogen is the lightest of all the elements, the volume that it occupies even when it's liquid is still large. It means that you have to provide in, say, an aeroplane or a motor car a bigger volume of storage for the fuel than you do for petrol. But undoubtedly it will come, and every day the techniques for transforming the sun's rays into electric power are becoming more and more efficient, cheaper and cheaper. It won't be very long now before it becomes commercially a practical proposition. Well, when that happens, Australia, especially South Australia, could export enormous amounts of energy as hydrogen gas, in the same way for instance as North West Cape is exporting liquid natural gas, which has a boiling point not much higher than that of hydrogen. It is exported in enormous thermos flasks on board vessels to Japan, and it's proving to be quite an economically practical proposition — so it would be for hydrogen.

Have you involved yourself at all in looking for a solution to the storage of solar energy?
I've done a number of experiments myself and I'm still doing odd experiments — getting ideas and trying things out.

So you're active as a scientist although you're aged over 90.
Yes.

And solar energy is your area of interest.
That's right, yes. But it's slow. I have no one. I haven't got research assistants and workshops and so on to help me. I have to do everything myself, but still it's fun.

The war left Mark Oliphant with a determination to do what he could to see to it that science was used in a positive way to benefit mankind. This enhanced sense of responsibility and his strong desire to make a constructive contribution probably made him particularly susceptible to the approach of Nugget Coombs who, in his position of Head of Post-War Reconstruction, was busy recruiting distinguished expatriate academics to help set up the Australian National University. Coombs persuaded Howard Florey (who had been involved in the discovery of penicillin), Keith Hancock (the historian and social scientist) and Mark Oliphant to form a small committee in England to help with the process. The three of them were invited to head the respective Research Institutes that formed the basis of the ANU. In the end Oliphant was the only one in the group who actually came.

I said I would come because I was, and still am, a very loyal Australian, and thought that I owed it to Australia, which had been very good to me and helped me to get this scholarship to go abroad. I felt, to use an American term, obligated to some extent to return to my native country. Secondly, I thought that it would be better for the children if they were to grow up in Australia. We had at that time two children, both adopted, and we were anxious for them to have the best possibilities of life. And it was for these reasons that I said yes. But at Victoria Station, where the boat-train left to join the *Orcades* at Southampton, Howard Florey came to see us off. We walked up and down the platform, he and I, while he told me what a 'b' fool I was to do it, and tried to persuade me to change my mind. He said: 'It'll be the end of your research career! You'll just find yourself so involved with setting up this new university that you'll have no proper time to devote to your scientific work.' He used the words: 'You know, if you leave this country you'll be committing scientific harakiri.' And he was right — I did. He also said to me: 'You know what you'll find when you get there?' I said no, and he said: 'A lot of promises and a hole in the ground!'

And that was exactly what I found. I'd been promised that there'd be a house for us to live in — there was no house for us to live in. We lived for nine months in the old Hotel Canberra before there was a house available for us to live in. And what's more there was no laboratory of any kind, we were housed in some old hospital buildings on the site of where the university is now; wooden buildings dating, I think, from the First World War or something of the sort, and I had an office there. But all I could do was to try to recruit people. So I spent a lot of time travelling around the world trying to persuade people to come to this unknown place in the Australian outback, to do scientific work, which most of them of course felt was an impossibility.

Were you offering them a lot of promises if they came?

No, I was careful not to over-expand, but I was pointing out that there were advantages in living in a new country, that the life was perhaps somewhat more exciting than the dull life of Britain, or of Germany or of America. The great problem that I faced was finding colleagues. I got Ernest Titterton to come out to head up the work on nuclear physics. He'd been my first research student in Birmingham, and had done very well, and he accepted the chance to come out with his family. But it took me an awful long time, for instance, to find a Professor of Mathematics. Mathematicians felt that Australia was the end of the world, but I was lucky enough to persuade Bernard Neumann and his wife to come. And there was great trouble about that because Bernard said that if he came, his wife, who was a mathematician also, had to have a job in mathematics as well. He said: 'It's like the butler and the cook housekeeper, you've got to have both together.' Of course, this was against the rules in Australia then, that a man and his wife should both be appointed to jobs, and I had to get this through the Council. There again Nugget Coombs was a great help. He was a very farsighted man. In the end Neumann and his wife did come, and that transformed mathematics in Australia. I think that was one of the really great things that we did.

In addition, the government gladly handed over the Mt Stromlow Observatory to us, but we then immediately realised that it was the wrong place for an observatory. Bart Bock, who became the Professor of Astronomy, immediately started to look for a better place. He settled on Siding Springs in northern New South Wales, where we were joined by the British with a British–Australian telescope which has done a wonderful job. It's become one of the big and famous observatories of the world — it played a major part in the observations that were made during the moon flights, for instance.

So gradually things took off, and things began to work. But it took a very long time. It took, I should think, 15 years to really feel that the Research School of Physics was a going concern. And we've always had to battle the problem that our special arrangements meant that we were regarded with envy by the other universities. Right now we're fighting a real battle to retain the Institute of Advanced Studies. It may be that all that I did will disappear in smoke, and that the National University will become just another ordinary university.

The present difficulties at the ANU reflect a broader questioning of the place of universities and the place of research and what scientific enquiry is actually for, which has become something of a national debate. What are your thoughts on the value of pure research?

Well, if I may say so, it's not only a national problem. It's a worldwide problem — the belief that what goes on in universities should be obviously useful, that nothing should be done or be financed by governments except something that leads directly to advances in technology or the standard of living, or something of that sort. So they demand that one should only do in universities the things that will produce useful people like engineers and so on — or economists, who for some reason or other are supposed to be useful. The real problems are still unknown in the physical sciences, in chemistry and so on. We're just beginning to understand the chemistry of the life process. You've got an animal, it's alive one moment, it's dead the next. Chemically, physically, it's identical when it's dead with when it was alive — and yet something is missing, this thing we call life, and we just haven't got any clue about that.

Now, despite the fact that even as we talk you're demonstrating an active interest in scientific research, all those years ago at the height of your research career you made this decision to take a more administrative role in coming home to help set up the ANU. Do you regret that move in coming here? And do you think you made an important contribution by helping to provide opportunities for others?

For myself I regret it. I realise each year when I go back to Cambridge just what I gave up in leaving it. And when I came out here I found myself, for such a long time, just an administrator, which I'm not good at and I don't like. I don't do it well, but it had to be done, and I hated it.

Was it too late for you to change your mind?

Well, no, I could have changed my mind, I suppose, and I was tempted to by Florey particularly, but I did give my word to Nugget Coombs that I would come out, and so I thought I ought to stick by it.

But you did undertake some of your own scientific research nevertheless, during that time?

Oh yes!

What was the major thing that you were involved in scientifically during your period in Australia?

I set out to try and bring Australia into the age of modern physics, and that meant trying to do experiments that were of the kind that were going on in Europe and America. But it turned out to be too difficult a task. We didn't have in Australia the engineering companies to make the sort of equipment that was really required. I had to abandon that. But I stuck to my old last — which I'd begun in Adelaide before I went to Cambridge and which I continued in Cambridge for a time, before I joined Rutherford in nuclear physics — which was the effects of the collisions between positively charged atoms and a metal surface.

*Your efforts to build a really big cyclotron here were largely frustrated,
and you also received some very bad press from people who called it the
'White Oliphant'. Was that a very big disappointment to you?*

Well, I don't want to talk about the bad press because that was
mainly generated by people from physics departments at other
universities who were jealous of our setup at the ANU. But in
relation to the other frustrations — they became apparent slowly, so
that in the end when I decided that it wasn't worthwhile trying to
do this in Australia, it wasn't as great a disappointment as it might
have been if the thing had been cut off suddenly. I only slowly
became aware of the fact that we weren't getting very far. And there
was a very nasty accident that led to the blinding of a man. There
was an explosion and he lost the sight of his eye and was terribly
disfigured in the face. It was terrible.

*Is danger always part of research? Were you yourself ever involved in a
dangerous situation with the work you were doing?*

Oh yes, I was knocked unconscious in Cambridge when I put my
hand on 10 000 volts. It burnt a hole in the sole of my shoe, because
I was standing in an old building with a stone floor, and the stone
floors were never quite dry — so I really got it! I woke up lying on
the ground to find my colleague bending over me, saying: 'My God,
my God, what have I done? Have I killed him?' [He laughs at the
memory.]

*The feeling of obligation to Australia and the same strong sense of
national identity which had brought Mark Oliphant back to help set
up the ANU came into play again when Premier Don Dunstan
came to see him in Canberra and asked him to become Governor of
South Australia. He remembered his childhood and youth in that
State and thought that it would be good to go back. He was
Governor from 1971 to 1976.*

I warned Mr Dunstan when he asked me whether he could put my
name forward to the Queen that I wasn't prepared to be a military-
type Governor. I would only go there if I was as free to speak on
public questions as I had been in Canberra.

And he accepted you on those terms.

Yes, and indeed he seemed to want me to do that.

Do you think he lived to regret it?

Yes, I'm afraid he did!

Can you tell us something of how that came about?

Well, I'd rather not go into it because personalities were involved.

Without going into it in too personal a way, what was the essence of the difficulty you found yourself in when you were operating in that job?

I found myself utterly opposed to some of his views on social questions. I admired him enormously, he was a great orator. To hear him do a bit of Shakespeare was really a delight, and he did that sort of thing so perfectly. He had a great appreciation of the arts. It was during that time that the Festival was opened in Adelaide, and of course I played a part in that, which gave me great satisfaction. In that sense I have a great regard for him. He built up art and appreciation of music and of drama in South Australia in a way that'd never been done before. But he had views about life in general with which I was not in sympathy.

What was the main philosophical difference?

When I really parted company with him was when he admitted on television that he was a homosexual. I thought that was a pretty bad thing for a Premier to do. I didn't think that it mattered from the general point of view. But to be a sort of advocate of aberrant behaviour seemed to me to be ... I was old-fashioned I suppose. And I didn't appreciate it.

The job itself — did you enjoy it, did you enjoy being Governor of South Australia?

For the first two or three years it was fun, meeting all sorts of people. Of course Government House is a sort of government hotel, and so one had to put up distinguished visitors — not only Australian, but the Royal Family. And this was quite good fun, and one got to know them very well, in a different sort of way from otherwise. It also enabled me to get about the place. You see, I could go wherever I wanted to, explore every corner of the State. And I was able to go to other States because of the connections between them and South Australia.

And what did you think of the Royal Family?

Well, I liked them all very much indeed, with one exception — I won't mention that ...

And were you impressed with the job that they did?

Very impressed indeed. Prince Phillip in particular was a great favourite of both my wife and myself. He was always a welcome visitor and we had him three or four times to stay with us.

So I take it I'm not speaking to an Australian republican.

No, you're not. I can see no advantage in having an elected President because there would be party politics involved. It's better to have it where the person has a duty to do that is clearly defined and not mixed up with politics or political decisions.

What's been suggested, of course, is an arrangement in which you would have somebody operating rather like the Governor-General does now, and not being a political President. Would you feel more comfortable with that sort of arrangement, or would you feel that the loss of connection with old Britain was a negative?

I don't think it would have much meaning under those circumstances. I mean, what would be the job of the President, why have him?

I suppose it would be a bit like your job as Governor of South Australia.

Yes, but what's the point? No, at least in the name of the Queen you do things, you sign laws, and they're not laws until you've signed them. In the name of the Queen you do various other things — you could always, if you felt like it, do a John Kerr, you see.

Were you ever tempted?

No. Despite the fact that I didn't get on too well with Don Dunstan in the latter part of my time, I respected him too much.

Despite your attitude to the Queen, I understand that when you were first offered a knighthood you refused it.

Yes.

Why was that?

Because I felt that the work we'd been doing for which it was offered, the war work, was the work of a team and not of me, and to honour me without honouring the rest of the team was wrong.

But five years later you did accept it.

Well, Mr Menzies got me into a corner at a party at the National University, in University House, and persuaded me that I should accept — that it was my duty to accept [he laughs]. I admired Mr Menzies very greatly, because he was a great admirer of the Westminster system, and I think rightly so. And so, in the end, I told him I'd have to talk to my wife first. She was a bit reluctant but agreed in the end.

When you were Governor was there any aspect of the job that you really didn't like?

Yes. One of the first things I discovered was that every lease on a piece of Crown land in the State had to be signed by the Governor, and that this lease had already been signed by nine people — the Minister and the various officials in the department that were involved in the land transaction. There were hundreds of leases every week, you see, and I felt this was just wasted time. I asked first of all whether I could use a rubber stamp. I pointed out to the government that each lease was already being signed by nine people who knew what they were doing, and for me to sign it knowing nothing about the place or anything else was just being a rubber stamp, so it might as well *be* a rubber stamp!

Did it do any good?

Oh yes, I was let off in the end. The Attorney General decided that it wasn't really essential under law for me to sign it.

Did your wife enjoy the time you spent as Governor?

I don't think she ever enjoyed it very much. She found it rather a chore. She enjoyed some aspects of it and I must say she was a wonderful wife to me as Governor. She did what was expected of her, and she was a marvellous hostess. She knew how to seat people at dinner, for instance, which I didn't understand — who should be next to whom and so on. And she also was a very gracious person, so that it really worked out from her point of view, and mine, not too badly. But I think she was as glad as I was when we left and it was over, the formalities were over.

The formalities bothered you?

Yes, in the end, they bothered me very much. Some of it seemed rather ridiculous, like standing absolutely still for one and a half hours while the Anzac Day parade went past.

As Governor you represented the major power in the State. Did you feel that you were in charge, or did you feel at times that other people were in charge of you?

No, I felt that I was a puppet after a time. [He laughs.] And I was, that's all I was. In the morning we always had breakfast in our own room upstairs. There was a foolscap piece of paper headed 'Orders of the Day', which told me exactly what I was doing, and that at 10:10 the Rolls would be at the front door, and I would be going to such and such a place to do this or that — give a speech or open a building or something of that kind. That sort of formality got me down a bit.

You weren't used to following orders.

No, and nor was I used to being on time. I liked to turn up at things when I felt I wanted to.

So finishing that time as Governor was something of a release?

That's right, yes.

Throughout his life Sir Mark's wife supported him through all his activities, completely relieving him of any domestic responsibilities and even assisting him in ventures about which she was less than enthusiastic. He valued her opinion on everything to do with their joint life and always consulted her in relation to any major decision. But theirs was a traditional relationship and it was his career that determined most of their major life choices. Especially during the war they were often separated for long periods and even when they settled back in Canberra his work necessitated a great deal of travel. She had full charge of family matters and did that difficult thing — raising small children — virtually in his absence. Sir Mark is hugely appreciative of her contribution to his life and especially of her uncomplaining acceptance of the difficulties she had to deal with unassisted because of the demands of his career.

We were married for 63 years, and I can say with my hand on my heart that there was never any problem between us at all in the whole of that time. Mainly because she was such a wonderful mother and delightful wife.

Were you aware, when you were away for long periods pursuing your work and your career, what that meant to her, holding the home front?

Oh yes. Of course I wrote a very great deal. I wrote letters and she wrote back and sent me snapshots of the children when I was living in America, and things of that sort, that kept things rolling . . .

Because men of your generation often just took it for granted that the woman was there holding the fort.

Oh, I don't think I did, because I'd been brought up in a family where the mother was a very important person indeed, and for the children much more important than the father, so that I had no feelings of that sort at all.

Were you always on hand when there was a crisis at home?

No, unfortunately. We had a baby of our own, a boy, who at the age of two and a half died of meningitis while I was away in Europe. John Cockroft, one of my great friends, got them to broadcast this on several of the stations in Europe as a message for me — of course there was no television or anything then. It said, would I please return home at once. A waiter who heard this message came and spoke to me in Cologne, I think it was, and I immediately went and found an aircraft and went back, but by that time the little boy was dead. My wife had to go through that on her own. But it was very quick; he was all right the previous day, and all right when he was put to bed, and then it developed during the night.

What impact did this personal tragedy have on your life?

Well, it was very tragic for me, but it was of course most tragic for my wife. I was so upset that I hadn't been there to help her at that time. I don't know . . . when one cares for somebody . . . we always shared.

Did you have more children after that?

No, unfortunately. It didn't work. As a matter of fact the first one was born four or five years after we were married, and there were no children after that, and then we decided to adopt. We adopted first of all a boy, Michael, who was a great success. And then I thought that it was wrong to have an only child, so we adopted Vivien, our girl. They both turned out wonderfully. Unfortunately Michael's no longer with us, but Vivien is a great tower of strength.

So you've lost two sons.

That's right. It was a terrible blow because once again . . . when Michael died . . . I was in Canberra. He was in the Walter and Eliza Hall Institute for Medical Research in Melbourne in his last days, and he died there on the night when I was in Canberra.

As a public man with major obligations all through your life, you always had a public role or a job or a war that had to be attended to. Did you feel ever that you neglected your personal life?

Yes, but one had to, you see. I'm afraid that's part of life. In scientific work you can't abandon an experiment right in the middle, just when it's showing promise of success, particularly when there's something exciting turning up. You have to work long hours and you have to be very dedicated in order to do such work and be a success. It's rather like being a musician really; you just so rapidly get stale if you're away from it for any time. So that of necessity it does mean a full-time job.

One has vacations, of course, and we took advantage of those, particularly with the children when they were young. We spent a lot of time exploring England and the Continent with them. Once I was invited to give a lecture at the Sorbonne and I decided that we'd all go to Paris. When I told the children that we were going to Paris Vivien burst out crying, and she was inconsolable. I couldn't get it out of her for a time. I said, 'What's the matter?', and she said, 'There mightn't be a loo on board!' That's the sort of thing that children worry about.

Is there anything in your life that you really regret?

Yes. I think the thing that needles at the back of my mind is, first of all, the fact that I never saw as much as I should have of my wife, and of my children when they were young. For so long I was an absentee father, as it were, except for short visits and writing to them. The second thing is that I still feel very unhappy about having been involved in the development of the nuclear weapon, and all that it means for the future of mankind if it ever gets out of control. We always hoped after the last world war, when the United Nations was established, that at last we were going to have a united world, a world that was going to work together, and we were going to have no more of these bloody wars. Then the nuclear weapon came along and changed the whole situation. But not only did that happen but the world, instead of being united, becomes more and more fragmented. Now Russia is broken up, we've got troubles in the Middle East . . .

So you don't feel very optimistic about the future.

I don't feel optimistic about the future at the present time. There's too much evidence of this grasping attitude of mankind. Always this desire for money and profit, for possessions, for being not the user of the wonders of this Earth but the master of the whole of the wonders of this Earth, and even of the whole universe.

Do you think this is fundamental to human nature?

I don't believe it is, you know, I don't believe it is. I mean, one sees so much of kindness, of decency, of pity amongst people towards other people whom they know, even though they are racially different or something of that sort. But one doesn't see that attitude between governments. This is the trouble, I think — so long as we have separate nations and governments, with people doing the governing who have ambitions, we'll be in trouble.

Do you have any vision of how that might be overcome?

Only by, I suppose, some sort of world government, by some sort of agreement amongst the nations, the peoples of the world, that they will live in peace. By the complete banishing of weapons of mass destruction, war as a whole, and indeed the outlawing of all forms of violence — because we breed violence, you know, we breed violence. There's no place more violent than the rugby field. And we're obsessed with toys that we invent and then abuse. We use them for the wrong purposes, and this is what makes me pessimistic about the future. I do believe that the increase in our knowledge of nature, both of dead matter and of living matter, has been disastrous because of the uses that are made of it. The knowledge itself is wonderful to think about. Take for instance the understanding of DNA, beautiful! But when you start mucking about with it, it's a different story.

If you had your time over again, would you be a nuclear physicist?

No.

What would you do?

I think if I was starting out today I'd either be an astronomer or a biophysicist.

What would your interest in biophysics be?

Well, I was always brought up in a do-gooder family and started out with the idea of being a doctor. I've retained a deep interest in biological things, expressed nowadays in my feeling that we've got to try and preserve some of the natural ecology of this wonderful country. The whole of the natural fauna and flora of this country are rapidly disappearing. We're losing something like 300 species of plants every year, and an even greater number of insects, and something of the order of 40 or 50 different kinds of animals and birds. They just become extinct as a result of our activities.

You said you felt that we interfere too much — that as human beings, when we get knowledge, we want to use it to interfere in nature. And yet in a way that was the exciting work you were doing during those years with Rutherford — you were interfering with the atom in order to create something additional that wasn't there before.

Oh, but you've always got to interfere with something. That's totally different from what I've been talking about. We weren't trying to make money by poking something into the middle of a nucleus, and the nucleus of course is a bit of inanimate matter. One wasn't destroying life by investigating the interior of the atom. No, it was curiosity about the whole structure of the universe that motivated us. It was like exploring the galaxies.

So you see connections — what you were doing with the atom connects with astronomy and with molecular biology — all helping us to understand the underlying patterns of life and the universe.

Yes. That's right.

And yet, in that exploration there are these dangers, the dangers you encountered in the way that knowledge was being used to make the bomb.

Yes.

But wouldn't you see similar dangers in the exploration of DNA?

Oh, I think much more far-reaching dangers. I mean, it is possible to imagine ways of getting agreement between nations not to use nuclear weapons, because after all they're destructive of everything. Whereas with DNA we're interfering with nature in what I might call unnatural ways — producing species of animals that are completely new; cloning animals that we find useful. Beef cattle, for instance, can be cloned quite easily and one can have a thousand cattle that are all identical 'twins'. I hate the idea! It's so against nature. One's interfering for the wrong reasons.

You're an individual who stood out from the crowd, you've succeeded beyond the level that most people succeed. How do you explain that? What do you think it is about you as an individual that's enabled you to do these things?

Cussedness! Determination, I think, is the only thing. I often wonder about old age in my nineties, but I realise the only way to live is just to keep on keeping on. Once you give in you're lost, and the wonderful thing, I think, is that I've managed to keep my curiosity and to keep wanting to learn all the time. I'm still a student, in other words, and I hope I remain so until I die.

What are you still most curious about?

The fact that we haven't the faintest idea of the difference between living and dead matter. What life is is something that's still completely unknown. Why there should be life on this one planet Earth in the solar system and not on any of the other planets that circulate around the sun, as we know now from our space exploration, is something that's strange. It does make this Earth something unique — there are probably other Earths somewhere or other, around other suns in the universe, but they're all so far away that it's difficult to imagine making any contact with those other living beings. The other thing that I often think about is this phenomenon of consciousness, of being aware of one's surroundings.

Science, of course, is only about 300 years old in its present form. However, we are living in a world that's moving so rapidly towards understanding that I feel that some day, perhaps, we might understand the difference between living and dead matter. But at the present moment it is *the* big puzzle.

Looking back with hindsight at the pattern of your life, are there any basic principles that you feel you've brought to bear on decisions or problems?

Only, I think, respect for the truth; that it's absolutely essential in scientific work. Once you begin to fake things or mess about, you're lost.

You say that, in old age, you think the recipe is just to determinedly keep on hanging in there. Do you think at all now about death and about what that's going to mean, and whether there's anything beyond it?

No. Death doesn't worry me. For one thing, I have experienced so much of death during the war and of course I've had the tragedies in my own family. But in addition to that I keep remembering that I'm the oldest of a family of five boys and I'm the only one still alive. And it amazes me at times — worries me sometimes too because it seems so grossly unfair — that I should be here and they, who were younger and could be doing far more for the world today than I can possibly do, are dead.

Do you think there's an afterlife?

No.

You feel quite sure about that?

I feel quite certain about it. I am prepared to believe that there are things that we don't understand about nature. The beliefs of Buddhism, for instance, rather attract me — the idea that there's a reservoir of life and that, when you die, as Fitzgerald says in the last line of his poem about the Buddha, 'then the dew drop fell into the silent sea'. And I rather like the idea of the dew drop of life joining all the rest of life in the universe.

How would you like to be remembered?

I'd like to be remembered just as 'a good Aussie bloke'. Shakespeare had Antony say in Julius Caesar: 'The evil that men do lives after them / The good is oft interred with their bones'. Well, I wouldn't like somebody to dig up some dirt; there might be some dirt in my past that I'm unconscious of, having being concerned with the development of the nuclear weapon, and I might be cursed for it. I hate that idea. I don't want to be cursed by anybody! [He laughs.]

What good do you most want to be remembered for? Would it be your contribution to society as a whole? Or would it be your contribution to science?

My love for the whole of nature. Right from the universe down to the nucleus of the atom and even the constituents of the nucleus of the atom. I have an innate love and care for that — particularly for anything with life. I think life is such a wonderful phenomenon that I'd want to be thought of as somebody who would like to see people taking care of living creatures, rather than killing them.

Sir Mark Oliphant continues to live independently in a flat behind his daughter's house in Canberra. His large frame is beginning to feel the effects of age and he gardens less than he used to. His reading is still wide and thorough and he keeps up to date with the latest scientific work in his field. But he complains that his own original thinking in the subject, which is still his greatest delight, is now impeded by a growing inability to maintain for long periods the intense concentration and purposive thinking that once came so naturally to him. However, this in no way precludes the pursuit of new ideas or his ability to converse about them with clarity and intelligence. And he is as determined as ever not to let go of the intense enjoyment that he gets from learning and discovery. He attributes his continuing good health to his lifelong avoidance of over-vigorous exercise.

$\mathcal{D}$onald Horne

The Clever Country Boy

$\mathcal{T}$he idea that our personal selves are derived from the groups to which we belong is implicit in the way Donald Horne describes himself. In the vast amount of auto-biographical material he has penned, a clear portrait of his psychological self eludes the reader. Instead, his descriptions of his own experiences are set firmly in their social context and are often used to illustrate the insights that he wishes to express about the broader reality they reflect.

This is a curious fact about a man who has sometimes been accused of being egocentric or egotistical. Perhaps it is the confident assertion of his opinions that attracts these adjectives to him. Yet a consistent characteristic, displayed throughout his life, is a great relish of opposition and a thorough enjoyment of *the cut and thrust of public debate. Indeed, controversy is the crucible in which his ideas have been refined.*

His mind is of a type that operates well in a social context. He gleans, absorbs and analyses a wide range of material — the facts, opinions and arguments of others — and integrates them into a broader overview which often penetrates to the core of the national psyche. This has meant that his contribution as a public intellectual has been not only valuable but possibly crucial in the formation of contemporary Australian attitudes.

In the following encounter Donald Horne uses his analytical powers to help evaluate his contribution to Australian public life. His life as an individual is brought under similar scrutiny, uncovering a Donald Horne whom few have known.

Donald Horne was born on 26 December 1921 and spent his early years in the town of Muswellbrook in New South Wales. His father was a schoolteacher and his mother an active participant in the social life of the town. Donald remained an only child throughout his time at Muswellbrook.

DH I think one of the most formative things in my early life was living in Muswellbrook. One gift given to me from that is something that I simply wouldn't have got by being brought up in a suburb, and that was a sense of a whole society. I think it came to me partly through my mother's social membranes, as it were. She was very sensitive to snubs and insults and so forth. But it also came from the fact that I lived in a society in which the big landholders were the Whites — Patrick White's cousins and others — and they were on top. At the very bottom were people who lived on the Common and whose children went to school without shoes. All of the intervening parts of that structure — middle class, lower middle class, upper lower middle class — all of those layers were present. It really was a microcosmic world. It's the reason, I think, why I would almost like to have written a nineteenth century novel. Not the rather tedious novels of sensibility that many people write now — but just to have once again that sense of all these people having these social relations to each other.

RH *Where did you fit in? Where did your family sit in that hierarchy?*

I remember, when I was writing *The Education of Young Donald*, I looked up the *Muswellbrook Chronicle* over a period of years to see who was invited to the different balls in the town. The big top ball was the Picnic Races Ball, and school teachers weren't allowed to go to that. Bank managers were, for obvious reasons, because they were keeping the whole racket going. We were in the next top one, which was the Golf Club Ball. Some of the big landed families played golf when nobody else was there, but school teachers were just about as low as you could get at the golf club [he laughs]. Then, after that, something that my parents worried about was the Anglican Ball. And they'd look at the Catholic Ball as pretty well near the bottom, because Catholics were not really seen as being part of ordinary human existence.

That was the town. What about your home? How did that shape you?

My father bought me a thing called Cassell's *Children's Book of Knowledge* and he was somehow or other — I don't know whether encouraging is the right word — but he was certainly complacent about my buying books of my own, which I would save for out of money I got from selling newspapers and things of that kind. I sold old newspapers, not new ones, to butchers. I think it was Cassell's *Children's Book of Knowledge* that gave me this great desire that I really would like to know everything. There are also memories of belief, which in our case were entirely secular. Anzac Day was very big in our house. My father would put on his medals and they'd all walk down the street, then the non-Catholics would go off to the Church of England and the Catholics would go off to their Mass, which seemed a pretty un-Australian thing to do, to their specific ceremony. The School Empire Day was big. I still have a copy of the speech I made for School Empire Day.

The Great War hadn't long ended, of course.

The shadow of the Great War — well, shadow's not quite the right word because it was also seen as redemptive in some ways — but the memories of the Great War were very big in our house. I remember, once, the movies had come to Muswellbrook and we went to see some movie about pacifists. When we got home my mother made cups of tea and we sat around with tea and biscuits in the kitchen. My father looked at me very anxiously, and then he suddenly said: 'You'd serve, wouldn't you, if there was another war?' We were in some ways getting ready for the *next* war.

How old were you?

I would have then been in about third class, but I was being signed up!

What sentiments did you express when you spoke at Empire Day?

I expressed idealistic sentiments about the Empire as a great brotherhood of nations — all that kind of thing. Ultimately even the natives, a few hundred years from now perhaps, could be in that brotherhood.

Was this the beginning of Donald Horne's multiculturalism?

There was no doubt that at that period people had an imperialist view of human existence, and Cassell's *Children's Book of Knowledge* certainly presented natives as different from the rest of us. In Muswellbrook we didn't have any multiculturals apart from Greeks. There were the Greeks who ran the steak and eggs place, the cafe, and that was it. There were no Aborigines. The census returns show there were a few Armenians and a few others, but it was really an English-speaking society divided most bitterly by the most important division known to humankind: the difference between Protestants and Catholics.

That was a bitter thing in the town?

People now who talk about a divided society make a considerable error. We now have a complex multi-ethnic society, but at that period there was a divided society. The difference between Catholic and Protestant went through most forms of life. I myself believed that Catholics were not really part of the human species like the rest of us. They had distinctive physical characteristics which made them different from us, although there were always individual exceptions. And, as we know, most business houses were Masonic and anti-Catholic and within government departments there were some Catholic and some Protestant. The police were bitterly divided. It was a divided society of the kind Australia perhaps will never be again.

And where did your family sit in relation to that? What part did religion play in your household?

Religion didn't matter much to us. We belonged to the Anglo-Presbyterian ascendancy in the sense that my father was born a Presbyterian but switched over to Anglicanism when he married my mother. We went to church once a year, for Anzac Day. We knew we'd been baptised in it, although actually I didn't get around to being confirmed. And we knew that we'd be buried in it, and it was there for that kind of purpose.

And for the Anglican Ball.

The Anglican Ball was not of such significance to us as the Golf Ball, if I might use that expression. But we did know that the Catholics were different, anti-British, superstitious, with priests drinking whisky all day. As it happened my schoolteacher, who had me for about four years, was a Catholic. But of course she was different, and the boy and girl next door with whom I used to play, they were quite different. Individual Catholics were human beings, but the idea of being Catholic was pretty repellent.

What about your parents as individuals — could you describe what kind of a person your father was?

My father had a nervous breakdown during my adolescence and that changed my attitude to him entirely, because he seemed to me to be a bit of a washout. My mother was, and continued to be until she died at the age of 92, in some ways rather superficial. But she was also an extremely generous and lively kind of person who felt that there should always be some fun going on in life. Her house used to be a great centre for playing pianolas, playing bridge, playing tennis — doing all of those things. Whereas my father had a somewhat more systematic view of life. I sometimes used to get beaten with a slipper because I'd broken one of the elements of this system.

What sort of things were you beaten for?

Oh, giving cheek to a shopkeeper, on one occasion. It didn't happen very often. I remember I once wrote 'shit' in indelible pencil on a chocolate box, and got a pretty fair hiding for that. I think the indelible pencil made it worse. On the other hand, my father used to be funny. He thought that one of the things in life one had to do was to do wisecracks, and make jokes and so forth, and I suppose that had some effect on me.

You used to engage in that with him? Was that part of your relationship?

No, I think the funny relationship was just him. He would be funny, we would laugh at him. But I came from a household in which it seemed appropriate that one should make little jokes, which is something I suppose I've continued and tried to do.

During these early Muswellbrook years you were an only child. Did that have any influence, do you think?

I don't know. I used to feel a bit guilty about being an only child, because it was spoken about like one of those menaces — diphtheria, cancer and things like that — that people spoke about privately. I could hear them discussing it at night when I was in bed.

With this great interest in learning you must have been a little bit different from your friends at school. Were you?

I was the kind of 'cleverer boy' in Muswellbrook District Rural School, I suppose. I remember, when I was in second class, one of the schoolteachers (with my father being a schoolteacher we used to meet them at home) came down to second class and asked me to read to her class, which was a fifth class, just to show them how stupid they were. Here was a second class boy, what a terrible thing to happen, ha ha ha, who could read better than they could!

Did you enjoy that? Did you enjoy being given the opportunity to show bigger boys that they were stupid?

I'm not quite sure whether I enjoyed it. But I was appalled once when I didn't come top in arithmetic. Throughout my period from third class to sixth class there used to be monthly tests and the results were all put up on the wall, and I came top in everything. [He laughs.] Except that on this particular occasion I think I came fourth in arithmetic and that seemed quite strange. I might say this know-all, smart-alec character disappeared later, in high school.

What made it disappear?

I don't know. I first went to Maitland Boys High School. By the end of the year I'd become number one in the Hunter Valley. Later, when I transferred to Parramatta High School, to my absolute amazement in my first half-yearly exam results in second year I failed French. I never imagined I'd fail in anything. It was associated partly with my father going through his nervous breakdown and with differences between city and country. And I think that I underwent a disturbance of some kind, which to some extent impeded or held up what you might call my 'natural cleverness'. It's just possible that if I'd stayed on at Maitland High School I would have ended up with, say, four first class honours in the Leaving Certificate, rather than two.

Why did you move from Muswellbrook to the city?

My father, being a schoolteacher, was moved. There was a great thing in my life called 'the Department' — and, mysteriously the Department would intervene in our lives. Once a year, it seemed, somebody called the Inspector would arrive at Muswellbrook, and schoolteachers' whole futures would depend on the Inspector. Suddenly the Department decided that my father would move to Sydney.

The move to Sydney coincided with a number of dramatic events in Donald Horne's life — his father's breakdown and subsequent retirement from teaching and Donald's loss of academic pre-eminence at school. He failed to develop new relationships to replace his Maitland and Muswellbrook friends, and during this same high school period a baby sister was born. These were, by any standard, significant changes to occur in the crucial period of early adolescence and they resulted in a dramatic shift in relationships within and without the Horne household. Today, when speaking of them, Donald Horne adopts a casual, matter-of-fact tone which distances him from the events and even seems to make light of them. But when he started talking about visiting his father in Callan Park, the underlying emotion almost broke through, betraying a depth of feeling that was otherwise concealed by his off-hand manner.

My father began to show signs of nervous disorder when I was in sixth class at primary school. In fact, he took two months off and went down to Bondi, and I spent a couple of months at Bondi Public School. He became more and more prone to anxiety and it was evidence in general of quite highly neurotic conduct.

Your sister Janet arrived when you were in your third year at high school. What effect did this have on your life?

I wasn't quite sure whether my mother was intelligent enough to have a baby [he laughs]. So I read all of the mothercraft books and we had big discussions about how she was to go through her early period.

Were you satisfied with the outcome?

Yes, she more or less followed my instructions. [He laughs.] The thing was that I felt responsible — we discussed it like two adults.

And at this stage your father was really a bit out of the scene?

Yes — my father was *going* out of the scene, then in the next year he was out. He was still at that stage really tense and difficult to get on with, but he became even more so. That behaviour ran through years six, seven, eight, nine; and in year ten I suddenly discovered that at the school it was suggested that he had put his hand on the thigh of one of the pupils. By this stage he was almost in a state of collapse. Nobody knew whether that was true or not, but he was then declared to have a nervous breakdown and for a while he spent a bit of time at Callan Park, which was, as we used to say in those days, a lunatic asylum. I can remember this great feeling of my mother's that one should always cheer people up, and we'd go there once a week and cheer him up. You know, we'd go along, have a talk about what was happening, and he'd give us a bit of gossip from Ward 6 or whatever it might be. We'd have a joke. He got better, but he was never much good. He'd been emptied out and he was living on a couple of pensions. I don't know that that had as much effect on me as the deterioration of the whole family atmosphere over four-and-a-half years.

After his collapse I kind of took over and helped. My mother had to write things about his condition in order to get the pensions and I remember I was going through that period at school in which you had to invert sentences. So she had to write this report on him and I was beginning sentences with 'Never have I known a man so agitated' — so that she could describe my father's condition to somebody who was then called the Master of Lunacy.

How long was your father in Callan Park?

He wasn't in Callan Park for long; he made very good progress. It was a bit like Muswellbrook School. He was a good boy and progressed rapidly through the grades and in no time at all was discharged. It was only a period of about three months or so. He used to say in his joking manner that he was actually one of the few people who had a certificate saying he was sane. In those days if you got out they wrote a thing saying you were sane again. But he was never the same again.

So your father had been a strong, coherent figure in your early childhood, and at a fairly early stage of your adolescence you actually almost swapped roles with him. You had to take on the role of the person who helped your mother with the new baby, and you organised things.

It was to some extent like that, yes.

What happened in your senior years at high school after this shift in your family had taken place?

I moved to Canterbury High School because we shifted house, and there I recovered a bit of spirit. It was a school which was devoted to only one thing, and that was getting good marks in the Leaving Certificate. On the whole I seemed to respond to that. But my secondary education was a washout, really, although I found a history teacher there who tried to interest us in social change, economic change, little bits of Marxism, things of this kind, which represented the most intelligent thing that happened to me in my high school days.

They had a school library too. I can remember picking up the *Oxford Book of Modern Verse* and reading Eliot's *The Hollow Men*. I also used to go into town, as we used to call the central business district back in those days, pretty regularly, about once a month, and I'd go to the Municipal Library and get whatever the total number of books was. My father belonged to the Teachers Federation Library, so I'd get another stack of books from that. I'd go home carrying this enormous stack of books.

So you weren't playing sport like other boys of that age?

I had no interest in playing sport. I used to play tennis when I was in primary school because we had a tennis court. After that I played nothing — no, there was cricket for a season at Maitland. That frightened me, I didn't quite understand why the ball wouldn't hit me. Otherwise in the summer I used to go swimming, which was quite easy. In the winter I used to try to avoid football. At Parramatta there was a cinema near the high school so it was quite easy to sneak off there on Wednesday afternoons.

Did you have any particular friends? Did you belong to a group?

At Parramatta High I just led a reclusive life because of our deteriorating home situation. At Canterbury I actually started having friends again and I remember that a great occasion for me, a liberation after all that anxiety, was when I went off with one of these friends to a boarding house in Kurrajong Heights. I had a good time, for a couple of schoolgirls were there, and some other people, so I began to feel that my great problems were over. In fact I had a diary in which I confided the fact that things were going to get better now.

When the young Donald Horne arrived at Sydney University in 1939 to enrol in an Arts course, his expanding world exploded with imaginative possibilities. His love of ideas, of debate and of public life found a natural home. Everything changed for him. He met slightly older people with similar interests. They included James McAuley, Harold Stewart and A. D. Hope, and these new friends introduced him to French symbolist poetry. He also began to read his way through the great nineteenth-century novels. A desire to understand more of the visual arts was kindled by the major exhibition of Impressionist and Post-Impressionist paintings that came to Sydney that year.

Within one year I passed rapidly from Marxism to Trotskyism to anarchism, which was my ideal position at the end of the age of 17. I was also entirely familiar with page one of Freud's *The Psychopathology of Everyday Life*, and had read *Ulysses*. I didn't turn up at lectures much. You had to do the essays, and you sat for an exam. The exam was 100 per cent of the mark. This gave me the opportunity to do this enormous amount of reading in my spare time. I'm sure universities are miles better now than they were then, but that kind of university suited me better.

Not all students took advantage of that freedom in the way that you did.

No, very few. Universities were mainly places where you got a degree so you could get a job. They used to call Melbourne University the Shop. It was the place where you bought a degree. And of course most of them *were* bought. At Sydney University there were 200 people on exhibitions who didn't have to pay their fees, but the rest were there because their parents could buy them university educations.

I take it you were there on an exhibition.

I was there on a Teachers College scholarship actually, much to my — not shame — but disgust. The Teachers College scholarship had attached to it £40 a year. It was pretty good money then, and it was the only way in which I could get through the university. I used to work in the vacations, mainly in bookshops.

Why were you able, do you think, to use the freedom and time at university to extend your education, when many other people found this an excuse for doing very little?

I'm one of nature's autodidacts in the sense that I believe the only education that thoroughly matters is the stuff you teach yourself. That can mean following a conventional course, but having a critical interest in it. I suppose it goes back to sitting there reading Cassell's *Children's Book of Knowledge* from front to back and then all over again and hoping I could know everything.

It was also prompted in my first year at Sydney University by the fact that some of the people I met opened up new doors. John Anderson, the then Professor of Philosophy at Sydney University, and a famous freethinker, had a special little library which was meant to offset the conservatism of the official library, and I was able to whip through that, or part of it, during the year. Anderson himself was one of those rare things, a university teacher who really can change people's ways. He had disciples. The word 'charismatic' is almost always wrongly used, but he did have a kind of semi-charismatic intellectual appeal, in which you felt that out of this Scottish mouth, with this Glaswegian accent, was coming the absolute truth in ethics, aesthetics, in general philosophy and in what we would now describe as sociology and psychology. He had an overall view, like Hegel, that a philosopher knew everything. This view appealed to me too. The kind of interest I've been trying to show in public intellectual life in Australia, many years later, is based on the fundamental belief that it's an error to imagine that human activity can be divided into economics, sociology, politics, anthropology and so forth. I think that humans don't exist in that kind of way, and you should see it whole.

Did you get involved in university politics while you were there?

My period at Muswellbrook had given me a sense of society. I didn't have any sense at all of politics until I was at Sydney University. My big breakthrough occurred when my friend Bill Pritchett, who later became head of the Defence Department, became editor of *Honi Soit*. He'd gone to Shore, the Sydney Church of England Grammar School, and at that stage only people who'd been to GPS schools of that kind were likely to become editor of *Honi Soit*. We'd become very friendly and I went in with him too, and then I entered student affairs almost fulltime. I abandoned most of my studies. During that year I got mixed up with all that business about the Student Representative Council and the National Union of Australian Students, and I began to philosophise about politics. By the end of the year I felt I knew really all that need be known about interpersonal politics — and I may have been right. [He laughs.]

When you became editor of Honi Soit *you really began, most publicly, your career as a stirrer. What do you remember about those days and about how you got into the business of stirring people up?*

I have been thinking about that lately, and I think that even when I was editing *Honi Soit* I had this idea that there's more to life than very careful, thorough statements. You arouse people's interest. You do that particularly by giving them a big shock, or by a loaded phrase. I regard life as hypothetical in a sense — I mean, it's all a theory about what existence is. And in some ways you can help people think by setting them something to think about. Looking back on *Honi Soit* — to describe it as 'technique' is slightly wrong, because I didn't sit down and think, now this is the way in which you encourage discussion. I just did it.

Didn't you also enjoy having a go at people, getting them ruffled?

I certainly enjoyed the whole idea of experimenting and mucking around. Of course, you get pretty frightened too at times. You think, God, I might be sent down, I might be expelled, or — later — I might get the sack. You bear that in mind as well. It would be wrong to imagine that it's just getting your enjoyment out of irritating people, although at that stage it might have been true. You can also get enjoyment out of people actually responding to what you're saying. I believe in making very positive statements and that's one way of finding out if you really believe what you're saying. It also has been my experience that I sometimes expressed things very forcibly and got reactions, and then changed my own mind. Setting the cat amongst the pigeons is a kind of sideline which still exists. You can certainly get a certain excitement in looking at the reactions. But the reactions do include the pleasure of some people actually being interested in what you're saying and not simply being affronted by it.

Do you remember any particular controversial issue that you got going in Honi Soit?

The most notable one, the one in which there were threats of sending me down, was that I wrote an editorial about sex — about which I didn't know all that much, actually, at the time — under the heading 'Sex, isn't it dreadful'. And this caused an enormous stir.

What was the thrust of it, if I may use that expression?

[He laughs.] I should really look it up to be quite sure. I think it was nothing much more really than that people were to talk about it a bit more freely. The one thing that especially irritated people was that I said that, really, for lots of people, the only written communication they have about sex is what they read on lavatory walls. And that caused an affront and then suddenly there was this great descent of letters, all complaining. So I thought, Oh gee, that's good, I've got next week's headline! I can remember it was in 60-point Metro bold caps: SEX LEADER CAUSES BIG STIR. And I think that filled up a couple of pages of *Honi Soit*. The Women's Christian Temperance Union went to the Vice Chancellor, complained, and he took me to afternoon tea and explained that he told them that it wasn't his business. And I said, 'What didn't they like about me?', and he said, 'Oh, you know, they think you've got a dirty mind'.

At this stage, were you thinking of journalism as a career?

No, I used to rather despise the idea of journalism. But I actually became the university correspondent for the *Daily Telegraph* when I was there. Three pounds a week, for God's sake, and here was I on £40 per year. It meant I could pay for my own drinks, which I hadn't been always able to do previously. I became a journalist entirely by accident. The *Daily Telegraph* earlier had had a very talented editor, Syd Deamer, and a full crew of liberal humanist journalists. It was very different from the *Sydney Morning Herald* which I considered to be a very conservative and reactionary paper. The *Telegraph* still had that tone about it in the early 1940s, although acquiring other characteristics as well.

While you were an undergraduate at Sydney University, were you aware of a pattern emerging in which authority had always to be questioned?

Yes, certainly. John Anderson was a great exponent of that. All authorities had to be questioned — apart from his own. That had certainly by that stage become crystallised, ideologised as it were — the idea of criticism.

Do you feel that this anti-authoritarian stand had to do with the ideas that you encountered at university or with the emotional experience of being disappointed with your father's authority?

Or maybe it began even earlier. My father, before he fell to bits, used to say you should think for yourself. I suppose lots of fathers say that to their children. But I seemed to be responsive to that idea, so that somewhere or other in those mysteries of personality development, even before my father went round the bend, I had acquired a certain kind of critical spirit. And a few schoolteachers I had, especially the history teacher, cultivated it. Then, at the university, the message was: criticism's good; that's what you should do.

When you were at university, you seemed to get a lot of fun out of the games you were playing. Is that how you saw it at the time?

At the time I certainly saw intellectual activity, and also politics, as some kind of fun. It had enormous ups and downs and reverses. One can overdo the element of fun. But I do believe, actually, in trying to avoid too much public whingeing and I think that, even if things aren't going so well, it might be better to put an optimistic and ironic face on them.

This was your mother's philosophy?

I would certainly have learned that from my mother. My father wasn't exactly a whinger, but he was a little bit of a whinger inside, I think.

You found yourself at university, for the first time having sufficient substance and style in your life to attract enemies and to attract people who were on your side. I get a sense out of your autobiographical writings that you really relished this.

Yes, well, I think I probably relished more enemies than friends when I was at the university. In fact, I didn't have much option towards the end — I'd pretty well run out of friends. I'm no longer in that situation in any way. But it made me aware of the fact that one can tolerate enemies. One shouldn't imagine that one's always going to be universally liked. Even people who are not in the public realm at all will walk out of a room and other people will start talking about them behind their back. It's characteristic of human behaviour, that we're all criticising each other. It's very disappointing, but nevertheless there.

You said you left university without any friends. Had you really alienated all your friends?

I hadn't, actually. I had alienated a number of them by that stage, but I seemed to be acquiring new ones.

Did you learn anything from that? Did that experience stay with you? Because you say that you can perfectly well do with enemies, but some people find it harder to do without friends.

The next thing that happened was that I was thrown into the Army, where one develops a different idea of friendship. The Army was dreadfully boring for me. I didn't understand the Army; I didn't get much out of it. But you could always find people with whom you could share experiences. So I passed from these highly febrile university relationships — a bit like a Dostoyevskian novel played fast for laughs — into the more traditional friendships of people thrown into similar circumstances who can find some accommodation with each other.

And did you get pleasure out of these new friendships?

I think 'pleasure' would be going too far, because they weren't exactly the kind of friendships I wanted, which would always have in them a certain intellectual quality. But I got a kind of solace out of them. They helped me get through a boring time, a time that felt highly artificial, in the sense that I was pretending that I was a gunner. Gunner Horne! It wasn't me.

Donald Horne left the Army to become a cadet in the diplomatic service. He was sent to Canberra, but resigned the next year because he was by that time involved in an intense love affair which demanded his presence in Sydney. He also felt that at that stage of his life he was unsuited to the restraints of diplomacy. He rather reluctantly commenced work as a journalist, mainly because it was work that was readily available to him. In 1948 he married his first wife, Ethel, an Englishwoman, and in 1949 went to England, intending to stay there for the rest of his life. He lived in a country village, worked in London, and almost gained preselection as a Conservative candidate for Parliament. His life in Britain after the war seemed to have nothing to do with anything that had gone before it.

You completely changed your life. Why do you think that happened?

Why did it happen? I don't know. When I wrote my auto-biographical trilogy I meant it to have certain enigmatic qualities about it. I think people can be over-clever about giving the reasons for why this, that or any of the other happened. My father going round the bend and things like that — you can see there's possibly a relationship. It was quite amazing, and when I wrote the book I just hoped that people would be amazed by that and, like me, think 'I wonder why that happened', and then not know.

You're perfectly prepared to be, as you say, 'over-clever' in putting interpretations on public things, on your attitudes and beliefs about the world around you. But you do have this reluctance which is apparent in your writing — and even as we talk now — to put similar interpretations on your personal and private feelings, thoughts and relationships.

I think there would be several reasons for that. One is that sometimes they affect other people. Second is that I frankly don't believe that a great deal of this self-revelation is altogether honest. Our minds are in such a muddle, with so many conflicts going on, that people fool themselves. They're making something up which is a more rational explanation than what actually occurred. When talking about myself I don't mind talking about the public stuff because in some ways that's more verifiable. I don't especially want to be enigmatic — I hadn't even thought of myself much like that. But it is certainly true that that was how I decided to write this autobiographical series.

Sometimes, of course, hindsight allows you to see patterns emerging in your own behaviour; for example, we've noted that by this stage a certain anti-authoritarian streak had emerged. Presumably that didn't sit well with looking to run as a Conservative MP.

Having been an anarchist at Sydney University, I continued to be what I would describe as a small 'l' liberal [*he laughs*]. I've always believed in abortion on demand, no censorship, the entire packet of works. I used to worry about whether people should be allowed to masturbate publicly, and I decided that if they wanted to do it there could be special streets where they could do it. So I had no doubt about being that kind of liberal. But I was also fervently anti-Stalinist, which in those days, for intellectuals, was sometimes a rather risky business, because you were usually seen therefore as a fascist.

What I was was firmly anti-planner. Hayek and others, now seen as great authorities by the economic fundamentalists, I read in the mid-1940s. I was never an economic fundamentalist to the extent that some of these people are now, but I saw what Hayek was on about.

You prefer 'economic fundamentalist' to 'economic rationalist'?

I use 'economic fundamentalist' because I think 'economic rationalist' gives rationalism a bad name. So amongst intellectuals in those days I was a bit anti-authoritarian because I had become anti-planning and anti-progressive in political terms. I moved into almost becoming a Conservative candidate through impulse and accident. I started a Conservative Party branch and one thing led to the other. For me that was an act of defiance of most of my friends. One has to go back to those days to understand how someone like me could be Conservative — I was anti the authority of my peer group's general approach.

During this period in England, how did you earn your living?

To begin with I decided I was going to be a great novelist. I'd saved some money, which was not very difficult because I was a successful young journalist, earning well. So for about 18 months we lived on that, and I wrote a novel which wasn't published until much later, under another name. Then I started to write another one, borrowed some money — and nobody was interested in the second one. After about two and a half years I had to descend to actually working again as a journalist on a newspaper.

Was that a good experience — working as a journalist in England?

I think I probably learned all that had to be learned about working as a journalist in the few years that I'd done it in Australia. I don't know that journalism is something in which you continue to acquire all that much. You may extend your range of interests and so forth, but it's necessarily limited to a few devices.

In 1954 Donald Horne returned to Australia almost by accident and with the firm intention of staying for no more than six months. Frank Packer wanted to start a popular magazine in Australia based on the format of the British Weekly Mail. It was to be called Weekend. During his period in London Donald had worked on the Weekly Mail and, although he despised it, he was outraged that Packer had not considered him for editor of the Australian version. Mainly out of resentment and anger at having been overlooked, he demanded and got the job of setting it up. He saw it as a buccaneer's adventure — to spend a strictly limited time successfully producing a

*magazine that he regarded as pure rubbish. But a number of personal
factors, including the dissolution of his marriage to his first wife Ethel
who had stayed behind in England, meant that instead of returning
to England after the six months, he remained in Australia.*

How did you relate to Australian society on your return from England?

Sometimes people wonder about who they are. What I knew,
fundamentally, was that I wasn't quite sure who I was. But I knew I
wasn't that rubbishy magazine, and it made me very unhappy and
frustrated. And then ultimately I got out of Packer this intellectual
fortnightly, the *Observer*, as part of my recompense. It started in
1958. Then a few months later Tom Fitzgerald of the *Sydney Morning
Herald* started another journal, *Nation*, and it used to come out in
the alternate weeks. This was a period when the cultural desert was
beginning to not so much bloom, as produce a few desert flowers.
There were an increasing number of quarterly intellectual
magazines. The theatre was developing, in what we now think of as
a primitive form at least. There was something called the Phillip
Street Revue in Sydney and they were into satire. It was the period
when Patrick White's books were getting praise and that cheered up
other people. It was also the period when the universities were
beginning to make some contributions to intellectual life. A lot of it
was rather skimpy, but it was a different kind of Australia from the
one I'd been a student in. In starting the *Observer* we were one of
the little flowers, or a cactus perhaps — a little part of that
movement in our previous cultural wilderness.

What happened with the Observer?

What happened with the *Observer* was that it died of indigestion. It
acquired the *Bulletin*. Frank Packer had been tipped off that Rupert
Murdoch was going to buy a women's magazine called the *Woman's
Mirror*. So Packer went down and bought it himself. Then he rang
me from a public telephone box, for some reason, and said: 'I just
bought the *Woman's Mirror*. They own a paper called the *Bulletin*.
Do you want to kill the *Bulletin* or kill the *Observer*?' And I said:
'I suppose we'll have to kill the *Observer*.'

So we took over the *Bulletin*. And not only did I take off its
masthead 'Australia for the White Man', but within about four or
five weeks I changed the magazine altogether. This was rather risky,
because all of its existing 87-year-old racist readers might have
stopped buying it without anybody else subscribing. Also, the entire

staff went. There were two I would have liked to have kept but the others had to go, partly because some of them were racists but mainly because they'd been in captivity for so long. They were so used to whingeing, so used to saying why can't we do this, that and the other, that when we arrived and said, 'What would you like to do?', of course they just wanted to go on whingeing.

Did you hesitate at all before you introduced all that change?

No.

It was obvious to you what was needed?

It was a bit like Whitlam crashing through. I had to do it quickly and it was an easy operation. I didn't really trust the ability of the Packer people to support my changes — I knew there'd be complaints all over the place and all kinds of people trying to bring pressure. I just had to change it irrevocably in no time at all.

And the Bulletin, *of course, really did have the banner 'Australia for the White Man'.*

Yes. There are a couple of generations of Australians now who don't realise that one of our really great and successful stories in Australia in the last few decades was changing one of the most declaredly bigoted societies in the world — White Australia. When I took 'Australia for the White Man' off the *Bulletin*, I didn't ask Packer or anything. I just went down to the composing room and said to the head compositor: 'Would you take that off.' It was in metal type, and I can still remember seeing it as he put his tweezers down and pulled it out. And I said: 'Would you melt it down' — that's what they do with type. Then the managing director who himself left a few weeks later, said: 'That's been the *Bulletin's* slogan ever since it started!' I said: 'No it hasn't.' To begin with they had no such caption, then they had one called 'Australia for the White Man and China for the Chow'. And of course 'Australia for the White Man' was a somewhat kinder way of putting it.

And how did you enjoy your stay at the Bulletin?

I enjoyed my stay at the *Bulletin*. I got the sack at the end of it, which was inevitable because I really kicked up such a stir that I put myself at entire risk. But by that stage nobody could put it back to where it was before. I *didn't* enjoy the fact that I was also bringing out this rubbishy thing *Weekend* at the same time. It was a great time of difficulty and strain, I suppose, although it was greatly helped by the fact that that was the period in which I got married a second time. I enjoyed really changing, indeed destroying, what I think was one of the most evil publications in Australia — which is what the *Bulletin* had become by that stage — and trying to turn it into something that could encourage a bit of public intellectual life in Australia. At that period that included jokes and short stories as well as the comment.

Why did you get sacked?

I never quite found out. I have some theories about it. I think it was partly that Frank Packer had been in a very expansionary mood. He had the tendency to put his money on the table and gamble, then cut his losses. I think he decided just to cut everything down.

But the Bulletin *stayed, without you . . .*

That's right.

So it was you that he wanted to get rid of.

In a place like that there's no point being too paranoid or indeed inquiring too much. I had enemies, as people do, and I thought they may have finally succeeded in having a go at me. I explained to Packer that I would therefore resign, although I'd spend a year trying to fix up this other magazine. Then, when my resignation time came, I got a long cable from him, characteristically from Honolulu, beginning: 'Dear Donald, after our long and fruitful association', and so forth, 'I do wish you'd reconsider your decision to resign'. So I went to see him when he came back and I said: 'What would you do with me?' He'd put Peter Hastings in as the editor of the *Bulletin* and Peter had walked out of the room as I walked in. I said, 'You haven't got any jobs for me anyway'. He said, 'Oh', pointing to Hastings's departing back, 'you can have his job!' He was suggesting I should go back to the *Bulletin*.

Do you know why he reconsidered?

No. I have bits of clues and so forth. Those places are a bit of a court, with courtiers in and out. But it didn't matter much who did it — did it?

You've always had a certain contempt for authority, and it would be difficult to think of a more absolute authority than Frank Packer was. Do you think there'd been a bit of insubordination as well?

I don't think so. I had a very strange relationship with Packer. He saw *himself*, in lots of ways, as somebody who bucked authority. He had a gentlemanly feel about him, but also a larrikin feel. Fortunately he wasn't very interested in the things that I was doing.

The *Observer* and the *Bulletin* were far from central to his concerns. And I had maintained a kind of working distance from him, which somehow worked. But then it stopped working.

Just reflecting a little on your work as a journalist . . . What do you think makes good journalism?

My own experience is that I think I was probably most useful as a journalist when I became an editor. With the *Observer* we were able to help people to have a bit of a new think about Australia. I think I regard that as the way of being most useful as a journalist. Even when I was working in Sydney on the *Daily Telegraph*, under a very tough editor, the articles that I liked best were those feature articles that might make them have a bit of a think. This was amongst the ordinary people, not just one's intellectual mates. That is the area of journalism that I've been personally most interested in and that I feel I've been best at.

Are there other general principles you feel it's important for journalists to remember?

I think that for the moment I would like the parliamentary press gallery to imagine that there's more to life than the possible political effects of the latest economic indicator. I think that journalists have an enormous responsibility amongst themselves to set a very diverse agenda. While it's true that ownership shouldn't be too concentrated, that's only the beginning of the story; sometimes journalists themselves have a monopoly of approach, and that's been characteristic of the Australian media. Over the late 1980s and early 1990s what mattered in the world was limited, really, just to Parliament House gossip — how people performed at question time, what would be the effect of the latest economic indicators, and the leadership struggles within the Liberal or Labor Party. This has been a rather degrading and debilitating period for Australian journalism. Yet it has been an extraordinary period in world history. No Cold War, the old-style economics doesn't work, the old-style political divisions no longer work, Australia itself needs all kinds of new definitions. Unfortunately, the news treatments and feature treatments don't sufficiently take that into account.

In thinking about your life in journalism and in writing, how do you relate those two, and what do you feel is the real role in society of a writer?

One has to recognise that some people write because they *like* it. That doesn't mean that they necessarily get physical pleasure out of it. Lots of people like long-distance running, and it can be pretty hard and distressing but you can become obsessed by it. To me, one of the great delights of writing, in itself, is that it can give you a sense of freedom, which is something we don't have all that much of in our lives. If you happen to be a formula writer who's hit on something which means you make a fair bit of money, you lose that freedom because you've just got to produce the same stuff. But you're sitting there and you're wondering, 'What will I think ... I wonder what I might do next'. Certainly some of the books I've written have been enormously interesting to me in that way. There's also the pleasure of handling words in a great number of ways. I think that's why all writers write, apart from perhaps the formula addicts.

Then you think: 'What would be the possible effects of this?' The first book of mine that was published, although it wasn't the first one that I wrote, was that thing *The Lucky Country*, and I had imagined that that would make people have a bit of a think. Of course, it ended up as a great commercial success, and was photocopied in schools and all over the place. It had various kinds of effects and it reached a much wider audience than anybody at all would have anticipated. When I started the *Observer*, which only sold about 10 000 copies an issue, I didn't know who was going to buy it. But it was putting up some new ideas about how one might see Australia in the world, and there were 10 000 people buying it. God knows who they were. But in both of these cases what was happening was that I, and the *Observer* generally, were articulating for people something that was already in their heads. I think that writing is always influential because it's telling people something they half know or want to know. It may sometimes simply be confirming them in old stuff, or it may be leading them on to a new kind of realisation.

As an editor you were dependent on the writing of other people. Did this ever irritate you — that you couldn't write the whole paper yourself?

It used to sometimes, but I wasn't bad at briefing people and also I was pretty quick at rewriting their stuff.

Did they mind?

I can't quite remember! [He laughs.]

Were you a good editor?

I wish there were a few more editors like that now. Editing a magazine is like producing a movie. You're trying stuff out, a lot of it's wasted, but finally somebody creates it. An editor, I think, should be doing that.

The journalists who worked for you didn't ever complain about the way you treated their work, or how detailed your briefings were?

[There is a pause.] I'm struck by a case of false modesty here. I think that it can sometimes be useful, if you're fulfilling a role like that, to be an interesting personality. The people can hate you but nevertheless be interested in what you are doing. I suppose in some ways that — this is terrible to say, but I probably put on a little bit of a turn in throwing copy out the window and so on. And also in praising people. I used to hire all kinds of people nobody else would hire, some of whom have managed to survive and who rather respect my judgement.

When Donald Horne left the Bulletin *he was offered a job with Jackson Wain, which at that stage was the third largest advertising agency in Australia and which handled the* Bulletin's *advertising account. During the period of his editorship of* Weekend *they had been particularly impressed by his scheme for gaining uncomplaining public acceptance of a price increase from threepence to fourpence. It included the unashamed use of a heading saying 'Here's wonderful news for you'. He was soon Creative Director of the agency. He couldn't raise much enthusiasm for his work in advertising, but it was during this period of his life that a significant turning point was reached. Over a period of six weeks during the Christmas/New Year period, when things were quiet at the agency, he wrote* The Lucky Country. *Much of it was written at the office while the other executives were on holidays. It was written quickly because, as several commentators have pointed out, it had all been thought through in articles prepared for the* Observer *and the* Bulletin.

The publication of The Lucky Country *really brought you very much into prominence in the public eye as somebody who was interpreting Australia, and emerging as an intellectual leader. What do you think the book's primary significance was at the time?*

I think the primary significance of *The Lucky Country* was that it articulated a number of things which a number of people half believed, or were ready to believe, when I said them: the criticisms of the White Australia Policy, for example, or the criticism of our treatment of Aborigines; the inadequacies of political life, for example the somewhat over-subservient approaches we had to both the British and the United States; and also the fact that our traditional puritanism and oppressiveness were undesirable characteristics. All of those things have actually changed. The other example, unfortunately, is one which is still on the agenda, and that was the unsatisfactory and highly derivative and non-innovative nature of Australian businesses. So all of those things were kind of talking points for people. One should remember that there wasn't a useful book on Australia then. *The Lucky Country* was a very successful literary creation, I think. It really is in some ways a series of essays, held together by a final thought about what it was all about. And it was photocopied in tens of thousands, and given to kids in classrooms.

Almost everything that it called for, analysed and criticised has been responded to in the intervening period, but, as you say, one of the significant exceptions has been the critique of business. Why do you think there's been a lack of response in that area?

I think that Australian business management had a colonial frame of mind. The important original thing that Australia did was to bung commodities out into other countries — and be very good at it. But the British provided the banking system. Our business sector didn't have to be all that good at manufacturing because, in the first place, the British were good at that, and secondly, when we started having our own manufacturing, we just took other people's ideas and used them. This is one of the reasons why I've taken symbolic representations of Australia's independence as being of enormous significance, because I think we still need to kickstart Australian business management. And it's getting pretty late now. They have to understand that when you talk about the factors of production you're not just talking about raw materials, labour and capital. You're also talking about knowledge, skills and ideas, about having a highly educated and lively people who can learn to do new things.

Your suggestion was that we don't lack innovation in our scientific and intellectual areas — the lack is in applying it in a business sense.

Enormous harm is being done in Australia by people talking all the time about something called macro-economic policy. By talking about economics in this most narrow sense, which is one that most good economists don't share, we cannot see what the real problem is. Australian business management is one of the least innovative of the modern industrial societies, and that is the basic problem. It's not trade unions, although there are things wrong with them of course. It's not banking policy, it's not interest rates, for God's sake. What on earth is wrong with these people? Now there is evidence that something is going better. It's a bit hard to find out though, because the people who control the media don't seem to be able to go much beyond the latest economic indicator — the meaning of which they may not understand — and tell us what is actually happening in the *good* businesses.

The title of your book — The Lucky Country — *has entered the language but has been very widely misconstrued. That has irritated you, hasn't it?*

Sometimes people ring up on radio and their first question is: 'Is Australia still the lucky country?' And I tell them off. I say: 'I've heard that question asked 250 times, and if you don't know the answer...' What I would like to say now is that a great number of Australians, tens or hundreds of thousands, knew what I meant. At the time there was no doubt about it — all the reviewers, everybody, knew that I was being ironic. It was quite clear that what I'd said in the book itself was that Australia was a lucky country run by second-rate people who shared its luck.

A couple of years after that there was that now-forgotten minerals boom, and a great deal of flatulent overpraise of Australia for being so clever as to have minerals. It was at that stage that people, who very largely hadn't read the book, began to speak of Australia as being the lucky country, as if it was a gift from God, as if the Australians were particularly clever at being lucky. At the same time there was a new lot of lecturers coming out of the universities who wanted to push old rubbish like me away; and they misrepresented the book too, and used the expression as if I'd meant somehow that lucky was the greatest thing that a country could be. The perpetuation of the misinterpretation of the phrase came almost entirely from lazy subeditors on newspapers. I remember one headline, 'We are indeed a lucky country for surfboards'. I'm sorry that that happened. But I think that there are still a lot of people around who understood what I meant. And the very use of the expression made a lot of people think, even if they misinterpreted what I meant — can the luck last?

The Lucky Country was a book of social, economic and political analysis, of cultural analysis with a broad scope. You looked at Australia

*in the round. How do you stand now, in the political sense, in the way
you look at your country?*

The Lucky Country's entirely out of date, thank God, in regard to its
political analysis. That was the age of Menzies — and I got stuck
into him. I got stuck into the Labor Party too. The place has
improved very considerably since then. I think I would apply, to an
analysis of Australia, some of these Australianised characteristics. I
would like to see some kind of a revival of the idea of a fair go. By
'fair go' I mean the idea of equal rights, of tolerance, of a pluralist
society, of a society in which the government was not making all of
the decisions. You could build up a whole 'fair go' ideology in
Australia, expressing the finest expressions of European liberalism. I
think, in Australia, a quite natural style is that not only of liberalism
but of liberal humanism.

Although the human condition contains great disasters, with 50
or 60 million people killed in Europe this century through political
disasters — we could certainly see it as a highly evil century — there
are also potentials for what I would describe as good in human
beings. I think human beings have cooperative qualities, as well as
the opposite. And I think that human beings have a great talent for
curiosity, which is their distinguishing characteristic from the other
animals. A little bit of that kind of humanism, associated also, for
Australia, with the kind of laconicism and irony summed up in the
idea 'give it a go', is what I think makes the only sensible basis for
action. You can never be sure about what you're going to do, but you
can give it a go. When John Kerin had his unfortunate period as
Treasurer, somebody asked some silly bloody question and he said:
'Your guess is as good as mine.' Now, if the press gallery had
understood, if they were truly Australian — laconic and ironic —
they would have praised him for it. It was the best answer given by a
Treasurer in the whole history of Treasurers, because most of what
people say about all these things is, to use a technical term, bullshit.
Instead, they attacked him for it. The idea that you don't know
everything but you try things out, you give them a go, and then react
to them, is true pragmatism. So in that we could be developing a
more Australian political approach.

In the party-political sense, where would you place yourself?

Oh. I try to avoid all discussion about party politics in Australia
because I feel that everybody else in public life is busy doing that,
and I don't have to do it. I have occupied various kinds of positions.

I passed from Trotskyism to anarchism and then subsequently I became a conservative, although a liberal conservative. I've always decried racism and sexism. Eventually I moved to a position in which I could finally end up voting Labor again. In 1972, which was my last year at the *Bulletin*, everybody was getting so much onto the Whitlam bandwagon that I put in a little bit of irony about it too, but I certainly was very pleased to see Whitlam win that election.

But when you saw a lot of other people on that bandwagon it made it less attractive to you.

Just a little bit, yes.

You don't really like being with the majority, do you.

I feel that if there's a majority they don't need me, do they.

On 11 November 1975, Donald Horne temporarily abandoned his individualistic political stance in order to join the 'Whitlamites' who were publicly denouncing the action of Sir John Kerr in dismissing the Labor Government. Shortly after the event the retina of one of Donald's eyes became detached, and while he was recovering from this he wrote a book called Death of the Lucky Country.

I actually used my retinal detachment as one of the metaphors of the book. It was an unusually written book. I thought it up while my eyes were still bandaged. I couldn't bend over, so then I lay on my back and wrote this book at the rate of three thousand words every three days. I'd be correcting the proofs of one chapter, and revising another chapter, and starting another chapter — it was a kind of workshop. I took Christmas Day off.

When you say you thought it up in your head, do you mean you thought up the words?

I thought up the overall structure of it, entirely. What are you going to do, when your eyes are bandaged? You can listen to music, which I also did — *Death of the Lucky Country* was thought up to a background of baroque music. Then when Myfanwy, my wife, came in I dictated the overall structure of it.

Could we turn now to your other books? You've been a very prolific writer. Is there anything in that whole body of work that you would particularly like to draw people's attention to?

People see my books quite differently; they get puzzled because they've been very different kinds of books. What I think unites almost all of the books is the belief that we *invent* reality — that we don't represent reality, there isn't a reality out there that we represent. We create, we construct, systems of belief and values and all that kind of thing. I've been getting into that in some more recent books — *The Public Culture* and *The Great Museum* — and in one I'm just finishing writing now. That's been a characteristic of most of them. I've also written more theoretical stuff about it. And I wrote a novel called *But What if there are No Pelicans*, which sold poorly, but I always hope that some day a few people might look at it more seriously. It's concerned with this theme about the ephemeral nature of reality. I think that, in a sense, life is hypothetical. Of course it is possible to prove things and you can take into account the evidence that what you believe is untrue — but most of us are not capable of doing that. Everything is in that sense theoretical.

Are you suggesting that non-fiction writing is just as imaginative a form of writing as fiction is?

I think it's very important to realise that the imagination *isn't* confined to fiction. A lot of fiction is straight formula stuff, as worthless as straight B-grade movies or that rubbishy magazine that I once produced. When I was Chair of the Australia Council I found it important to get rid of the expression 'non-fiction'. Non-fiction to me made as much sense as non-gardening books, or non-philosophy or non-history. There is nothing particularly literary about fiction. There are some things that fiction can do that history can't do. There are things that history can do that fiction can't do. For example, Manning Clark, when he sat around and thought up this enormous six-volume thing, *A History of Australia*, was surely involved in a great imaginative act. He was imagining Australia, and he was doing it as if he were writing a nineteenth-century novel. He imagined a whole society, he imagined that personalities were important, he wondered about the meaning of life. Edward Gibbon's famous work, *The Decline and Fall of the Roman Empire*, is one of the greatest acts of imagination produced in the eighteenth century. I could go on for some time, but I'm just trying to establish that imagination is not limited to fiction and that a lot of fiction is not imaginative.

Between 1963 and 1966, while he was with the Jackson Wain advertising agency, Donald Horne was also co-editor of Quadrant, *an intellectual journal. In 1966 he left the agency and from 1967 to 1972 he was back for a second stint as editor of the* Bulletin. *It was a vigorous period in the Bulletin's history, reflecting the profound political and social changes that were occurring in Australian society in the lead-up to the Whitlam years. But Donald had done it all before. He was ready for a new direction.*

Young Donald Horne wrote in his diary that he'd like to be a writer or a university lecturer. In the end you became both, didn't you. The writer, we've heard about. The university lecturer was a little bit more unpredictable, because you didn't ever complete an undergraduate degree.

I didn't ever complete *two* undergraduate degrees — in the sense that I was at Sydney University for three years and later at Canberra University College for two years. So I actually received a university education without benefit of degrees. Then the University of New South Wales invited me to go along there as a Research Fellow for a couple of years, and while I was there, I gave some lectures.

Why did they invite you to do that?

I had decided to resign from the *Bulletin* — I got sick of it because it was my second editorship there — and a couple of people in the Faculty of Arts just thought it would be quite good for a university to have somebody like me. It gave me a chance to settle down to some steady writing, and I thought its enlightened approach should be more widely adopted. While I was there as a Research Fellow I gave some lectures which the Dean sat in on, and then they decided to advertise a position which I applied for and got. There were still plenty of jobs at that stage.

That was a position as a lecturer?

I found nothing odd about this, in the sense that I'd published all these damned things which I thought were some kind of contribution to Australian public intellectual life. The kinds of techniques that I'd learned as a writer, as it turned out, worked quite well in lecturing, so I was relatively competent in that.

What did you think of academic life?

I thought it was wonderful. I really enjoyed the various kinds of lecturing. The function of first year lectures was simply to inspire people's interest, and to hope that they would learn something from reading about the topic and thinking about it intelligently. The upper level lectures could be related to one's own interests more fully. The MA courses had a third kind of interest. I loved them. They brought together different kinds of people and they were also related to books I was writing. I enjoyed writing *The Great Museum* and *The Public Culture* and I partly worked them out in establishing these courses. I thought it was wonderful to be able to relate one's work so fully, one part of it to another part. It was from then on that I began to be happy with my working life, which I hadn't been thoroughly happy with before. It was now all out of the same cloth.

And all related to ideas.

All related, certainly, to thinking and providing expositions. I liked students — with a few exceptions, I suppose — but I didn't have that kind of detestation of students that some conservative people have developed. I remember many years ago having an argument with one of those conservative people, and at the end of it she said to me: 'Oh, Donald, you're speaking like an undergraduate!' I think that was a funny comment on her approach to university life. I loved the life.

Donald Horne's period at the University of New South Wales lasted from 1973 to 1987, when he retired from the university with the title of Professor Emeritus. Over the years he had taken a leadership role in many different cultural organisations, including being President of the Australian Society of Authors and chairing the Copyright Agency. In 1985 he became Chairman of the Australia Council, a position he held until 1990, during which time he oversaw a restructuring of the Council.

I'd always had an enormous regard for the importance of the Australia Council and the overall high quality of its work. I never imagined I'd be any good as a Chairman, because I'd always been the one who went along to a committee meeting and interrupted it. When I became Chairman of the Faculty of Arts, at a rather difficult time in that Faculty's history, I discovered that as Chairman you can interrupt a meeting — and also be Chairman as well. I was actually, one way and the other, quite a good Chair. If I hadn't established that, I may not have accepted the Australia Council position, but I felt confident. Being a Chair's more than just conducting the meeting I think, it's connected with the agenda, it's connected with the follow-up and it's connected not really with leadership but with setting a bit of an example or expressing corporate aspirations. I applied that in the Australia Council and I felt honoured to have been given that situation, and on the whole I enjoyed it.

What do you think was your best achievement there?

One never knows that until you see what the final result is. I was connected with the restructuring of the Council, which I think was very important, and we made it a better body. I was also connected with the idea of extending the Council's imagination, and range of conduct. I don't know that that's been carried on now so perhaps that wasn't an achievement, although the idea is still around and I would hope it will come again. Thirdly, I spent quite a lot of time in building up ideas for sustaining the idea of the importance of the arts. When I came to the Australia Council there had been a tendency to feel that the arts were a self-evident truth, the arts were good for you, good in themselves, which is a silly argument. What does 'good' mean? But it seemed to be quite easy to explain the social and public benefits of the arts — not in terms of export earnings but in general terms. I think I worked out arguments in relation to that, which I also related to the general benefit of intellectual life. I was also, as the university acknowledged, very good at actually chairing meetings.

Did you attract much criticism in the time you were there?

I did attract a lot of criticism, especially over the period when we were restructuring the Boards of the Australia Council. It's what I think of, looking back at it, as the great civil war of the Boards. A lot of people had such an enormous affection for the Australia Council Boards they didn't want them to be changed in any way at all. I can remember appearing in Perth one day, Brisbane the next. The same arguments had to be recycled. That was an unpopular period, and there were some difficulties for a while with certain management questions. But over the latter part of it, I may be mistaken, but I think on the whole that what I was doing was relatively popular.

I get the feeling whenever you talk about being under attack that you're reflecting on what was really an enjoyable experience.

Well, I suppose so. As I've got older I've also begun to enjoy not being under attack. It's not so much being liked but, you know, feeling I'm doing something useful. When I began writing I used to imagine infuriating people.

With glee!

With glee — that's right, yes. Well, that disappeared quite a long time ago. Writing *The Lucky Country* was indicative of that. I started to write it like that, and I changed it at the end. *The Lucky Country* was, as we all know, a very popular book, and that was partly I think because I tried — and continued, I hope — to use a slightly more persuasive style.

But people are supposed to get milder as they get older. I have the feeling that there's still quite an element of larrikinism and mischief in the way you go about things.

Yes, well, people have often said there's an element of larrikinism in me, and I don't mind them saying that. I sometimes jump on top of the dining room table and do imitations, and I suddenly cause strange scenes in restaurants. I don't mind that — that's an Australian characteristic that I'm quite happy with. So long as it's not a kind of loudmouthed vulgar boasting, as it can sometimes be.

Donald Horne's time on the Australia Council had given him the opportunity to preside over the increasingly strong expression of Australia being conveyed through the arts. It also meant that he could see more clearly the need for the nation as a whole to engage in some more organised form of public thinking. His own personal experience demonstrated the real value in bringing academic thought and work into the public arena. His concept of 'unlocking the academies' was influential and in 1991 he commenced a program of public discussion and debate called 'Ideas for Australia'. This was a forum in which his own evolving ideas about the nature of Australia, its position in the world and the need for it to develop more thoughtful and responsible citizens could be advanced.

Some people think that the task of defining Australia is a matter of defining how its economy will operate, who it will be friends with internationally, what kind of defence arrangements it will have. But you have the more abstract notion of creating a set of ideas for Australia. Can you tell us what they are? And where you're coming from?

I think it's really important that Australians should think about their economy and about their strategic relationship to other countries, about their politics, their society — all of those things. But I think they shouldn't think about them in isolation, because they're connected. In universities these days there's been this tragic specialisation of knowledge, which means you chop a country up under different headings as if it didn't exist as a whole. What is of great importance to Australia is a thorough cultural analysis of the kinds of values and ideas that we have and which are often expressed not by what we say but by the way we act. I don't think all this other stuff about economics and so forth is going to be quite successful unless we know a little bit more about the different kinds of values and habits of Australians. I've written more books about Australia than I ever intended to because what interests me above all is that you can see the world quite differently, from one society to the other. What Australia needs is more overall theories about what Australians are and what the world is, and that would be a realistic way of going about solving Australia's problems.

What are the most distinctive things that we ought to be conscious of?

I think it would be an enormously important thing for us to get rid of all this claptrap about rating ourselves and our living standards in terms of something called 'per capita GDP'. We should learn ways of estimating what it is we've got going for us. What things are there about Australian life that we like? Do we want to have gardens, do we want to have relaxed manners, are we interested in holidays, do we want more libraries? Things of this kind can provide a much better vital basis for economic policy than looking at all these damned figures, which are infinitely reinterpretable. You can't base a whole policy for a society's future by looking up its so-called per capita gross domestic product, especially since you can reinterpret the figures in several different kinds of ways, according to what measure you use. Why don't we think more about who we are and what we think is good about ourselves, and how that might be strengthened?

Would the clever boy of Muswellbrook like to see Australia become the clever country?

I thought it was quite good that Bob Hawke used the expression 'the clever country', but I thought it was unfortunate that character-istically he forgot he'd used it the minute after he'd used it. Cleverness is essential but not sufficient. After all, the opposite of clever country is stupid country, and one can't really base a successful modern society on stupidity. But cleverness is a basic need — and also needed is capability, which is a slightly different thing. Also needed is imagination. And finally wisdom. But cleverness is the entry key, and then after that you're imaginative, you're capable.

You are a prominent supporter of the move to an Australian republic. What is the reason for your republicanism?

My republicanism wasn't always there. When I was a liberal conservative in England I was what you might describe as a Whig royalist. I thought the Royal Family were a lot of German imports and not much good, but they performed a very useful functional role, which in Britain might still be an explanation for them. I never thought of being a republican. But when I was starting to write *The Lucky Country* I was ticking all these things off, like the White Australia Policy, Aborigines and so forth, and the author Geoffrey Dutton had written an interesting article in the journal *Nation* on Australia being a republic. I thought, 'Oh God yes, why not? That's a good idea'. And I took it up as well. I think we need kickstarts to imagine that we are really an independent nation. But also the Cold War's over, and what the hell's the use of our traditional foreign policy? Loyalty to great allies? Which great ally? Just as I provided a kind of reconceptualisation of Australia in *The Lucky Country*, I think it's time for us to do some quick reconceptualising now, although lazyminded people don't like to do it.

I know that you like to be optimistic, and not to whinge, but for a moment let me invite you to be pessimistic and outline what could happen in Australia if we get it wrong.

It would be a very unfortunate thing for Australia if we continued to develop this mechanical approach to economics in which almost anything that matters shows up as a measurement on a gauge. I think that could really wreck the whole place. For the moment I don't think there's much danger that Australia will alienate itself from its immediate neighbours. I feel that possibilities of that are greatly exaggerated. The political difficulties of Australia in the world environment for the moment are close to nil. I mean, we're in South East Asia and at the moment, relatively speaking, it's a nice peaceful area, isn't it. I would also hate to see a reaction in Australia against the general liberation that is occurring in it. I think that Australians are quite good at being tolerant. It would be shameful if occasional expressions of racism, which can sometimes be exploited by a political party, should be exploited in Australia. It would be economically disastrous, and what a shabby way for us to go. And I can't imagine we'd really try to undo some of the changes that have occurred in the position of women. I know there are some conservatives in Australia now who would like to put Australia back to some imaginary past. That would be disastrous too.

What circumstances can you imagine in which our basic democratic approach to things might falter?

I believe that more important than democracy is maintaining a liberal humanist value in society. That, after all, was what the whole collapse of communism was about. In theory, any country can become highly authoritarian and repressive. The Bjelke-Petersen government in Queensland had some of those elements. I can't quite see the circumstances in which they would take over in Australia, but they could, certainly. Economic catastrophe might produce some kind of change of that kind. If there were any such thing, there would be a lot of yabber about free enterprise, combined with 'let's bash the boongs, the poofters and get the sheilas back into the kitchen'.

Donald Horne's position on various issues has meant that he has often been at the centre of public controversy. His capacity to mock human folly in witty and telling ways has been used effectively against many with whom he has had public differences. This same talent has provided a kind of smokescreen of self-mockery that has enabled him to write several autobiographical books without revealing much of the private Donald Horne. I did not want to conclude this interview without finding out more about his real view of his own life, personality and close relationships and without attempting to discover what he has valued at the personal level.

When did you meet your present wife?

About a week after we started the *Observer* Michael Baume, who was a member of its staff and is now a Liberal senator, held a party and I met somebody called Myfanwy Gollan — and a week later I proposed.

You make up your mind quickly.

Apparently, yes, although successfully in this case. At that stage I wasn't divorced, so that produced a delay of a couple of years, one way and the other.

And what part has Myfanwy played in the rest of your life?

Myfanwy, and subsequently our son and daughter, Nicholas and Julia, make up for me the essential part of my life.

When you say the essential part of your life . . .

I can't imagine their not being around.

They represent the main personal support and emotional connection for you in life?

I'm not quite sure about that. I think I'm somebody who doesn't necessarily always require a great deal of emotional support, unlike lots of husbands and fathers. There've been all kinds of worries I have in the office that I don't bring home. The four of us are on the whole very great companions, we can still go away on holidays together and things like that.

So by human support you mean companionship.

I mean companionship and trust, familiarity, affection and so on. My family life has been central to me so far as human relationships are concerned.

And in a lot of your work as a writer, Myfanwy's played a supporting role?

Myfanwy's a very good critic.

Do you take your family's criticism well?

I don't know. Like most people I explode now and again. I'd sooner have an exploder than a brooder, and I think in all human relationships people sometimes explode.

If you're good at exploding, are you also good at apologising?

Not earlier in my life. I've got better at it.

But you don't hold grudges.

I don't believe in holding grudges. There are one or two people I decided I'd never speak to again. One of them was John Kerr, whom I would now have a very small possibility of speaking to again. A couple of others, and that's it. There may be some quite bitter relationship, then later you've shuffled the cards, you have different hands, and you find other sides of people.

In relation to friendship generally — you say that there'd been a progression from a period, in adolescence, of intense loneliness in which you were operating quite separately from any intimate companion.

At high school I was very lonely. At the university I was intensely preoccupied with my relations with people, whether they were enemies or friends, and this was bound up with my expanding intellectual world. The important part that friendship has played for me has been that of intellectual experience. One of my favourite intellectual forums now is a lunch with one person, so that that one person and I can talk about things in ways that we mightn't be able to do with other people around. I can't think of any friendships I've had with people that haven't had, to some extent, that element in them.

So you look to your friends for intellectual stimulation and exchange more than the traditional things of loyalty and emotional support. Do you have anybody you confide in?

I lend myself out in various bits to various people. There are a whole lot of things that I don't consider all that confidential about myself. I don't have much in the way of secrets apart from those inner things that one hasn't even thought about oneself, some of which you may only be bringing out now. The questions about loyalty: those are more related, to my mind anyway, to practical situations — that loyalty's extremely important if you're engaging in something. But I don't live in a world in which I have some sense that I'm defined by and depend on the loyalty or lack of loyalty of friends. I don't want to use them that way.

You've said that you have friends that you use for intellectual exchange, for stimulation, to kick ideas around with. But there's another level of friendship that has to do with an emotional relationship with somebody.

I think what I was saying is that, in my case, the first is essential and the second might also exist. They're not contradictory.

Who have been your great friends in life?

I wouldn't like to specify names. I wouldn't like to make a list.

Throughout the course of your life, whatever you've done — because it's tended to be strongly said, arresting, out of the mould, often against the crowd — you've attracted both supporters and enemies. Thinking first of those who've liked you, and like what you've done, what do you think they like about you?

I think there are two lots of things there. There are all the people I know, and we just like to talk to each other and exchange views and be funny and tell anecdotes and swap theories and in general have a good time over lunch or dinner or whatever it might be. Then there are all the other people who come up to me in the street, and what they like is simply — they like the books, they've given them some ideas. Of course, I've written so many different kinds of books that people get quite uneasy about it. I always like it when somebody comes up and says, 'I really like your book', and I say, 'What book?' — thinking, 'if it's *The Lucky Country* I'll knock your bloody head off' — and they say, 'Oh, *The Permit*' or something, which is a satirical novel that I wrote. I enjoy being outside of Australia because there people say, 'I really like your book', and they mean this thing *The Great Museum* — they've never heard of *The Lucky Country*. After all, for a writer it's not altogether displeasing to have one's books liked.

The people who haven't liked you — what kinds of things have attracted the criticism or dislike?

Oh, God knows. I've changed around a bit myself, being radical conservative and all that kind of thing. I've had all kinds of dislikers. When I was at Sydney University I was disliked by the conservative element and also by the people I used to call the Stalinists, who disliked me for different reasons, I think. In my army period I was just a gunner — I don't know that I attracted any great emotions. When I was a feature writer on the *Daily Telegraph* I was disliked intensely by a whole section of the left wing because of my attacks on what I saw as the authoritarianism of the left, and I was also disliked of course by conservatives if I wrote liberal articles. And so the story's gone on.

Are you aware that there are some people who have said that they're really quite afraid of you? They're afraid of your ability to ridicule them or make fun of them. Are you conscious of your power to induce this feeling in some people?

Probably a great deal less than I used to, I think. I don't know whether that means that I've learned to suffer fools in silence more, or whether I've acquired greater diplomatic technique. I mean, when I was — as A. D. Hope used to call me — 'Young Donald', I had an extremely belligerent and destructive style. There were some people for whom I had extraordinary veneration, I kind of amused them by speaking softly and saying funny things, but the others I really got stuck into. I certainly would now have tempered that fairly considerably, although not altogether. I don't mind on occasion becoming quite angry with people, as long as I don't any longer feel inwardly angry — because that can put you off. Instead I sometimes use the techniques of anger. I can remember, for example, when Geoff Blainey was going around with all of that criticism of immigration policy, I made some quite bitter attacks on him, but I had the advantage of not having any personally bitter feelings towards him. This was even in his presence — it was his arguments that I was attacking. That invective after all is part of the general discussion of things. Attacking things you consider to be grave error is sometimes a very useful thing to do, especially because it can encourage others. But it's better to do it, insofar as you can, without doing your block.

Another accusation, seeing as we're touching on rude words you've been called, is that you're overconfident, even self-satisfied, about your own position.

Self-satisfied I'm certainly not. I mean, I wake up at 3.30 every night thinking what an idiot I am, how I've mucked everything up. Not every night, but sometimes I wake up and I think, what'll I worry about this time? I'm not self-satisfied and smug, in fact, in any way whatsoever. But at the same time I don't think one has to go through life saying, 'Look at me, I'm an idiot'.

You've indicated that you believe in keeping your problems to yourself, that you don't complain about things or confide in people, not even your family — and yet things wake you at 3.30 in the morning.

I can see myself as being constitutionally optimistic but also, by intellect, pessimistic. I mean, I've read so many books and know so many things about the hideous potential of human beings — who could not be in some ways pessimistic? And it seems to me that that comes together quite well as an ironic style. If you are an optimist you have to be an ironist, and it all goes backwards and somehow you see how funny it could be. But when I wake up at 3.30 in the morning, there's no optimism. I think it does me good, to sit there in the depths of pessimism. On the other hand, if it's about myself I can't stand it for too long. I say to myself: remember trench warfare, remember the Holocaust, remember this, that and the other — for God's sake, what are you whingeing about! And I will sometimes end up trying to tell myself some instructive stories.

So your mother taught you well about the 'brave face'.

I think so, yes.

If you could nominate one really valuable idea about how one should live one's life, something that you've learned from your own experience, what would it be?

Corny as it may seem, and meaningless as it really is, I think I would continue to say, 'The unexamined life is not worth living' — Socrates' famous dictum. I think that human curiosity is one of our really noble and useful characteristics. And if I were to offer any advice it would probably be: for God's sake don't whinge.

Would you like that for your epitaph? — He Never Whinged.

Well, I think epitaphs are really something more than that. I'd just like a simple statement, something like 'Writer and Critic'. That'd do me — 'Writer and Critic, Keep Off the Grass'. [He laughs.]

'*Keep Off the Grass*' *seems right to me. I have to say, at the end of this long interview, that I have rarely talked to someone who is at the same time so open and so closed. When I've asked you to construct a picture of yourself, you've been very ready to do it about your public life and about your role as a critic and so on. You've been more guarded with your description when it comes to the things you think privately. Do you have a view that the sociological, the public, domain is more important than the psychological, the private one?*

Oddly — it just occurred to me — it may be partly because I haven't thought about it very much, I don't have much faith in really internal introspection, and I just don't think I've conducted it. I think that one's existence on the public stage is more easily examined, and what one thinks about it can be checked and if necessary refuted from the public record. When I wrote all that autobiographical stuff, as far as possible I tried external checks, which is something one can't do, of course, in relation to internal examination.

So you were looking at society in the individual rather than the individual in society?

Yes. I mean, I don't believe that we're entirely socially determined, and I do believe that in a sense there's a kind of free will, that individuals can be of enormous importance. But all individuals are social. We work within the limitations and the potential of being social — beyond that we don't exist.

Well, taking up that idea, would you care to talk about those characteristics of Donald Horne that you think are significant, and tell us something about the process by which you've become who you are, and what you are, in our society?

One of the three autobiographical books I wrote was called *Confessions of a New Boy*. The 'new boy' idea was that I'd been a bit of a gatecrasher. It wasn't all that evident, in the cultural wilderness of 1958, that an intellectual fortnightly like the *Observer* would sell 10 000 copies per issue in Australia. That worked because there were 10 000 people to whom that meant something. I didn't know who they were, and I didn't care much at that stage; I just happened to be saying these things, and there they were. *The Lucky Country* came about because Max Harris said to me, 'Why don't you write a book about Australia, because you've written some good stuff in the *Observer*', and I thought, 'Oh yes, why not?'. London Penguin said, 'Australians won't read that', but Geoffrey Dutton — the editor of Penguin Australia — took a risk on it and of course it sold a great deal more than anyone had expected. In other words, what I've done is some things which most people thought wouldn't work — but they *have* worked because there've been people in Australia to whom they meant something. But I think, above all, yes, I've kind of crashed in at times. And I seem to have been more accurate than not in estimating a potential in the Australian people to be interested in what I'm doing.

The old Australian attribute of being as game as Ned Kelly?

I suppose sometimes it's foolish. But I'm glad you mentioned Ned Kelly. During the Bicentenary celebrations they produced a book on the 200 Australians who 'made Australia great'. The *Sydney Morning Herald* wrote an editorial that Saturday saying it was a rather pompous list, that they should have included rebellious people like Ned Kelly and Donald Horne! [He laughs.]

Have you usually found that you're right about things?

I have changed my mind about quite a lot of things. For example, the White Australia Policy. To begin with I was never racist, but I thought Australians were such a lot of bloody snobs that they would never agree. I thought that perhaps it was too dangerous to change the White Australia Policy because of our fellow Australians and their prejudices. Then I read a pamphlet produced by a group called the Immigration Reform Group — it was titled *Immigration Reform: Control or Colour Bar* — and I thought, this will be a lot of nonsense, these bleeding hearts are overestimating the possibility of change. But I went through it twice with a pencil and then thought, they're right! That was like reading the article by Geoff Dutton which helped me put republicanism into *The Lucky Country*. Reading this pamphlet made me feel that it was really a practical and possible thing, that the White Australia Policy could be reformed.

At times you've been accused of intellectual arrogance, and I wonder if you recognise or accept that label at all?

In the sense that if characteristics are to be carried to excess, I'd sooner be arrogant than over-humble. It's not a personal matter, it's a question of how on earth does one encourage discussion amongst our fellow creatures. One way of doing that is to state something quite confidently, in a way which might spark off a debate, and of course that can be arrogance in excess. It becomes arrogance if you assume that you're absolutely right. I'm prepared to make an idiot of myself. All kinds of people are preparing their footnotes or qualifying everything or turning it into jargon, and here's this idiot who stands up and says: 'I'll speak up, okay?' Which means, of course, that you may be knocked down.

There's another paradox in you — you're very strong in your egalitarian stance and you talk a great deal about a fair go and equality, and yet you're also something of an elitist in that you have very little time for people you regard as stupid.

But I do have a considerable regard for their right to be stupid. I believe in toleration. In a liberal society you don't have the government deciding everything and you don't expect everybody to be the same. So if egalitarian means everybody is the same, I'm not an egalitarian. If it means that in our kind of liberal democratic society a diversity of beliefs and values and ways of behaving are tolerated, as well as what all these idiots are saying that we don't agree with, well then that's okay.

Irony is something that you've used quite a lot in your writing, in conversation and in public life generally. It's a characteristic of Australian humour that's often been commented on, that we're an ironical lot, but it has also been the basis of quite a lot of misinterpretation. Do you feel that your use of irony has got you into difficulties, or led to your being misinterpreted?

I think that my use of irony *has* got me into difficulties — and that's bad luck, finally, for the people who misinterpreted me. One can't deny a style. In some ways I have a kind of intellectualised version of an Australian style which is intended to be ironic and laconic. I wish that more people would join me in that. I really think that Frank Moorhouse's little book *Conferenceville* is more use to me than, say, Patrick White's *The Solid Mandala*. I think a lot of Australian fiction writing has become over-portentous. Australians can be really remarkable when they're adopting a laconic and ironic style, or sometimes a light 'realist' style. That can also apply to a lot of academic discourse. We shouldn't have just sociology about Australia but an Australian style in sociology. Lamentably, although we did once have an Australian style in economics it's been pushed aside, although perhaps it will come back again. We shouldn't deny the kind of intellectual benefits that might be obtained by raising, to a higher intellectual level, characteristics of our citizens who are not necessarily professional intellectuals.

So you think the recognition of bullshit might be useful in academia as well as in the pub?

You find academics talking amongst themselves and they'll say 'that's bullshit', in conversation, but they won't express that when they write. I thought the publication *Nation Review*, now deceased, had a splendid way of bringing into words intellectual conversation around dinner tables. It was a great achievement to put into intellectual language a kind of vernacular wit and insight.

You acknowledge a reluctance to talk about very personal matters and you've said the reason is that you feel that such self-revelation is often contrived and can even be a bit self-promoting. I wonder whether another reason is that you're a very well-defended person, and that not putting yourself forward is a way of avoiding pain?

That is always possible — I don't know. In my 3.30 in the morning moods, when I wake up and recall my follies, that certainly wouldn't be the case. I certainly do believe that a fair bit of this kind of very interesting inner sensibility stuff is not true. I just don't believe that anybody is quite as sensitive as appears written up in novels, for example.

But you've already said that you feel that when you write about anything, it isn't exactly the absolute truth — it's a version of it — and you're happy to do that about public things. What's wrong with doing it about private things?

Because the private things purport to be a representation of how things feel in a way that is entirely different from externalities. I'm a very great believer in the important intellectual attributes of superficiality. First of all look at the surface of things. You're likely to talk less rubbish that way; often the rest of it is somewhat mysterious. For example, I start saying something or other, and somebody says *why*? And I say, that's a silly bloody question, let's first of all consider *what*?, and then we might consider how we can change it. The 'why' may be unanswerable.

Maybe there's another way of looking at it. In your study of Australian history, you've looked at patterns, at shapes and meanings. In your life, if I may be so bold, I see a certain repetition of a pattern of someone who's had periods of withdrawal and loneliness, and who's perhaps made a virtue of that ability to stand alone. There was the period in your adolescence during your father's breakdown, but even before that as the boy in Muswellbrook who liked studying. Then later in your life you've talked about your friendships, you've talked about your relationship with your family — it seems to have a pattern in which you've guarded fairly carefully against making yourself too vulnerable to situations.

All I can say is, that may be so. But the motives by which we act are really so confused, mysterious and contradictory, yet we come out making these great pronouncements about why we're this that and the other. It can nevertheless be a perfectly tenable intellectual position that an excessive sensibility and introversion may be unsustainable.

You started life with small regard for authority and authority figures. Has this changed with age?

I believe that there can be periods when there are people who do provide a sense of liberation and leadership. A lot of it may not work later, but those are pretty important matters in intellectual or political life, and that kind of authority which is not the authority of having power to regulate people but the authority that appeals to intelligence or conscience or reason, those are great moments of authority.

Have you ever believed in God?

I ceased to believe in God early in high school, I think, and my belief earlier was never very intense.

What do you think's going to happen when you die?

I think I'll just simply cease to exist. That was something which used to terrify me earlier. I've discovered with great delight that as one gets older it becomes something one can contemplate, and I hope that when the time comes I'll behave with a certain amount of decorum. You never know, of course, because of the pain and disturbance that can happen to people when they're dying. It's entirely out of your control. I would like to make what used to be described as 'a good death', but of course I don't know whether I'll be granted that possibility.

Have you ever been afraid in the course of your life that you'd disintegrate in the way your father did?

Not really, no. I've gone through periods, especially when I did all those jobs I hated, in which I'd sometimes be unable to move. I'd go home, have a headache for a day; think, oh God, this is terrible. But no, I think I probably have outlets in living which mean that I wouldn't, in that sense, disintegrate.

Do you think your life has had the kind of effect that you hoped for?

Oh, probably not. It's the kind of question I've ceased to ask myself now. For a large part of my life I thought I was the most alarming failure. I can remember at the age of 35 I thought 'my God I'm 35, what a waste, here I am mucking around with all this rubbish', then

I thought, 'I'm not 35, I'm 37'. [He laughs.] I think that was about the time I started on the *Observer*.

So you've really achieved more in the last few years of your life than you ever did before?

Well, the last half, I suppose. I've been a late starter. My first book wasn't published until I was aged 42. I hadn't learnt that I could chair meetings until I was aged 62 or something. I was an early starter, and then there was this long puzzling bit of my life which was almost an utter waste. That's the part that I've written about mainly in the autobiographical trilogy.

And you still find it puzzling.

I still find it puzzling and I wrote it deliberately so that people could puzzle over it if they cared to, rather than provide slick answers.

Donald Horne and his wife Myfanwy now divide their time between their Sydney home and a house in the Blue Mountains. The value he places on the role of ideas in creating a desirable and vigorous society is evident in all that he does. He continues to fight for the right of all citizens, even those whose opinions attract his withering contempt, to be allowed their part in public debate.

He is at present working on three books and from time to time writes bold and pithy newspaper pieces designed to stir up controversy and set people thinking.

Dame Joan Hammond

Deceptive Ease

ome people seem to be born with the kind of well-coordinated and energetic body that gives them grace and confidence from the very beginning. Dame Joan Hammond was such a child. As she grew she quickly and effortlessly became a natural athlete who loved to practise and perfect whatever skill she was interested in acquiring. In this way she became both Australia's champion woman golfer and later a singer renowned throughout the world.

Her secure and privileged childhood and her natural physical prowess provided opportunities for her to develop her many talents. In speaking of her life she emphasises the good fortune she has enjoyed, yet, like the ease and naturalness of her singing, this might well deceive the listener.

In fact she has encountered considerable misfortune throughout her entire life and has worked with great determination to achieve the high standards for which she has been so admired. She overcame the legacy of a major accident and various other disasters, she made choices between the paths offered by her many different talents and she managed her international singing career with an energy and confidence that made up for a rather narrow education. And in relation to both her golf and her music, the natural easy style for which she was well known was in reality the product of endless hours of practice and care.

Dame Joan calls herself a fatalist and believes that the pattern of our lives is predetermined, but she herself has shown great determination in every one of her many endeavours. Her natural gifts have been physical rather than intellectual, but they have given her a certain confidence which means that she has been able to act with decisiveness when the situation demanded it.

This interview is about a life focused on the development of great skills. It explores the personal discipline and the capacity to perform for the public in all circumstances that such a life entails.

Joan Hammond was born in 1912. Her family was well off during her early years and she had a pleasant, comfortable childhood with a supportive father and a musical mother. She attended PLC Pymble, a school in Sydney's North Shore. When the Depression came, her father's business interests were affected and the family fortunes fell. But while things were good she had been steadily developing some outstanding skills. She attributes much of her early confident growth to the fortunate circumstances of her family.

JH We grew up in a lovely environment, in a family that was united. We had our troubles later, but in the early days of my youth we were a happy family. And my parents did everything to encourage us musically.

RH *What did your father do?*

He was what he called a general merchant, but in London, where he was born, he was in the electrical trade, and he used to do very fine work too. He and my mother came out via New Zealand, where I was 'dropped'. I was conceived in England, born in New Zealand and brought up in Australia. I think that's the only way I can put it.

My father went on working in the electrical trade when he came here, and then later branched off to become a general merchant, which seemed to cover a multitude of things that he was involved in. And he did well. So I had a wonderful youth up until what was known as the Lang Government. In our household Mr Lang was called the Liar. Ha! I can remember that so well. And my father came in with unfortunate business results in that period and we suffered. We had to sell up the home at Killara. I was about 17 or 18.

But when you were at school you started developing some remarkable abilities, didn't you? It became fairly obvious that you weren't a run-of-the-mill child. And you showed great physical coordination in relation to sport. How did that first emerge?

That's a rather difficult question because it was a natural thing. I played all games at school, and loved them. I should have really loved doing more homework and studying. Instead I was often swimming in the pool at PLC when I should have been at class. I think it was nearly always maths — I hated maths. In fact one day the teacher sent for me and another girl had to find me. I was in the pool. So this came back on my report, and was read out at the breakfast table with all the reports. And my father wasn't very pleased!

And eventually, in relation to sport, you settled on golf. How did that come to be chosen out of all the rest?

Well, we had a weekend place at Palm Beach, north of Sydney, and there my father gave me a little set of golf clubs — a miniature set to try. Our place was right on the golf links. It was a short course, only nine holes. The ninth green was right by our front verandah — our old home is now the clubhouse — and I used to just hop over and practise on the ninth green, putt and chip and do those things. Then I got a full set. Not only a driver, as we called it in those days — you don't call them that today, they're numbered one, two, three and four — but I also had a putter, a cleek and a mashie.

Eventually there were three very well-known Sydney men, friends of my father, who used to come to Palm Beach. I can remember them now. There was Percy Hunter, Alan Box and a Mr Moses; I never knew his other name. These three men called over one day and said: 'Would Joan like to join us and make a four?' So I did. And from that time on I made a four. I never had a lesson, but I learned from watching them, and hitting just as they did. Alan Box was a very good golfer, so was Percy Hunter — not that I knew it. I just knew that Mr Hunter and Mr Box played the game and enjoyed every moment of it. And that's really how I learned to 'hit through' and put some oomph into it.

Did it reach a point where you were beating them? How did these men take it when a young schoolgirl started beating them?

Well, it was wonderful really, because once I left school I was at the Conservatorium in Sydney and playing in golf matches for teams and doing very well at it. And our foursomes at Palm Beach gradually had to stop because my life had changed so tremendously. But these three men used to come out and watch me play at Royal Sydney when I became a champion.

And you became a champion despite the fact that by this time you had a physical disability.

Yes, it was a car accident. I was on a bike and we had a collision, and I pulled the handlebars around to the right and somehow my left arm got caught in those old-fashioned spoke wheels of that period. I'm very lucky to have the arm because the first doctor was going to amputate it straightaway, but evidently the pulse was beating. The second doctor called in was a surgeon and he said he'd try, which he did. I was out of everything for a year. It all knitted up, but it's much shorter, my left arm.

How old were you when it happened?

Twelve, I think, 12 or 13.

Do you remember whether you felt that this was going to be the end of all the things you enjoyed?

I just knew that I was in a lot of pain at that stage, and of course I had several operations to my arm. In those days it was called a skin graft; it was taken off my thigh here. The surgeon was a Frenchman who was called in to do this skin graft — which was a separate thing from what had happened in the first place with the surgeon who had to connect all the tendons and everything. Both bones were broken, of course, and they had to wait for the bones to knit before doing the graft to try to cover the scar a bit. I always felt very embarrassed, when swimming, about the graft site on my thigh.

And I didn't know then that my hand movements would be permanently restricted. In order to help me get the movement back they had to pull the hand up with a glove glued on it and rings at the end and a contraption on my bed, and I was so fearful when all this was happening. They don't explain. I think it would've helped me tremendously if they'd just said: 'Look, with these weights here and those weights there, all that we're doing is trying to open up your hand.' Then worse was to come in trying to get it moving. The massaging of the fingers was more painful, because at least with an operation you were put out to it — but this was something I had to sort of sit and watch. And feel!

Do you remember when it was that you became really interested in music and started learning?

I think I used to sing right from the beginning almost, at my first kindergarten and then at school. They'd always ask me to sing for them — I didn't know why — but the teacher would have me stand up and sing a song or give a tune to the others because I sang in tune and had the good fortune to have a natural rhythm. I think those two things combined to make the teacher have me up in front of the class.

So you were singing first and then you started to learn an instrument.

Well, I had begun to learn the violin when I was very young. I loved the violin.

What was it that attracted you to the violin rather than some other instrument?

Now that is an interesting question! But I can't tell you, I really don't know. It may have been from listening to recordings of violinists, because Mother had one or two old records. And I remember hearing Kreisler and Heifetz, and Heifetz was my absolute joy and I thought, I'll aim at being a Heifetz! He was my first violin idol. I thought, oh yes, I'll even practise. I spent a lot of time practising the fiddle, and this stopped me practising singing. I was very lucky really, because all the hours that I put into the fiddle I might have been putting into my voice — and ruining it at the same time, tiring it. But I sang whenever I wanted to and if I was asked to. But I did put all those hours into the fiddle and into learning my theory and harmony from that. The only prize I ever won at school was to do with music, never anything else. [She laughs.]

Except for sport.

Oh yes, I was the swimming champion.

Trophies for sport and prizes for music. What about the rest of your schoolwork?

I wasn't all that interested, except in geography and history. But I found when I was sitting at a desk I wanted to be outside and bursting my boiler on the hockey field or somewhere like that. I really found sitting for a long time at a desk quite a chore, and a bore.

These days we quite often tell children that they need to specialise a little bit. You seemed to do such a variety of things — you had all these sports, you had your violin which you were developing to a very high standard, you had your singing. Was it ever thought at the time that maybe you were trying to do too much?

No. No one ever suggested that. Just as well, because I don't think I would have taken any notice.

The fact that Joan Hammond had so many different talents, all of which were developing in parallel, allowed her to rise above the legacy of the bicycle accident. In golf she mastered an unorthodox but perfectly effective grip. But her violin playing was more directly hit. Although determined and often painful practice meant that she improved sufficiently to resume playing in the Sydney Symphony Orchestra, her fingering hand was so seriously impaired that eventually she had to give up the violin altogether. Her natural musicality would have to find another outlet and her ambitions to be a performer another vehicle. Fortunately an alternative talent — her remarkable singing voice — did not depend on a dexterous left hand.

I was studying singing at the same time as the violin, but not seriously. I was just a natural. When I was in my late teens at the Conservatorium the orchestra, for one of its symphony concerts, was doing the Vaughan Williams. It has a difficult solo, only a couple of pages or so, but unaccompanied. I was a complete amateur then; I hadn't started any professional work. But the conductor could not find a singer who could start this piece in tune and end in tune. It was the shepherd's little solo, and the voice comes in off stage. You're not seen, and of course the orchestra has to pick it up so it was very important for the singer to start it in tune and end in tune. And they were getting rather anxious because the time was coming on and they still hadn't found anybody. And someone suggested that they ask my teacher if one of the students could cope. So they asked me to sight-read it on the spot while they were rehearsing in the main hall.

I just did it because I was asked. I finished in tune, and the orchestra came in and there were claps in the hall and I didn't know what it was for. And I waited there in the wings having sung what I'd been asked to sing, and the conductor said with great excitement: 'She'll do it, she's the one!' It was easy, easy sight-reading, and easy for me to learn. I didn't realise what it all meant but it was my first appearance of any importance.

Were you earning your own living at that time?

Yes, because I had to by this time. Things had gone all wrong with the family. Fortunately I was asked to cover the golf for the *Sydney Morning Herald*. I was only on it for a short time because I went on to the *Bulletin* to write up the golfing results. Of course, I couldn't cover my own matches at all… someone else had to do that. But I covered all the local club results throughout the week. I had to ring them all up and get their results in. If there was a championship on then I was given a column. They gave far more space to golf in the paper in those days.

Yes that's true, it was big, wasn't it.

Well, it was really not big until I came on the scene, and my friend Odette too — young women didn't play golf then. It was an old person's game, and I only came to play it because of my three men down at Palm Beach. It just wasn't a game for youth.

So these two young girls brought a bit of glamour to the scene.

The papers were full of it! We had tremendous publicity [she laughs]. And the golfers didn't know that I had anything to do with music, just as the musicians didn't know I had anything to do with golf.

Did you cover the men's games?

No. I didn't stay long at all with the *Bulletin*; I went to the *Telegraph*, which offered me a very good salary. I was only learning then what a salary was and I just went along with it. I used to cover the hockey, or any of those sports that I knew about — they would send me out on occasions to cover them. I was once sent out to cover a social event. That meant writing up what the women were wearing and I hated that. I thought it was so rude to be looking at what jewellery they were wearing and so on. Of course, it came to me later on that I was looked at in the same way. I could see a reporter looking to see whether my jewellery was diamanté or a real diamond, so it all came back to me [she laughs].

By her late teens Joan Hammond's many activities were producing real opportunities. Shortly after she stopped violin lessons the J. C. Williamson Imperial Opera Company was touring with Italian principals and local singers for the minor roles. Joan was engaged at £3 a week. She won the NSW golf championship while on special leave from the opera company granted her by its owner, E. J. Tate, who was a golf lover. She was doing well at her sports journalism and those around her felt that she would soon have to confront some difficult choices.

I certainly didn't choose things. I'm a fatalist. The pattern was already being made out for me, and I think events just led me. I have a strong feeling that that's why one shouldn't really regret anything, because what's meant to happen is going to happen. I loved whatever I was doing. I really enjoyed studying music — I never had to be told to practise — and I always enjoyed practising golf. I would be seen just hitting balls and practising when no one else would be thinking of doing it. I never saw it as a chore.

But that wasn't how you'd felt about your schoolwork, so what was the difference?

I think it had to do with the fact that I didn't have to be in at nine o'clock or eight-thirty or whatever and I didn't have to go and sit at a desk. And I was studying or practising things that I really loved.

Did golf and music ever come into conflict for you?

Not really at all. In my youth, when I was playing a lot of golf, I played in the daytime, and I had my music at night.

And found the energy for both.

Ah, yes, I had boundless energy, obviously. And I never thought really that I could be tired; I think that thought didn't reach me till many years later. It's reaching me now, though!

What do you think it was that really made the difference in giving you an opportunity to develop as a world class singer?

I had a wonderful fairy godmother. That's the only way I can describe Lady Gowrie, who was at that time Lady Hore-Ruthven, the wife of the Governor of New South Wales. She gave me my big opportunity, the most wonderful opportunity that could have happened. It happened like this:

One day there was a soirée put on in Lady Gowrie's honour. The lady who always accompanied me when I sang was at the committee meeting when they were deciding who should be on the bill, and she thought, this is an opening for this young girl Joan, whom I play for. So she spoke up and suggested me and of course she was told that there wasn't a hope because everybody else was professional. But she went on pushing and in the end the committee decided that they'd let me go on and just do one little group in the first part of the program.

After I finished my performance I was very unhappy backstage because the other singers had shown me all too clearly that, as an amateur, I was not one of them. I couldn't mistake their looks and behaviour, and I was very sensitive. Somewhere towards the end of the first half I hurried off, stuffed my music into the funny little bag I carried, and as I was going out the door a lady came running up to me and said: 'Oh Joan, they'd like you to sing again. Will you go back? The request is for you sing "The Green Hills of Somerset" again.'

Lady Gowrie was at this afternoon soirée, of course. She said that it was a very hot day, and where she was sitting she could hear the bees and the flies humming around. She was almost dozing off when she suddenly heard what she described as a peerless voice. It was she who requested that I be asked to sing again. Afterwards I received a note asking me to go to Government House, where she told me that she was so struck with my voice that she was determined that I should be given a chance to be sent overseas to study. So she put all her feelers out. She knew that she could manipulate people from her position. And do you know who she got to support me? The golfers! They didn't know that I was a singer until she got them interested.

At that time there was no alternative for a promising singer other than to study overseas. This was a costly business. As well as the fare, a living allowance for a substantial period had to be found. The Joan Hammond Fund was launched with two major dinner parties at Government House. The sum of £1250 was raised eventually, a very large amount at that time. She had many well-wishers and supporters — including some who thought she was mad to be leaving her golfing career in favour of singing.

I was told I was a very silly girl to think of giving golf away at a stage when I was at the top, on the lowest handicap in Australia. I always remember Mr Tate of J. C. Williamson's because he had asked me to play in a mixed foursome with him, and after the game he took me aside and said: 'You know, Joan, I've been in the theatre world for a long time, and you're making a great mistake, going overseas to sing. You should stay here and play your golf.' But there was no professionalism in golf in those days, it was all amateur, and I was wanting a career. I had an absolute love of singing, I had a determination to make a profession, and I wasn't happy doing anything but singing by then. But I thought it was very kind of him, because he knew I was as naive as could possibly be, and I suppose he saw all kinds of terrible things that could happen to me in the career that I was choosing. Later on I realised what he was hinting at, but I didn't at the time — and again it wouldn't have made any difference.

Where did you go to study in Europe?
Vienna. In 1936.

And how did you choose Vienna?
I didn't choose it, it was chosen for me. The Vienna Boys Choir was out here at that period, and the Director was having interviews with everybody in Sydney who had something to do with the musical world. The committee that had been formed to look after my trust fund discussed the matter with him and decided that it would be a good idea for me to go straight to Vienna. This also helped my finances, because I went and lived with the Boys Choir up on the mountain behind Vienna, a lovely position. It was one of Prince Rudolf's old hunting places and had only one bathroom in it! It was a nightmare for me. The very first day I was shown in, and the two big rooms that I was allocated looked lovely. I just thought there would be a bathroom and toilet, everything there. Not at all! There was no bath or shower, no toilet; just a little washroom. I thought, how funny, and I went looking for them and couldn't find them anywhere. So I had to ask the Director where they were.

I was the only young girl, but it turned out there was also a countess living there. And the countess had the prince's rooms which were very beautifully set up, with a huge, lovely bathroom — but that was the only bathroom in that house. I don't know how the boys washed; maybe they didn't! Well, the Director certainly got a shock when I said I must have a shower every day. His face changed colour and he didn't know what to say at first. Then he said he'd have to have a word with the countess. I got to know her quite well. She was a charming person, and she used to help me with my German. We'd sit in the garden and she'd talk with me all the time. And she gave permission for me to go and use the bath. Not every day, though!

What about your singing? Did Vienna turn out to be a good place to go?

Again, that was fate. The castle was wonderful because I had plenty of room to practise in and the Director played for me and I did a lot of work up there with him, because I had the time. However, going to a teacher was very difficult because I had to go into Vienna by tram, which took 40 minutes. I had to leave the tram at the heart of the city, opposite the Opera House, and walk right down a street called the Kartnerstrasse, to the river. Then I had to go over to what was called the Second District and that's where this teacher was that the Director fixed up for me. I didn't know whether she was good, bad or indifferent. She turned out to be not very good but she was a very sweet person. That makes it hard — when you know you're not progressing and you've got to go on, but your teacher is so sweet.

So you knew enough to know you weren't progressing.

Oh yes, oh yes.

How was that so? You really hadn't had a great deal of exposure to anything that would have given you a standard to judge by.

No, no. I've always said that nature is the best guide of all, and I knew that if my muscles were aching something was wrong and I was not singing correctly. And sometimes after a lesson I'd find I had aching muscles and I thought, this is no good. So I had to make that decision to tell her that I was not having any more lessons. It was very hard, but I knew that I had to do it. I knew she was very upset, and so I told her it was because of the cost and that I wouldn't be able to go to anybody for a while.

There began then a difficult time for Joan Hammond, because winter came and she had unsuitably thin Australian clothes with no warm boots or heavy coat. Having patrons who are paying for you and supporting you can be a mixed blessing. She felt accountable to her trust committee for her finances and kept a record of all she spent in a small account book. She had to write to a member of the committee if she wanted to buy something special. She created a furore when she wrote saying that she needed to buy a fur coat. The committee, not realising that she was seriously cold and that fur coats were standard wear in central Europe, thought she was developing the luxurious tastes of a prima donna. In fact, it was during that initial ill-clad winter in Europe that she first became susceptible to the colds that were to affect her throughout her career. At the same time, other more sinister and serious changes were occurring around her. In advance of the Anschluss the Nazis were becoming a significant force in Austria. Joan recalls that she had little awareness and no understanding of what was going on.

It had already begun really before I arrived in Vienna, as I discovered later on from the boys at the castle, once I could begin to converse with them. Just as I was naive about so many things, I was about politics. I wasn't interested in politics, not a scrap, and this was going on under my nose for a long time before I realised that many of the boys I was talking to were all Nazis.

What made you realise that?

Well, because the question of the Jews kept coming up. The teacher I was learning from lived in a Jewish district. She was a Jewess. That fact never occurred to me. So this idea of politics didn't hit me until nearer the time, when Hitler came to Vienna while I was there. The full thing didn't really hit me until later, because I wasn't interested.

It must have been a very strange time for a politically naive girl to find herself in Vienna. What did you make of the Nazis?

Oh, I must have had so much contact with so many without even knowing! I couldn't tell at first, of course — no one could tell who was and who was not. However, my singing teacher in Vienna had a son and daughter. On occasion her son Karl would talk to me after my lessons. He was in army uniform, and I didn't realise that he was what they called a Mischling — half Jew, half Christian. But he was so anti-Jewish! That was my first sort of realisation of how they felt, and how vehement they could be.

Was this self-protection for him?

I don't know, it could have been. He used to complain about the family upstairs, about the noise they used to make. They were very solid homes, which was really wonderful for practising and playing music, but Karl would go mad at times about this family up above, saying that they were 'Juden' — Jewish. It was all foreign to me.

What did you think of it, what did you feel about it?

I thought he was a bit peculiar, quite frankly. I didn't understand why he was making such a fuss about a Jew and a Jewish family. Again, of course, it was my naivety. At the time of Anschluss, the invasion of Vienna, nearly every shop in the famous Kartnerstrasse was under Jewish control. After the changeover I noticed a difference in the Jewish-owned coffee house that I used to go to. I liked it because it didn't cost me very much and the daily papers were there for me to read. A couple of weeks after the Nazis came I went back to my old haunt and the nice, lazy atmosphere had gone. Everything was very brisk: you had your coffee and that was that. There was no sitting and reading a paper then. The lazy life vanished, I think, almost overnight.

But when I went back in 1946 — I suppose I was one of the first of the foreigners to go back to sing in Vienna — one of the first things I did was to walk down and go over the bridge. But the building that my teacher's family had lived in had been destroyed. I couldn't find anybody who knew anything about them. So I really lost all contact with them.

Did you ever hear Hitler speak?

When I was singing with the Opera Company — this was early in 1938 — they put an announcement of a general rehearsal on the noticeboard and everybody, but everybody, had to attend. We all sat in the auditorium and I can remember there were three Norwegians and myself, a Greek, and I think a couple of Yugoslavs — the foreigners with the company. I was in the eighth row back in the stalls, and one of our conductors was sitting along from me. Then it came on the screen. Hitler delivering his speech, and we all had to listen to it.

What did you think of it?

I thought he was mad! I mean, his voice would go rising up here and there and his hands would go up and then he'd drop them down. And he had a funny voice. I was very surprised to see this conductor getting so excited — they were all sitting on the edge of their seats looking at this face on the screen with absolute adoration. It was just as though he was an idol — a god. They all obviously felt this. But I thought he was raving too much about Chamberlain and the British and of course I wanted to sink down lower in my seat, as he really raved on about it. And the thing was, they were all looking at me to see what my reaction was, looking along the row.

And what was your reaction?

I just felt embarrassed — I was wearing a little British flag on my lapel, one that the consulate asked us to wear. But it was all so quick that night, the night of the Anschluss. They just sort of walked in and took over. It was so well organised, and everything very military. The very next day the difference was so noticeable. You know, there was not a shot fired but the whole city took on a different atmosphere, a different mood. But I had no fear whatsoever.

So what made you leave?

I had three very important engagements offered to me in London. I'd already been there for a holiday when my fairy godmother, Lady Gowrie, had arranged for me to go for the Coronation of George VI. She had a little bit of money put aside to pay for my fare and I was given accommodation in London. While I was there I gave an audition for the BBC. As a result, I was sent a contract to sing the soprano solo in the *Messiah*. Also, the BBC booked me for a part in *Pagliacci*. I'd sung *Pagliacci* in Vienna, in German of course, but they offered me the contract if I would sing it in English. That was my first opera in English, you might say. Finally, in '39, Sir Henry Wood booked me for the Promenade Concert. He booked me upon hearing me, which I was rather surprised at.

It was a bit extraordinary, wasn't it. You hadn't really had any very good training up to this point, but nevertheless you were being booked for the best engagements.

Yes, that's true.

And so you went across for the Proms, in 1939.

I had not thought of the imminence of war because I was reading the Austrian papers. Perhaps if I had got the *Manchester Guardian* or something, if I had seen a copy somewhere in a coffee house, or if I had been reading my own country's papers, I would have known that things were very serious.

The British Embassy didn't do anything to suggest that you might get out?

Oh no, no.

So you were in London for the Proms — why didn't you then return to Vienna if you had no sense of danger?

I'll tell you why. When I arrived in London, I went to the rehearsal and I heard all the chat going on about war and what was happening, and my ears were like antennae because I had no idea of the situation. None whatsoever! I suddenly realised what was happening, and it was like pulling a horse up at a gate or a water jump. Then I had a cable from Lady Gowrie who said, 'Don't go back to Vienna, don't go back'. But I had only been given two weeks' leave to carry out my engagements. I'd got special permission to go to London from Vienna, and I felt guilty because to me a contract is a contract. So I cabled Vienna and said that I'd got a very bad cold. The fact that I was lying so blatantly upset me — but of course things happened very quickly after that.

So, in retrospect, given how naive you were, it was just as well you had a fairy godmother.

Oh, in so many ways, and right throughout my career, she was always behind me. Wonderful!

The lucky chance that took the unsuspecting Joan Hammond out of Austria on the very eve of war strengthened her feeling that fate was determining her life. Had she remained in Vienna she would have been interned. She would not have made the recording of 'Oh My Beloved Father' that so increased her popularity all over the world. The war years in England were another turning point for her. They consolidated a network of contacts and support that were to stand her in good stead after the war was over. They also offered her the opportunity to extend her somewhat limited life experience.

You spent the whole of the war years in England. What was your contribution to the war effort?

My contribution? I tried to join the Women's Royal Naval Service first, because of my love of the sea and yachting — but believe it or not I had what was called a disability, my arm. Mind you, towards the end of the war they would have taken any or all of us, disabilities or no disabilities. I remember the sweet person who interviewed me saying: 'Perhaps it's just as well, you can get on with your singing.' But of course the theatres were closed. Nothing in the world of entertainment was going on at all. Once the war was declared all my engagements were cancelled.

What about entertaining the troops?

That came later. Nothing really happened in that first year. The first big thing that started up was ENSA — that was the organisation for entertaining the troops. They started doing concerts in the most incredible places — a big block of flats down by the Thames, cellars, the Underground, basements. If a bomb had hit it would have been like a pack of cards coming in on us. Those air raid shelters, with sacks of sand piled up, were all so rushed. I'm sure nothing really would have saved us. But there we entertained some troops. And we went out to gun sites. They were not good environments to sing in [she laughs].

But in that first year everybody was happy because there was no fighting at that stage and nobody really thought of bombing. It seemed a sort of farcical situation really. I was asked to sing 'Roll out the Barrel', which of course I wouldn't. I said: 'I haven't been trained for that.' But once the war began in seriousness, and we were being bombed, everything suddenly changed. Opera didn't really return to Covent Garden until about '46, '47. But the Carl Rosa started up, and that's how I first got back into singing opera. They were the only company that went on tour.

And you also began recording, didn't you?

That happened in '41 or '42, I think. I auditioned for EMI and was turned down. But then I got a contract with Columbia. So there you are! It was one of those things. My first recording was, I think, 'The Green Hills of Somerset'. It was later that I recorded 'Oh My Beloved Daddy'. Funnily enough, Mr Legge, who was in charge of the recording, didn't want this little song on the record. The selling side was going to be 'Love and Music' from *Tosca*. That had been settled; it was what was going to sell the record. But we had to find another short song to go on the other side. And I suggested 'Oh My Beloved', but he thought it was not well known enough to even go on the flip side. Anyhow, it got nearer the time of the recording session, and although the conductor was quite happy to have it we still couldn't get Mr Legge's approval. Then in the end he had no choice; time had beaten him. Fortunately!

Why do you think it was such a phenomenal success?

Because it was sung in English. Daughters and sons would make presents of it to their father. I suppose it became a sort of family thing. Everything, by the way, during the war years, had to be sung in English. Everything. And remember, for me that wasn't that easy because I'd had to learn my whole repertoire in German. You might be amused to hear something. Once when I was performing *Tosca* at Covent Garden, I had finished my aria and as the applause was dying down a voice shouted from one of the galleries: 'And now let's have the other side of the record!' — meaning 'Oh My Beloved'. The audience burst out laughing. It was so funny. In the middle of the opera!

Did you have a sense at this time of being very much loved by the audience?

I was getting it. In the concerts that I was doing around the place, I knew that I was gathering a following. You can tell. You have a rapport somehow with an audience, you sense it when you go on stage and you first bow to them. In fact everywhere in the British Isles I always knew I had this wonderful warm applause, and I knew that I had that love from them, but in a lot of foreign places it was tougher. I knew I had to make it, I had to earn it before they acknowledged that I could sing.

What does it feel like to have the whole audience rise up in a standing ovation?

It may sound strange but I hardly ever realised then the great noise of the audience clapping. I stood there and acknowledged it, but I didn't realise the depth and the sound of that applause. I remember one occasion in Liverpool, on the 11th of November at a special Armistice concert — I'd finished singing 'To The Fallen', an Elgar piece. When I'd finished and the conductor's baton was still, there wasn't a sound. It's the only time that I've had that feeling where there was no applause, absolutely nothing, still, so still. And then suddenly they all jumped up. That was one of the most amazing moments of my career. It was very emotional. And so it is when the audience stands up and comes right down to the stage to you.

Did it ever go to your head?

I think I could quite honestly say no. I went through a period when I wasn't very happy with myself and I thought I was better than I was, but I knew that I was going down the wrong route, getting a bit swollen in the head, and I pulled myself up in time.

Well of course a lot of people assume that that's how prima donnas are going to be, don't they?

Do you know, I put it down to the fact that I was insecure, and I think that was the entire secret behind my behaviour. I was insecure because I wasn't very happy with my voice. I wasn't happy with the way I was singing. I realised that it was the emotional strain of the war years; the nights of the bombing when, I must admit, I was pretty frightened. I think it was taking its toll and I was trying to get myself back — my voice was not how I wanted it. I wasn't eating as I used to eat. In Germany and Russia singers got full rations, but of course we didn't in Britain.

During the war you didn't just sing, did you. You were an ambulance driver at one stage. How did that come about?

Oh, I'd joined the ambulance service straightaway, when there was nothing happening. I was first in Clerkenwell near Sadlers Wells, then I was stationed down in the East End. There I saw a side of life that I didn't think existed. I had to go to one call where there was only one tap in a building of seven floors, where everybody in that building had to go to get water. To get the stretcher down was a nightmare; there were only two of us girls. I was the driver, but I had to help out on occasion with the stretchers, and that's when it really upset me because of my arm. I wasn't meant to do that. But then there are many things that you're not meant to do that you have to do on occasion.

After the war Joan was offered the opportunity to return to Australia to do a concert tour for the ABC. Ten years had elapsed since the Joan Hammond Fund had sent her overseas. She was returning having achieved just the kind of success her benefactors had hoped for. For some time she had not needed their financial support, but she retained a sense of their interest and backing and was looking forward to the Australian tour as a way of thanking them. Lady Gowrie and the others were all there to meet her on her arrival back in Australia. The question was how the rest of the Australian public would receive her.

The big problem was that I had no idea of my popularity out here until I arrived. I came out on one of the flying boats and landed at Rose Bay, right opposite the Royal Sydney, my old golf club. The number there to welcome me was absolutely overwhelming. I couldn't believe it! Then it was down to work because I had to give 12 recital programs to be put over the air on the ABC. The programs were entirely up to me. The translations too. If it were German or Italian or French I had to do the translations. It takes some planning, a recital program. You've got to have a change of mood, a change of key. It's wonderful work, fitting it all in and thinking: what would I like here or there, how fast and how slow, and the words I want. When you're doing it you become so involved. I had a very favourite key, F major — why, I couldn't tell you. Everything that I was choosing happened to be in F major, so I had to find variety in other ways.

So with this great optimistic feeling, you set out on what was a very arduous schedule of work for you. Was the tour a success?

I'm sure for the ABC it was, but for me it brought about a physical tiredness, and eventually a vocal strain. I had to take it easy towards the end of the tour. I was worried, vocally, and I left here not feeling good at all.

Seeing my family again was especially draining. There was a great deal of friction at the time. It had been ten years since I'd seen them, and there were so many things that I had to pick up, so much to find out. It drained me without my being really aware of it. These things happen so slowly and silently that you're not even aware of your bodily reaction until it eventually begins to show.

I see. You'd left a very happy family behind when you departed but it wasn't quite the same when you came back.

Yes, there were tensions everywhere. I left with a very unhappy feeling family-wise.

In presenting an account of matters that she considers to be personal Dame Joan displays her very well-honed social skills. She is charming and apparently open in manner but she tells you no more than she wishes to. Not for her the public confessions of contemporary stars. She is a model of charming restraint. It is clear that she is very conscious of her public image and vigilant in protecting it. As with her appearance, to which in her old age she still pays careful attention, so with her dignity. It is an important part of the way in which she presents herself to the world and she is far too skilled and practised a performer to be caught in what she considers to be a bad light.

In Australia, although many people took you to their hearts and you had this great welcome, there was also some criticism, wasn't there?

With all singers there's always criticism; the higher you go the more critical they become. I think this is a natural way for people to react.

I learned more from critics then, in Australia, than ever before, because in Europe you didn't get much criticism of what you wore, how you looked and that sort of thing. But here, as in America, it's very important for the singer to remember what dress she wore. Right throughout my career I kept a little book of every dress I wore for every concert. Oddly enough, men were more critical about clothes than women — if you wore the same dress twice it seemed to be the men who picked it up.

So they went along to look at you as much as to listen to you?

I used to wonder which it was at times! [She laughs.]

People were ready to criticise your dress. Did they criticise the music?

Yes, my programs were criticised. First of all, in Sydney, they were 'too highbrow'. They didn't get 'Oh My Beloved Father', and they had Hugo Wolf and Richard Strauss to contend with. In reaction to this, two bands of people started up in Sydney — those who thought them too highbrow, and another lot who were saying: 'We love them, we appreciate them.' I suppose it was good publicity. I couldn't understand why some didn't like the programs, and then I realised that I'd gained all my popularity through 'Oh My Beloved Father'.

When you were on the Australian tour there were people who criticised your dress and people who criticised your music programs, but what was worrying you yourself was your voice. What was actually happening to it?

I am overcritical of my singing voice and I always have been. For me it wasn't vibrant, it was losing its tonic. I use that word, tonic, a lot. If I said that my voice was not tonic, I would meant that it wasn't ringing, the tone was not there — that it wasn't resonating as well as it should. I always got it back on the rails by practising and singing certain scales. The voice cannot be in the throat. That's the most important thing of all. A throaty voice is a sick voice, and if you go on singing when it's there then it gets worse and worse. To my ears this was exactly what was happening to me and it was really worrying me. I was so relieved when the tour was over, because I knew that when I got back home I could finally rest. Rest is one of the best things for the human voice.

When I got back to England I discovered I had bronchitis. I kept very quiet, and I tried to be patient. But I started singing again too soon — which is always a fatal thing, you must let the vocal cords really get back to normal. That's something that you have to try and drill into singers: not to use their voices when they are sick. Of course, the one thing singers want to do when their voice is sick is to use it, to try to find out if it's still there. The whole process made me realise that, for the future, to stop the illness coming on again, I had to know exactly what I was doing. You might say I took my voice to pieces and built it up again, in my own way. Although it was a long and unhappy time, it was a wonderful period in that I gained tremendous knowledge through that. I knew that I had to know my own instrument.

After Joan Hammond rebuilt her voice she launched herself on the major part of her career. Based in England, she travelled to almost every country in the world, singing recitals and occasionally opera. She travelled to Africa, Asia, the United States and of course throughout Europe. She went to places where no recitals had ever been given, and everywhere she went she realised just how popular she had become. It was a stimulating and satisfying experience and demonstrated the value for a singer of becoming identified with a well-known and well-loved song.

'Oh My Beloved' went everywhere and as a result I went everywhere. There wasn't a place that didn't know that record, and of course I always sang it at the end of the concert. I'm sure all of the people only came to hear that, and were bored with the rest of the recital. No, I don't really mean that! [She laughs.]

But the Australian tour had taught you that there was a certain element in the audience that you needed to please.

Yes, indeed. I designed a different type of program as a result of my Australian tour, because in going to places like Tanganyika — you'll note I use the old names of these countries; they keep changing their names, don't they — I realised that I must make sure that I put in something for everybody in my programs. I'd put in material that I knew would please the serious concert-minded person, and I'd put in a more popular group of songs.

Some parts of Africa were quite dangerous at that time. Did this affect your concerts?

Oh yes. It was the height of the awful Mau Mau period. Whites could not possibly leave their children or anybody in the household alone. Wherever they went the whole family went and if it was night-time the youngsters just slept, whether it was in a hotel or at a concert. But the most interesting thing at the concert was their clothes. They were beautifully gowned, but they all wore a belt with a revolver, which will show you what it was like for them living in Nairobi at that time. They never knew when they were going to be attacked, or from where and how. Standing on the platform, looking down at these beautifully groomed families, and then to see this grim thing attached to their belts really jolted me. I had to make myself concentrate on what I was doing, which was to sing and remember my words and music. It's like someone fainting in an audience. I see them, but it's my job to continue as if nothing is happening.

How did you get on in America?

The first tour was all right, but I think what killed me eventually was the fact that I had to cancel another tour because I had bronchitis again. The extraordinary thing was that in Europe it is understood that there will be occasions when a singer has to cancel, but my agent in New York wrote to me saying that she couldn't book me at the same places, because they won't have any singer who turns them down once! That was a strange lesson, and I had to go and get engagements in all different places.

It wasn't the only thing that you found yourself having to turn down in America. Wasn't there another time when you turned down an engagement that you were asked to do?

Ah! Mrs Roosevelt, the First Lady, asked me to sing at a luncheon for her. It happened to be on the day of my opening night of *Tosca*, and I had the orchestral rehearsal in the morning and the performance at night. I realised that to say no would be like rejecting the Queen, but I didn't want to spoil my performance — *Tosca*'s not the lightest of roles, it's not like it's just a few pages. So I declined as gracefully as I could. I thought perhaps she'd ask me another day. But not at all. I never heard again, and I realised that I had slighted her, which was surprising and upsetting. I was very sorry about it and I wrote and told Lady Gowrie, who had helped set it up, exactly what had happened. But those were my principles. You save your voice as much as you can for the performance at night.

I have regretted that since, but I think if I were in that situation again I would do the same thing. Nonetheless, I feel that I never did quite as well in America as perhaps I could have, and I blame myself for that, I really do.

You've told us how your voice was like an instrument that you carried around with you and that you'd learned a lot about how to look after it after the Australian tour. Did you ever again have difficulty with it?

It would be very silly of me to say I didn't have anything happen after that in such a long and full career. I can recall one very unhappy incident, something that was quite beyond my control. I was in Manchester, singing away, and suddenly for some unknown reason my voice went. I had come to the end of a group, so I went backstage, and my voice was completely croaky. I had to go back and apologise about the rest of the program and say how sorry I was, that I had a cold. I had no cold at all, but I felt I had to say something.

But then suddenly my voice came back again, so I went on with the program and everything was quite normal. But the following night the same thing happened. Of course, now I really was getting concerned. The voice kept on coming and going, coming and going. I thought it was most peculiar, because I didn't really feel sick. I rang my specialist friend in London and he said: 'You must have some sort of cold or something.' I said: 'No I haven't, not a thing.' When I got back to London I went straight to see him and he looked at my vocal cords. He told me that they were perfect, that there was nothing wrong with them. I didn't understand, and asked him what was happening — why my voice was so croaky. 'Joan', he said, 'could you be becoming nervous?' 'Not a chance', I said. 'I'm always a little nervous before I go on, yes, but that's normal.'

Well, it was a puzzle for him and a big puzzle for me. I had to go off the following day to Amsterdam to sing the *Verdi Requiem*. I got to Heathrow feeling fine, everything all right, and then suddenly my voice went again. Thank God it was before I got onto the plane. I telephoned my specialist immediately and said: 'It's happened again and I'm about to catch a flight to Amsterdam.' Suddenly, he said: 'Are you on any pills or anything?' And I said: 'Yes, I am, I damaged my knee up in the woods the other day; it gave me a terrible jolt because I was doing *Madame Butterfly*. It was giving me trouble during performances, and the local doctor came and gave me some cortisone pills.' On hearing this, my specialist told me that I must cancel all engagements and not sing until my next period, when I should go and see him immediately. I didn't understand what a woman's period would have to do with all this. But I hung up and rang my agent to tell them they'd have to get someone else to go over and sing the *Verdi Requiem*. Then, within an hour of my next period, my voice was absolutely clear. It was a case of cortisone reaction so unusual that it came out in the British medical magazine.

That really brought home to you the fact that the instrument you play is dependent on your whole body.

Oh, indeed. Everything you eat or drink and the atmosphere you're in all passes down near the larynx. So anything too hot can make your voice slightly muffled and unpleasant, and anything too cold — when you come offstage and your system is all hot from singing and you drink an icy drink — that can produce an effect like burning. You know when you drink soup and the tip of the tongue gets burnt? That's just what happens to the larynx, it just burns for about 12 hours and then it's gone. But if you don't know what's caused it, it can make the singer very unhappy and anxious, wondering whether they've got laryngitis. So you have to watch your food, your drink, and naturally you have to keep yourself in jolly good condition, because of the breathing. Breath is our lifeline.

Singing is clearly a very physical activity and I suppose it's easy to form a picture of you as a strong, sporty girl, very good at golf, very gifted physically. Yet you did have quite a bit of ill health and physical trouble during the course of your career. What do you think it was that undermined your robust good health?

I often suffered from hayfever and I had asthma from time to time. Fortunately I always believed that one could sing one's way through it. Singing helped most of all with the hayfever. It kept my sinuses dry. But of course I couldn't sing all day and all night.

I can remember one dreadful Sunday down at Brighton where I had a recital to give in the afternoon, and my nose was just streaming — so much so that I thought I couldn't go on. But of course I did, and the more I sang the drier it became. It's wonderful, because all the little mucous membranes dry up in the nose. But the moment I finish, back it comes! I've been surprised to read from time to time of singers saying they couldn't sing because of hayfever. Although it was an irritant it didn't affect my larynx, so I knew that I could go through with an engagement. I had to put up with the runny nose until I went on stage, and then I was right.

Now, in relation to the musical side of your career, what have you enjoyed singing most? You've sung opera, you've sung concerts. What aspect of the music has appealed to you most?

My simple answer to that is that I sang what I loved, and I loved mostly everything. I enjoyed opera, I enjoyed concert work, orchestral concerts. I say 'enjoy', but *on the day* one wouldn't think it was enjoyment, because there's always a certain amount of concern until one goes on that platform. For me this concern meant making sure of my music. I always thought, I mustn't let the composer down, I mustn't forget anything, my voice must be tonic — in good form — and I mustn't let the audience down. Those are the sorts of things that you worry about all day, on the day of a performance.

Did you have a favourite opera role?

Not really, no. All the roles I sang I loved. Although *Madame Butterfly*, perhaps, was slightly ahead of the others.

'Oh My Beloved Father' was a great success and an aria that has been associated with you all through your life. Was it something you sang from the heart because of your relationship with your own father? Were you particularly close to your father, in a family of boys?

Not at all. In fact I never thought of my father while I was singing it. In the opera she's pleading with her father because she wants to marry this young fellow, and if he said no she would throw herself off the Ponte Vecchio. Well, of course, I knew the Ponte Vecchio very well, having lived and studied in Florence. I think that aria was closer to me because, unlike other operas I sang, I could see all the places where it occurred. That brought another side of it to me. But I didn't think of my father at all, not when I was recording it.

You'd had that period of being very poor, which you said had taught you things about taking care of money. Later on when you became famous and you got a lot of bookings you had a lot of money to spend. How did you feel about that? Was that something that gave you a great deal of pleasure — that suddenly you didn't have to pinch pennies any more?

Yes [she laughs]. I enjoyed spending it so much that I was inclined to have it come in one hand and go out the other. But I had a careful side to me, and always had a little put away. And I had the wonderful support of my great friend Lolita Mariott and her father. Mr Mariott was the first one that kept saying to me: 'Joan, you have to put money aside for the time when you may not be earning it.' And he was the first person to get me some shares and he looked after my affairs for quite some time.

Dame Joan never married. For most of her adult life, until 1993, she lived, worked and travelled with Lolita Mariott, who managed her household and all her personal affairs. Both completely dedicated to Joan's career, the pair organised their lives around it. When I interviewed Joan in their house by the water outside Melbourne it was clear that Lolita had assumed responsibility for all the practical arrangements of their joint life. Again, although Dame Joan was restrained in discussing the details of her personal life, she wished very much to pay tribute to her partner.

Lolita has played a tremendous role in my life. Some unfortunate artists go through their lives without having anyone to trust, but I can trust her, and this is where I consider that I have been more than lucky, more than blessed. I mean, many husbands and wives cannot trust each other — it's an extraordinary thing, but it happens. In our world you learn not to trust people, because you're let down so often. I first met Lolita before I left Australia in 1936, so our relationship now is well over 50 years old. Our friends say: 'What on earth do you find to laugh and talk about?' I would say that she's one of the greatest godsends I've been given. Someone with whom I could discuss everything. After a performance I naturally would turn to her and say: 'How was the voice tonight?' Among the hundreds that would come around and say, 'Oh darling, you were wonderful', I could rely on her to tell me if something was not quite wonderful.

Lolita actually started travelling and living with you in 1946, ten years after you met, and she has supported you professionally as well as personally.

Oh yes, indeed. She was my personal representative, and she would go ahead of me. She went to America first and she did lots of things like that. The whole thing was intertwined very very closely. I can only just repeat how blessed I have been in that regard.

You've described yourself as a fatalist, where at times something good came out of a situation that looked bad. You have said that you felt that things were meant to be and that you had to accept what fate dished out. However, on the other hand, you've been a very determined person and you've gone after your goals. How do you reconcile these two attitudes that you have, of being both a fatalist and somebody who is very determined?

But don't you think a fatalist can be somebody very determined? It must be — otherwise I couldn't exist, could I! To be fatalistic doesn't mean that you're not a determined person. I say that determination could well go hand in hand with fatalism.

There have been some crises in your life. There was the time you lost your voice, and then, towards the end of your career, you started having some health problems. Could you tell us what happened at that stage?

It's a stage that I have tried to forget about because I wanted to feel that it hadn't happened. You might call that part of my determination as well. It was something that came on slowly. I just got these pains and they kept coming back, and when I lifted my arms or wanted to lift something it hurt. In the end it was diagnosed that there was something wrong with the heart. I had to carry around little white tablets — you put one under the tongue and it immediately gives relief. I still carry them. When I found out about it, I was booked to sing in York Cathedral, to record with the boys' choir. We were doing a lot of Handel, a program quite unlike any I had recorded before, with organ. It would've been a lovely, lovely experience and it broke me up completely when I found I couldn't do it. I was rehearsing and, bang, I got this blessed pain which meant that I had to stop singing. The doctor said that if I wanted to go on living I had to give it away, that it was obviously too much for me. So that was really the end of the story for me.

I came back out to Australia on a long sea voyage and for a year, I think I can honestly say, I thought I would never get well again. I felt complete lassitude and didn't want to do anything. Then slowly I began to pick up, and I began my teaching career. That has been like another career. It's very demanding, very tiring, but it's not so emotional. It was the emotion of singing, expressing myself through my voice, and facing the public that I just couldn't cope with again. And having to cancel. Really, having to cancel took a tremendous amount out of me. I always thought I was letting down the people who'd paid to come to hear me.

You're still working. Could you describe what your working life is like at the moment?

Getting up early, going for a walk first thing, then going to the College. Taking my little packet of lunch with me. I was Head of Vocal Studies for many years and I worked long hours, five days a week. I'm cutting things down a bit now, just three days a week, but that's quite enough. As I'm also writing, and wanting to get another book finished, my days are long. But in fact they're not long enough! I find that each night I think: 'Oh dear, I haven't done all that I wanted to do today.'

I love teaching. I taught for a time during the war in London. I always tell my students that they must ask me whatever they want to, any question at all, because I've gone so thoroughly into my subject and I know that I can help them. I know where their weaknesses are, because I've been through it myself. I can tell them if they're heading for danger vocally, because I've been through it. I think that not everyone can teach — teaching is a gift. When I hear a voice I can almost see the vocal cords and I know exactly where the trouble is. They only have to come through the door and speak to me, and I know what to expect when I hear them sing, because their speaking voice already has told me whether it's tonic or sick, forward or back.

Joan Hammond has a profound belief that always, whatever the circumstances, one must put a brave face on things. Throughout her life, even when things were going badly for her, she always managed to put on a good performance. It seems to have been a belief that she absorbed at a young age and it has stood her in good stead in her career as a performer. It has also shaped the way she has responded to personal misfortune. Her biggest setback of all came quite late in life.

At the personal level, has anything ever happened that you found it difficult to put a brave face on?

A very juicy question, this one. The worst thing that ever happened to me was the 1983 bushfire that raged along the coast to the west of Geelong. I was in Melbourne, lunching with the Director of the College. It was a terrible day; the sky was black and getting blacker. I left to go back home, down to 'Jumbunna', near Aireys Inlet. The journey down was terrible. We'd heard that the fire was along at Lorne; it had gone through the mountains there, and was fierce and dreadful. The wind hadn't changed, so we just didn't give it a thought. We got home at about half-past five. By the time we got in I wanted to go for a swim straightaway. I was in the process of undressing when the phone went, and it was our local doctor. He said that I had to leave the house immediately. He knew by my voice that I wasn't taking any notice, so about ten minutes later he rang again and said: 'Look, I really mean it, you *must* go!' I still didn't take any notice.

The next thing, he came to the front door and said: 'You've got to get out, you've got to go now. And I mean *now!*' And he went off again. I went out into the courtyard and I heard this terrible roar — oh, it was frightening, in fact I froze. Then, of course, I was galvanised into action. I shouted out: 'Look, we've got to leave! We've got to leave!' Lola got into one car and I got into the other. It was an exodus! The road was packed with people fleeing from the fire.

We got accommodation in Geelong for the night. It was a night of sitting and thinking and listening to the news. Next morning we set off to go back home. At the base of the hill that led out of Anglesea we were stopped by a policeman who recognised us and said: 'I've got bad news for you. You're burnt out, your home doesn't exist.' I think even then I didn't believe it had gone. So we went on and we got to where the gates used to be. We turned in and there was nothing there. Only this big, long, burning log that was our house.

There was no sound. Not a bird, not an animal, not a sound. And it was a beautiful day, that following day, absolutely beautiful. It was still, and so quiet. I suppose we were stunned. All my clothes had gone, and I was still in the old slacks I had thrown on when we left. And I had to go into Melbourne dressed like that, and I just hoped and prayed that no one would see me.

But that wasn't the worst of it, was it.

No, I'd lost my life. I felt I'd never existed.

What about your photographs?

Oh, they were all down at 'Jumbunna'. Everything went. Everything I treasured. My Russian scores, my letters, my address book. Every single record of my life.

How did you deal with it?

I just thought, well, we've got to get something to live in, we've got to start building again. But it was a very slow coming together. If I had had my passport I think I would have got on a plane and gone back to England. But I had no current passport, and that took weeks to get.

How did you deal with it emotionally? You came very close to death — how do you feel about death?

Well, I know it's inevitable. We all realise that. I also know there are times when I think I haven't completed what I'm here on Earth for, I haven't got time left, I must hurry — that's how I feel at this very moment. Can you understand that? And also when it all slowly seeped through, when I began to realise the enormity of losing all those things . . . It's amazing what that fire did. In the cellar all the bottles had burst. It was a very deep thick-walled cellar, well built. Completely burnt.

Did this experience alter your values at all — did you start thinking differently about material possessions?

Yes, it did. And I swore to myself that I would never collect anything again. But after the fire it was wonderful how quickly people reacted and started sending things. The Brotherhood of St Lawrence and the Salvation Army were wonderful. And quite frankly, I think I've been living on the articles of clothing and the blankets and sheets which came through those organisations, even now.

Can I ask you how you feel about Australia and being Australian, because of course you had to go overseas to make your way and then many of your golden years were spent in England as a British artist. What made you come back to Australia at the end of your career?

The British always think of me as being one of them, as a British artist, I know that. The feeling is, when I'm there, that I'm not Australian. I think having spent the war years there has made a big difference: there's this sort of link, something that would always be there. What made me eventually decide to come home was my health, that was the prime reason. They told me to go to a warm climate when I wasn't making very much progress after the coronary. And I was suffering from quite a number of bad chest colds that forced me to cancel engagements time and time again. When they said a warm climate, I naturally thought of Australia. But really our climate is very unpredictable, isn't it? I think of that Dorothea Mackellar poem, 'I Love a Sunburnt Country'. Well, 1983 was a bit too sunburnt for me!

Have you felt appreciated, professionally, in Australia?

Oh, I don't know. That's a difficult question. I had a bad time when I first came back; I certainly wasn't acknowledged then. But I feel that's just universal. I don't think it's anything Australian in particular, but it's probably more exaggerated and one thinks about it more in this country because it's smaller.

It's clear from what has been written about you that you have the kind of voice that really moves people. It's a voice with great emotional expression — that's how the audience hears it. Now, when you're up there on the stage and singing, and this glorious voice is coming out, how does it feel to you?

It's strange . . . naturally the first thing I think about is 'tonic'. You know what I mean by that. Healthy and right, with all vibrations working. For instance, you have those lovely Verdi passages. Verdi and Puccini both wrote so well for the human voice! And this is important, because when you're a singer you can't get another instrument. You can't go around the corner and replace a string or something. A violinist saves up to get a beautiful instrument. It costs them a lot of money. We don't have that problem, but our instrument is irreplaceable. And this feeling, when you're singing and the orchestra's accompanying you, there is that time when the voice soars above everything else and you're getting those top notes and you know that they're ringing out; you know that they're coming as you want them and that you have that power, something inherent that you know nothing about, and yet it's there.

Whoever thinks about it realises what a mystery the voice is. How do we pitch a note? How do we know that it's a B flat or whatever? The feeling when the performance is going well, is one of inner joy; I think that's possibly the only way I can express it. You feel within yourself that you have a power, that you have the desire to express; and you know that you've got that rapport with the audience and you can tell, when you're taking a top note, that there is an immediate response down there, that perhaps they're getting goose pimples. You don't get goose pimples yourself, in that you don't feel any of those sorts of emotions, but you do feel that you've got something within, something that you're able to project. You feel that you're able to sing a lovely phrase — and there's nothing more satisfying than to be able to sing that phrase absolutely correctly.

In 1993 Lolita died. Dame Joan was not only emotionally devastated but also bereft of the companion who had looked after all her personal needs. In her life Joan had perfected many physical, musical and social skills. But because of Lolita she had never learned to cook — nor had she learned how to administer the insulin she needed for her diabetes. Shortly after Lolita's death she inadvertently injected herself with an overdose of insulin and went into a coma, from which she emerged with impaired short-term memory and deteriorating mental prowess.

She is now living in a nursing home where her charm and attractiveness still draw everybody to her. Every day she dresses carefully, taking great trouble with her appearance, and the staff are amazed at how skilfully she masks her mental limitations.

Jack Hazlitt

The Survivor's Tale

*T*he story of the Gallipoli landing has been told many
times. The annual national celebration of it gives rise to
reverence and remembrance and jokes about a nation that
celebrates a wartime defeat rather than a victory. The story of
Jack Hazlitt, survivor of the Great War, is the story of that
generation and of what they felt it meant to be a man.
Jack displays the qualities that made the Anzac legend possible.

In describing what happened to him during those years of his
youth, Jack's manner reflects the ideal of masculinity that
prevailed at the time and shaped his development. He relates
his stories in a modest, understated fashion that focuses on the
action and brings the listener vividly into the spaces he occupied
and observed during his adventures. His inclination is to avoid

voluntary introspection and he has to be pressed to speak of his own feelings and reactions to events.

His experiences in the First World War, and subsequently in the Great Depression, entrenched rather than displaced his commitment to heroic risk-taking, discipline, obedience and stoical endurance of pain and discomfort. His willingness to expose himself to danger and his practical and technical skills led him to take part in the pioneering days of aviation in Australia, and the risk-taking continued until he married at the beginning of the Depression. Like so many of his generation, he then rechannelled the courage and determination that had characterised his youthful exploits into providing a steady and secure environment in which his children could grow.

More than others in this collection, Jack Hazlitt's life is representative. He embodies the values that his generation most admired. This interview took place when Jack was in his nineties; the spirit that enabled him to survive and endure so many of the twentieth century's disasters was still strongly evident. In the course of the conversation we explore not only the events but also the attitudes that were crucial in shaping the idea of what it means to be an admirable Australian.

Jack Hazlitt was born in 1897 in Millswyn Street, South Yarra,
in Melbourne. His father was an actor and stage manager with
J. C. Williamson's, where he met Jack's mother. She was a pianist
and a teacher and she loved the theatre. Jack was the youngest of
three boys. The only girl in the family died before he was born.

RH *Was yours a happy family?*

JH No. Because of his job my father could seldom live in the family
house. J. C. Williamson played in theatres all over Australia, New
Zealand and Africa and my father was away most of the time. I think
he was a brutal man. He used to drink a bit. I can just very vaguely
remember some of the awful rows. On one occasion he hurled her
down the stairs in a blind rage — I won't go into any more of that.
Finally, when I was very young, he left the family home and never
came back. I never saw him again.

How did your mother manage?

Well, he was supposed to send her a money order every month for I
think £8. More times it didn't come than it ever came. In those days
there was practically no state-run dole or anything like that. If you
didn't have any money that was it! And I think we would have
starved, but what saved the day was that before my mother came out
from England she had done very well in her musical studies, and she
was qualified to teach piano and singing and that's what put butter
on the bread. Where we lived was in a little ramshackle cottage
down in Brighton Beach. I remember the rent was 12 shillings a
week. I remember that about three-quarters of a mile up the main
road was a school, Haileybury College. My mother was earning just
enough teaching piano around private homes and so on, but one
time, on a whim, she walked up South Road and went into the
College and asked to see the headmaster. And my mother put up the
idea that if he would permit her boys to attend Haileybury College
free of charge she would give music and singing lessons. So that was
agreed to and that's how we got there. The headmaster was very
fond of music himself, in fact he wrote music in his spare time.

*Despite this arrangement for your schooling, was she still short of money
for everyday things?*

Continuously, it was desperate. The main thing we ate was bread.
I don't remember ever anything in the way of biscuits. We had bread
and a very limited amount of butter, and a lot of dripping was used

in those days, dreadful stuff! We ate beef dripping to keep from using too much butter. The food was enough to keep us going, but very very scarce.

Do you remember being hungry?

Oh yes! And of course, in order for her to keep up this income from teaching, she had to go out to private homes and she used to have a little 15-year-old girl come in for a few shillings a week to look after me. That nearly finished me off right then and there because one day, when this girl was heating up some milk for me, when she was pouring it out, she bumped her arm in some way and the scalding milk went all over my front. And that nearly finished me off! And what didn't help — my mother told me all this later — was that she lost her head and went screaming outside instead of doing anything to try and get rid of this boiling milk all down my front. Anyhow, I survived that.

I was just thinking about your mother in this situation, having to look after you, leaving you at times with help that she couldn't have been very happy with — it must have been very difficult for her. What sort of a woman was she? How do you remember her?

Well, the older I get the more I appreciate what a tremendous personality she must have been, not to give up, or lose her reason. All her roots and so on were from England. We didn't have any wealthy family and relatives around here. They were old family from Somerset, Somerhayes by name. They go back for hundreds of years, but they never had any money. And I can't emphasise too strongly that in those days the amount of help from government and so on was always nil in these situations. It was only after many many years that welfare schemes were introduced. I think the family would have been finished off if she hadn't had this musical ability. She also started to organise concerts and musical plays, which earned a little.

Did you miss having a father or did you find other men to give you a lead as to how you should grow as a boy?

The nearest approach to that was my old headmaster. For instance, he was a very keen early-day motorist, in the days when you had two-cylinder Derdien cars chugging around. Very few people had cars, but he used to import them from England. He had a Humber and a Derdien at different times. On Sundays he used to take me out in the car, choofing around the bush. It was all bush around Brighton then. Well, that was really taking the place of a father, wasn't it.

What was Haileybury College like?

It was a boarding school for boys and I went there when I was almost eight, in 1905. It simply made our lives because, without any income to support us, boarding at that school saved the day and it became like our second home. The discipline was very strict there; it taught me a lot about the need for discipline in life too.

What form did the discipline take?

It started with the headmaster. Then there were the other masters who all lived in the school. There were the prefects who could penalise a boy if he had committed something he shouldn't have. And they could even cane him, but only one cane each from 12 prefects. If you were going to be caned by the prefects you got 12 stripes on your bottom. They were never dangerous, they were just little flicks with a thin cane. If the offence was more serious than that I was paraded around to the headmaster, and if he thought I needed it he'd give me another go! To this day I haven't got any hatred or any dislike of that or why they did it, because it was only done when there had been a fair trial.

Do you think that the cane was a good thing or are you glad to see that it has mostly gone now?

I don't like to open up too much on that because I know the public opinion — that in a school the teachers must never lay a finger on their pupils no matter how they're playing up, and I do know now that a number of teachers have a very bad time because they've got no control over some of these more rebellious kids.

Were you a rebellious kid?

Yes.

And do you think that the cane made you behave better?

Well, it established in you a respect. If you mucked up again you'd get another lot. That kept you going along the way the teachers wanted you to go. It's as simple as that.

Did you reach a point at the school where you weren't getting the cane any more, or did you manage to deserve the cane right to the end?

I was at my worst when I was about seven or eight, but by the time I'd got to 12 I had learned how to avoid anything like that.

What sort of things did you get the cane for — can you give me an example?

It sounds funny to say it now, but I got it over my brother. He was a pretty good footballer and his team were playing at another college — Caulfield Grammar School — and I was watching the game at the time. I thought he'd made a great mistake and I yelled out to him, 'Dick, you damned fool', and that was heard by a master. You couldn't say 'damn' at Haileybury. Oh no! And as far as some of the more trenchant language — one or two were expelled from that school while I was there, because of it. It was very strict.

And 'damn' was considered very bad language?

Oh yes!

But you didn't stop using it outside school?

Well, you had to be careful, because if you were overheard by a prefect or a master you were for it.

When did you leave school?

When my second brother Richard left Haileybury he went to study at Hawkesbury Agricultural College. When he graduated from there his father was still alive — I suppose I could say *our* father but I never saw him from the day he walked out, you see — well, the father knew the Minister for Agriculture over in the Western Australian Government and my second brother Richard went around by ship and was given a job to start there. My mother tootled off to Western Australia because she wanted to follow her favourite son, which I do think Richard was. My eldest brother was at Melbourne University and I was supposed to stay at Haileybury until I finished my education — what was called the Leaving Certificate, which was the entrance then to university. The headmaster had practically adopted me and he'd decided that I'd make a journalist. Apparently I used to write fairly good essays and that sort of thing. But when my mother and brother had left the eastern States I got restless and so noisy and rebellious that, after a lot of objection from the headmaster who didn't want me to leave, I was put on a ship and shipped off over to Perth, where my mother had again started up a musical connection. This seemed to be no problem to her. It was amazing how she got the pupils around her, and then concerts.

Jack's brother Richard was working at a little place near Bunbury just out of Perth and Jack joined him there. The Western Australian Government had established a pioneering experimental irrigation scheme, one of the earliest in Australia. Soon after he arrived, war broke out. It was August 1914 and Jack was not quite 17. About a month after war was declared Richard, his revered older brother, hopped on the train, went up to Perth and enlisted. When his brother went off to Perth, Jack quickly decided that he wanted to enlist too. Young men and boys like them were enlisting all over the country.

....

There was nothing very brave about either of us. In the early part, when the war had just started, there had been no casualties and it looked like a wonderful way of getting around the world. That's what got him all excited — the idea of travel and adventure. He got into the Army fairly quickly. Then of course I followed on. But I was only 17 and they weren't supposed to take us under 19. Everybody wanted to go, but they were very choosy at the beginning. They didn't know what this war was going to do to the population, you see. They even chose only six-footers! When we used to march through Perth, you know, they were all big men at first but as soon as the casualties started to really rock everybody that soon changed. I was just on six feet then. I said I was 19 and they didn't ask for a birth certificate so in I went, into the Army. But Richard had gone to Egypt in — I think it was December 1914, he was in the original 11th Battalion. I went into Blackboy Hill Camp in February. We lived in bell tents there. I was with the 28th Battalion, which was a unit formed over in Western Australia.

What was it like on the ship going over to Gallipoli?

It had no luxury in it. There were no cabins. The ship we went on from Fremantle to Suez was really a cargo ship and, on what were originally decks for stowing cargo, they provided hooks just like the Navy, where you slung a hammock. We were packed in. There was some attempt at ventilation down into the holds but it didn't happen too well. The air down there, I tell you, was unbelievable and of course we each got into a hammock. In hammocks you can't get straight, each end of you goes up and the middle goes down into a sort of U-shape — but still, when you are very young you put up with that.

You wouldn't want to sleep in one now?

Oh, I don't think I could last! Also, we had to eat there. When the reveille came on you had to get out and fold up your blanket and hook up the hammock, and then along underneath were board tables and trestles and that's where the food was served. So you ate underneath where you slept. It was no joy on that trip.

You began to get the idea that maybe travelling overseas on a ship wasn't such a fantastic idea after all?

We still thought that we were going to see the world; we still had the spirit of adventure in us. We lost a bit of that when we got to Egypt and we were stuck in tents out in the sandy desert and started training. We slept in Boer War type tents, 12 to a tent with your feet to the pole in the centre and your head out near the flap. If you were the last one to go to bed you would have to avoid treading over a lot of recumbent bodies which were already asleep on an oilsheet on the ground. There were no beds and no such things as mess huts in those days. We just fed in the front of the tent and cook used to bring around the stew and serve it out to us in our little dixies, just outside our tents.

How did they train you — what did they get you to do?

There were long marches across the sandy country carrying an 80-pound pack on your back. This held your groundsheet that you slept on, emergency rations and a little bit of underclothing and a blanket, and then hanging to one side was a waterbottle. On the other side was a bayonet. And hanging and flapping just above your posterior was a trenching tool. It was a pick on one side, when you put a handle in it, and a shovel shape on the other. That's what you used to dig down to the trenches.

So you were trained and shown how to dig trenches, how to use a bayonet, how to march and most particularly how to endure.

That's why they had most of us very young. I mean, fellows getting into their late thirties and forties weren't good material out there. A lot of them started to feel physical troubles out in the desert, in Egypt. It was sandy country with very little water. It was quite gruelling, the sand was so dry.

Did you get any leave? What did the troops do when they had leave?

In Cairo, when we got leave, it was a hotbed of prostitution and every other thing you could name in those days; probably still is. When we got leave a lot of the fellows would charge down into what they call the 'wazza', where all the houses of pleasure were, and I went with some of them once or twice, but the things I saw! I didn't want to see any more.

What kind of things?

Well, in one dreadful kind of music hall — the Eldorado — enormous coloured women, completely nude, would come on and they'd bring a donkey on. You can imagine what else took place! Well, that sort of thing revolted me. I'm no purist but I think that's carrying the thing too far — in front of an audience.

So you stopped going?

Oh yes. When we got leave I'd go into Cairo, because it was the only place to go. I would go to the museums and art galleries and to the Shepherd's Hotel, where they would only allow officers in to start with — but that broke down. You could go in there and meet somebody from another unit. It passed the time, when you had time off.

Were you laughed at by the other blokes in the unit because you weren't particularly interested in the fleshpots of Cairo?

Oh no. I think everybody minded their own business. A lot of them used to drink too much. They used to go and drink mostly beer, but they would overdo it. All it did was make me vomit, so it was easy enough for me not to do it.

So you were never really tempted by any of the things that got your friends into trouble.

No, I don't think I've ever been very strong on those sorts of activities. So it hasn't been any effort on my part to keep clear.

When did you hear that you were going to Gallipoli?

Well, we didn't know where we were going. There was still a strong expectation we were going to France, where the fighting was of course roaring along. Gallipoli hadn't been even heard of. Then my brother went off, and he was at the landing — I wasn't there for the first landing and I got a scribbled note from him saying what had happened. Of course, it was all very heavily censored but we knew we were bound to go there.

Jack Hazlitt and the rest of the troops who had been training in Egypt were taken to the island of Lemnos, not far from the Turkish coast. While he was there he heard that his brother had been wounded by a piece of shrapnel which had hit him in the left leg. He had been sent back to Egypt in the hospital ship and so, by the time Jack arrived in Gallipoli, his brother had already gone. It was not till much later in the war, in a fateful meeting in France, that Jack would see his brother again. The young men in Jack's troop were now somewhat more subdued than the eager bunch of adventurers they had been when they left Australia. But they still had no idea of what lay in store for them. It didn't take them long to realise that what they had to face was very different from anything they could possibly have imagined.

After the original landing, the only way they could land any fresh troops was in the dark. The Turks held all the high country. They had everything under observation except for the little valleys close to where Anzac Cove is now. So it all had to be done in the dark, with all its difficulties. And my unit, the 28th Battalion, in which I was a signaller, landed on the beach and tramped up into a little valley — Shrapnel Valley it was named, for good reason. The Turks had it constantly under shellfire. However, in the dark it was fairly quiet. We could hear a lot of rifle and machine-gun fire going on further up the hill, but we just lay back on our packs and straightaway our first casualty occurred. It must have been a stray bullet — I don't think it could have been a direct shot from long range — but I heard one of the fellas call out, and he'd got hit in the groin. And by the time they could stop the flow of blood he was dead. One of the main arteries was cut through. So that made us realise then that things were really getting serious! [He laughs.]

Were you afraid?

Oh yes. You had to really make yourself get harder and harder in your attitude. You know, it's perfectly natural for any of us — males or females — if you see a dead body with blood running out, say after a road accident, it's natural to get a shock. But my goodness, I could tell you what *we* had to see. You do become used to it. It seems strange, but there is a picture of me in the tent, in that camp at Blackboy Hill. There were 12 of us and most of them never came back. In those earlier battles the slaughter rate was terrible.

And another problem was of course the water supply. There was no natural water or rivers on Gallipoli itself. It was all just rocky mountain ranges and so on. They used to bring tanks of water in from the ships moored out in the sea. But it was never enough and we used to try and augment our supplies — through ignorance as we knew later. There were little creeks running down various parts of the ranges there. We used to go and scoop up water there and we didn't always boil it. What we didn't realise was, that water was trickling down through thousands of corpses which were still lying there unburied. And of course it was just a forerunner for dysentery. So a lot of us became casualties, but unless we were absolutely in the last stages there was such a demand for troops that we were kept going on our job as long as we could make it.

In your job as a signaller, what did you have to do?

Well, firstly, there was no radio. It was in its infancy and we never saw it. It would have made a big difference to the whole picture if we had. So communication from where our frontline was was by field telephones — Stephens phones they were called — and we used to reel off insulated landlines from the frontline, battalion headquarters, back to brigade headquarters to keep in touch. Well, this Turkish shellfire was so terrific that the lines used to get busted up with bursting shells. When that happened the only communication was by 'runner'. I was a runner. You had to take down an urgent message demanding some more help or reinforcements or more ammunition or asking them to collect some of the wounded.

Now the runner's life wasn't a happy one because you couldn't take time to go down and zigzag through the trenches to protect yourself. You had to hop across the top, and you were in full view of the Turkish snipers. The average life of a runner in those days was about 24 hours before he was knocked. I was just missed so many times I couldn't name it. The noise sounds like a bee flying past. It's a whizzing sound — you know. But of course the one that hits you, you don't hear. Well, that was the life down there. You know, we were trained as signallers to work with big flags like the Navy used and we found it absolutely absurd to put up a flag on Gallipoli. As soon as you went up above your mound of dirt it would get shot out of your hands. They were marvellous shots. They could knock anything at 1000 yards and that's a long way away.

Better shots than you were?

In many cases. Oh, of course, we had some good shots. They all became snipers on our side, but I would say that the average Turk that I remember was a much more dangerous man when aiming his rifle than the average Aussie was.

Did you feel that you'd been trained well enough for what you did?

Well, yes and no to that. I think we felt the casualty rates were mounting at such a rate that reinforcements were badly needed to keep propping up the frontline people. And I do think that more training would have helped. It wouldn't have helped on the health problem but it would have helped on the shooting side. An example of this was that rather unhappy Suvla Bay landing which was the last desperate effort by the General Staff to sort out the Gallipoli position. That was a few miles up the coast. It was largely carried out by the British Army and it was the horrifying part of the whole history, I think, because most of the troops were not professional soldiers. They'd been got together with that Kitchener's army in England, very young in most cases, and given very quick training. They were landed off these barges up there against the strongest unit of Kemal's army, professional Turkish soldiers. They didn't have a chance! They had to give up. That was the last chance to resolve that Gallipoli position. After that it was just stalemate.

So it wasn't just the Australian soldiers that were sacrificed?

Oh no. The British, the 29th Division which landed down at Cape Hellas — that was the end of the Gallipoli Peninsula — they took an awful pasting. I don't remember the figures, but the losses down there were much more than the Anzacs lost.

During the whole period you were there, was there ever any time when you could really relax and feel secure and safe?

Well, you see, without any bathing arrangements, when we could get leave we'd try and get down in the night-time and have a dip in the sea. That's where we cleaned ourselves up a bit. It's the only time, though, we had any chance. It was impossible to show in pictures — I've not seen any myself ever — but what were once army uniforms became rags. We became like a lot of ragged tramps in the end because it was hard to get any fresh clothing. We mostly wore shorts, and they were in rags, and khaki shirts, also in rags. Of course we didn't have tin hats then. We didn't get the tin hats till we got to France. And the cloth cap didn't last very long. So I think we really were a ragged-looking army in the last few months.

How did you relieve yourselves? You had latrines?

Obviously it's hopeless to have people relieving themselves in the bottom of the trench. It would have become even worse than it already was. So, mostly, just about 100 yards or so behind the front line, a 'T' party would sink a very deep trench as near out of any direct aim from the Turks as possible. They would try to find some little place behind a little hill or somewhere. It was all rocky country there. They'd go down about 10 or 12 feet and then they'd lay a long pole along it, on a trestle at each end, and that's where the relieving was done. You'd get as many as 15 men on that pole at any one time, but the Turks were a cunning mob and they found out what was going on. This didn't actually apply to the whole of the frontline, which was a pretty long one even on Gallipoli, but I know on our part they discovered that they could lob a bomb into that thing by sending up what we called a broomstick bomb —

with a big brass case full of explosive and a wooden tail on it. That's why they were called broomstick. And of course, if one of those fell in the trench when a lot of people were using it, it could cause some devastating results.

Did you get any warning?

Some. A lot got wounded, others got killed in the thing and there were those of us who survived. We could hear this whistling sound that the broomstick bomb made and, no matter what stage we'd reached that took us there in the first place, we'd pull up our pants and we'd go for our lives out of that pit. It's no way to live! The word 'dignity', of course, was abandoned.

They all had dysentery anyway.

That and bad water were the two main reasons why I think the Gallipoli campaign suffered so badly.

You think it played a real part in the failure?

It played a big part. Half the soldiers, within about two or three months after they had got there, were weakened, despite the good strong bodies they had had when they landed there, by dysentery caused by infected water and lack of proper food and vitamins. Mind you, of course the Turks had it pretty bad too. But it was their country and I suppose they were a bit more accustomed to it.

How long were you a runner?

Oh, well, I was there for several months — I think they carted me off in the last stages of dysentery about November, just before the evacuation.

That was a bit more than 24 hours!

Oh yes, oh yes.

Why do you think you survived?

Youth, mainly, I suppose. And I was strong. But I never saw a loaf of bread all the time I was at Gallipoli. We had tinned beef, very salty, which made you thirstier than you wanted to be, and so-called apricot jam which you didn't even need to open the lid of because you punched a hole in it and it would run out like syrup — dreadful stuff from some rascally English contractor, no doubt — and Army biscuits which were just like the biscuits I have here for these dogs. We used to try and vary the thing by getting an empty shellcase and putting a number of these hard biscuits in it and then pounding them down with a handle out of our trenching tool to break it all up. And then we would tip a bit of this so-called apricot jam in it, and a bit of water, and make a sort of dessert. Then you ate the beef supplied by another rascally contractor from South America, where they took all the goodness out of the beef there and tinned the rest. That's what the Army fed us on.

And that was it?

That was it! I remember I was on a mission down on the beach and there was a sailor off the ships there, and he had a tin of condensed milk. I somehow got wind of it that he had it poked in his tunic and I was so desperate I think I gave him a pound note for that tin of Nestlés Condensed Milk, and that was absolute luxury. But the food there was dreadful.

Did you ever get anything fresh?

Never, never once. And another thing is, of course, we got absolutely lousy because we hardly took our clothes off for weeks and weeks on end. We slept in the ground on the side of the little dugouts and when we had to go on duty we just got up with the same clothes on.

Did you have any very close mates while you were there in Gallipoli?

Yes. There was another young fellow who was about my age, I think, in that bell tent we slept in at Blackboy Hill. A fellow called Holmes. He and I were very friendly to each other in all the training; shared our feelings at times. He got killed in the end. I never had anybody as close as him.

He was killed at Gallipoli?

No, France. He got killed up in the Somme. I never had anybody very close other than that, though I had a lot of friends.

Is there anything you learned from your time in Gallipoli that you've never forgotten?

Before I got so bad with dysentery I was still battling along in the job with the Signals company and I had to go down to the beach frequently with messages. I remember on one occasion it was pitch dark and I was sitting on the beach looking out. The Turks never damaged the ships. The hospital ships used to moor about half a mile out from the beach and they were all lit up brilliantly — and the Turks never fired at them. This night I remember I sat on the beach and I could hear an orchestra playing on a hospital ship. The sound was coming across the water. Even against the booming of the guns you could hear the music. And like the rest of the mob I was unwashed, dirty, lousy and generally physically rundown and — I can't remember the exact words — I said this to myself, that 'if ever I get out of this hellhole I'll never do anything bad again'. And I tried to live up to that, but of course I didn't for too long. And I promised myself that I would never complain about anything else as long as I lived — and of course I've broken that one too.

You said you survived as a runner for as long as you did because you were young and fit. Didn't the dysentery have an effect on this? When you got dysentery and you were sick, it must have been harder to run so fast.

Well, yes, but it didn't stop me. I think that when people get into desperate situations they think differently. It was becoming more and more obvious — although we didn't admit to this there — that the various attempts to overcome the Turkish army were failing; Lone Pine, for example. The slaughter there for our poor old Light Horse was dreadful. And we began to realise that we weren't going to overcome them. And I don't think that any of the old veterans that got off there would ever admit to this, but there was a feeling of relief when the British General Staff decided to call it off, to evacuate. About three weeks before they did that I was carted off to a so-called hospital at Lemnos Island, which was about 60 miles away from the Gallipoli mainland.

Why do you call it a 'so-called' hospital?

There were no nurses as we know them — female nurses, trained. There were men. I don't think any of them had ever had any medical training and they were the ones that had to look after us. There were no proper beds. The beds were made of cane which, through constant use, had gone down in the middle and up at the end so that your bottom was down near the ground and your head and shoulders were up at an angle. You weren't very comfortable and that's where I was until — I think more by luck than anything else — I gradually recovered.

In the hospital Jack learned enough about the way in which the war was going to know that he would probably be sent next to France. The Battle of the Somme hadn't started but there was intense fighting already going on. When he had recovered from the dysentery he was sent back across the Suez Canal. Military Intelligence reports suggested that the Turks were planning a thrust down through Palestine into Egypt, where the troops were based. Jack was among the soldiers sent there to prepare for war.

We had to dig trenches there. The heat averaged about 120 degrees Fahrenheit in the daytime. And we had one army bottle of water issued per day per man and you could drink the lot in an hour if you let yourself, and if you didn't save a bit for the cooks you never got anything from the cookhouse. You had to give a bit of that water to the stew and other stuff that the cooks were making. So we were back to some extent on the old tinned beef and hard biscuit again. There was no bread and not much water. After a few months of that the General Staff must have decided the Turks weren't going to have a go. So they shipped us back across the Canal, via train up to Alexandria, and on to a ship and across the Mediterranean to Marseille. So that was the end of the Gallipoli Peninsula position.

And the start of your war in France.

We were taken right across France to Belgium. We were all excited because the train line took us within sight of Paris. We thought we were going to get leave in Paris and we'd all read about Paris [he laughs], but the train kept going right up and into Belgium and that's where we were deposited.

As the troops were moved about from place to place they had absolutely no idea as to where they were being transported or why. This they accepted as inevitable and lived from day to day — wondering when they would reach the frontline and also wondering how the fighting would differ from what they had already experienced in Gallipoli. In the absence of any real information, rumours (or 'furphys' as the soldiers referred to them) abounded. It was assumed that some of the senior officers knew what was being planned, but sometimes even this seemed doubtful.

Jack's battalion didn't arrive in France until 1916. The war had started in 1914 and by the time they got there there was a semi-stalemate on the whole of the frontline, right across France. The men were billeted in houses in small French villages. The owners of the houses were required to take in the soldiers whether they wanted to or not. The Army officers responsible for arranging accommodation would simply knock on the door of a house, find out how many beds it had, and assign soldiers to sleep there.

In one village a husband and his wife and two sons had to all sleep in the one bed, 'cause we had taken over the other beds. Well, that's the way the Army dealt with the thing and that's the type of war it was.

Did the owners of the house have to feed you?

We got our regular tinned stuff, and at least there the food was better than Gallipoli. We used to see a loaf of bread now and again and even a pat of butter and a bit of fruit from a nearby orchard. So that's where we were for a little while, but in the meantime the war had roared up further down the line. Down around Albert, near the Somme, they were having a bad time. So we all whizzed off down there again on a train trip. It had one advantage over Gallipoli. When you went into the line in France, after ten days you were pulled out and replaced with somebody else. You went back far enough to where you could still hear the guns, but you could have a bath or shower and get some decent food. But of course, after the ten days in again you went. The carnage down on the Somme battlefield was infinitely worse than anything I saw on Gallipoli. The Germans had far more machine-guns than the Turks and that's what did the damage. When our troops would try and go forward they would mow them down, you know.

How did this affect your spirits?

I can only say I do think that after the months became years you built up quite a capacity to be callous. It's just as well, I think, all in all. Otherwise I might have gone bonkers.

You were in Signals. Were you directly involved in killing people?

Well, strictly speaking, ours was a technical unit. We had rifles but we didn't carry them. If any man in the frontline unit was found without his rifle near him, even when he went to relieve himself, he'd get into trouble. But you see, we had to carry equipment, this telephone we used to sling around our knees — the Stephens phone. And we had lights and things like that, so we were not expected to carry our rifles. We had Webley revolvers. But we didn't have a bayonet, so I can't claim any great stories about sticking a bayonet into a man's stomach and trying to pull it out. Sometimes it didn't *want* to come out, you know — you had to boot them off with a foot! I've seen it all happen, but I wasn't into it myself.

In the Signals it was our job to keep up communications from where the actual fighting was going on to people further back who were directing things. There was a battalion headquarters right on the frontline, then back a bit was company headquarters — all in dugouts of course. And then it went from there back to brigade headquarters and then right back, some miles back, to divisional headquarters. Theoretically, communication was by telephones, but they were very unreliable because they were only laid across the dirt and were easily broken. It was our job to go out and find where they were broken and mend them — under fire. And if things got desperate at different times we became runners, as in Gallipoli.

Was that as dangerous as it had been at Gallipoli?

Oh, yes and no about that. Gallipoli was semi-mountainous country and you were able to hurry along. You couldn't go down into the saps — the trenches — that would have taken too long, but there was natural protection for some of the time. But in France, particularly around the Somme, it's undulating country, but you were completely unprotected once you got out of the communicating trenches and the Germans, I always reckoned, kept up much heavier fire. They had more machine-guns and there were more guns behind the line. So it was a toss-up between one and the other as to which was the more dangerous job. I've never been quite certain of that.

While you were in France, did your job in Signals require you to do anything besides mending the telephone lines and sending or delivering messages?

Oh yes. The need for improved communications was desperate, and all sorts of experiments were being carried out. Radio was starting to show up but it was extremely unreliable, always breaking down. It wouldn't work at a time when an attack was on, and then they had to resort to older methods. So very briefly, being in a Signals company, I took part in experiments to communicate by using planes to fly overhead and spot the positions of German guns and communicate back what the planes saw. Now of course this was very vital information that would enable our artillery to try to blow the German guns out, before they blew us out. Throughout the whole operation we had to communicate with unreliable radio, which didn't work more often than it did.

One of the attempts to work out a better means of communication, which is rather comical to recall now, was when they produced a large green and white striped thing, like a huge venetian blind, which used to be set up on the ground behind a little hill or somewhere where it was not in direct sight of the Germans. And it was so worked that it could send dots and dashes (with a lever) that could be read from a plane if it wasn't more than 2000 or 3000 feet above. The plane in turn would relay the information to the ground with a system of flashing lights in Morse. Information would be received on the ground and then passed on to the artillery nearby, about how to aim their guns. I took part in decoding the signals. The whole thing wasn't very successful, though. Other times, I went up in the plane as an observer to send the information down to the ground.

Was that more dangerous than being on the ground?
Well, planes flying along near a frontline, when they're only a couple of thousand feet up, are very vulnerable to attack from the other side. The fighter planes, they always flew at a much greater height. That wasn't as dangerous a job, I don't think.

Were you ever shot down?
No — plenty of bullet holes in the planes, though. They were only made of wood and wire then, you know. They weren't metal. Near misses, no doubt.

Were you excited, getting on the plane and going up?
No, I was frightened. In a blue funk, most of the time, but I kept my head about it — as the others did. None of us were whistling!

The excitement of war, that whole side of it that makes young men feel excited at the start, did you experience any of that?
Well, not when you're there. You're fighting off a feeling that the next lump of shell or the next bullet could be yours. A dismal thought, but you can't get rid of the idea because you can see what's happened to some of your mates around you.

What was it like being there — what did you see, what did you hear, what did you smell?
Sitting here in this comfortable room you could only say it was quite ghastly most of the time, because there was no chance to bury any of the people who got killed. If they were wounded, but not dead, they tried to get them back with stretcher-bearers, out of the line of fire. But if they were dead there was no time for burials or funerals or anything. A lot of them simply fell down in the bottom of the trench, where it was full of wet mud, and we were forced to carry on our work treading over people who were alive the day before. That's not very exciting. And the sounds? Well, hearing was almost at a standstill, because in France the shelling never stopped 24 hours a day from both sides. Sometimes the Germans had their trench line only perhaps 20 yards, sometimes 50 yards from ours. They had their machine-guns banging away and our side were banging away at them. And, as I say, you just toughened yourself up.

I can remember one day I was looking for places to hitch on this telephone wire — we had to hitch them on with a clove hitch —

when I came upon a place where obviously there had been quite a number of dead buried. A trench had been dug about six feet deep and here were the feet of the skeletons who'd been dead a month or two, sticking out on the edge of the trench — and I was looping the telephone cable around their big toes, the bone part of it. Well, you wouldn't do that in normal life, would you? But you get so used to people you train with being blown to bits and hit with shells and goodness knows what — I mean, although this wire was insulated it was better not to let it lie down, continuously wet. All the trees and shrubs had been shot away by weeks and weeks of shellfire, so there was nowhere much to hang it. I saw all these bony skeletons there and I just took advantage of it. I didn't feel any remorse or . . .

Did you think of them as human or simply a mechanical device?

Oh, well, I knew it was human, they were skeletons all right. It doesn't take long there, even in that climate, for the flesh to all disappear, leaving only a bony structure that of course lasts for years. And the bony part of the big toe was a very handy peg to put the telephone wire on. It's just an example of the attitude that I suppose one cultivated to avoid going bonkers. But it was hard on the nerves!

You said earlier that you caught up with your brother in France.

Yes, that was the climax of my time in France. My brother Richard was in a different unit and I hadn't seen him for a while. I was still in the Signals and our brigade headquarters had occupied an old German dugout which the Germans must have built before they were overrun by the British Army, before we got there. This thing was about 40 feet down, buried into the soft soil of the Somme, and that's where we had set up a little switchboard. We had these insulated lines going up to various parts of the frontline, and when the lines hadn't been busted messages used to come in. I was on duty and I heard heavy boots coming down the wooden stairs — and it was my brother! I hadn't seen him for months. He was taking a bomb squad up to the frontline. It was pitch dark outside and he just wanted fresh information about finding a way for his squad. He didn't know I would be there. Of course, we exchanged greetings and, you know, that's the last time I saw him alive.

When he went into the line with his squad, a piece of a shell hit him and wounded him, but didn't kill him. They got him onto a stretcher — I heard all this later when I got to England — they got him to England, to Cambridge, to a military hospital in Cambridge. I think he'd have been alive probably today, although he is three years older than me, but antibiotics hadn't been invented and this wound went to gangrene and they couldn't stop it. Three weeks after they got him to the hospital he died. I didn't know about that until sometime later, because Richard was in a different unit. But he's buried in Cambridge Public Cemetery. There is a memorial there.

And back in Australia, what was hard on my mother was that my eldest brother, who was a marvellous cricketer and had played for Australia and was a master at the Kings School at Parramatta, died there from pneumonia a few months after Richard died. That left nobody but me.

How did you feel when you finally heard the news about Richard's death? You said you'd become quite callous to death in the war. I presume this was different.

I suppose I was very saddened about it, because he and I were very friendly. We'd done a lot together, much more than with my eldest brother who was more distant from us at the time. But it is true that when you've been in a war like that you've seen so many mutilated bodies, alongside of you sometimes. I remember my close friend — the little fellow, Holmes — he was in a trench next to me in France and suddenly I found he had no head. They'd taken his head clean off, a shellcase. Well, that's enough to make one go mad if it happened in civilian life, but somehow or other you stiffen yourself up. You've got to!

And were you able to keep that up?

Well, I had an experience in France. I was sent from brigade headquarters because the line had been blown up. You carried a mobile phone with you and you used to tap in every now and again to make certain the line was still there. I found that, as fast as I mended the line on this night, the shelling from the Germans was so fierce that it made it almost impossible to keep it open. So I decided to take the message I had to send to the battalion headquarters, do a running job. A shell just missed me. It must have been a pretty big one, I think, because it blew a hole in the earth as deep as you could imagine and bombed me right out of where I was. It didn't do any damage to my structure but it certainly did a lot of damage to my nervous system, and I passed out. Next morning I came to and I thought, well, I've got to try and crawl back to my own side. But I knew I was near the frontline with the Germans and I didn't feel at all well, so I lay there.

This hole that the shell must have made was about as big as an average room and I was at the bottom of it. All of a sudden I heard voices, hoping it was some of my own mob or even a stretcher-bearer or two, but they were German voices and I knew then that in this tangle during the night I had somehow got pretty close to, if not on, the frontline. The frontline was just a chain of muddy trench holes. There were no forts there; the shelling was too fierce to ever keep anything like that. There was a rumour around, which was probably quite unfounded, that the Germans at some parts of the line didn't take prisoners because they were so overloaded with their own problems. Whether that's true or not I don't know to this day, but I do know the thought never crossed my mind with the Turks on Gallipoli. If you were captured by them, you were taken back as a prisoner.

Anyway, I decided I'd better lie doggo down there for as long as I could, until the next night. I lay in the bottom of that hole there, hoping another shell wouldn't go anywhere near me. I had the usual emergency rations which you carried in a little pack, and a waterbottle. So I lay there all that day, and the next night. In the meantime I think I'd recovered some of my damaged senses. I knew which way to go and as soon as it got dark I crawled out of the shell hole and gradually crawled back in the direction of the brigade headquarters. And I got back to the top of that thing, and the officer in charge of a Signals squad looked at me and I remember him saying: 'Good God, you've had it! Go on back to clearing station!'

From there I was ordered back to another place where I had to look after horses. We were a mounted brigade and we carried all our phone lines and stuff on horses, and they were tethered about a mile back from where this other situation occurred. I lived in a tent there, one tent, and I tried to keep the horses alive. It snowed there every winter and that was a sad situation. There were about 16 horses there and they were dying one by one from starvation, because the food to keep them alive wasn't arriving from base. And no food arrived for me either. But there was a mountainous pile of American tinned asparagus made by a big firm called Libbys. They were great big cans and there were stacks of them there that had been left behind when the troops went forward. They were there for the officers — I don't think the privates ever saw tinned asparagus. I practically lived on that and army biscuits, and in the end I recovered enough. I got a message back to Albert, where the divisional headquarters were, that I was a bit of a mess and they eventually came and took me back there. And then they apparently decided that I was more than half silly. I was sent away from the battle, under medical supervision. I wasn't in hospital, I wasn't in bed, but they decided that I was finished with the war. Apparently my speech and the general look of me was not much use on the frontline.

Jack, let me get this straight. You found yourself at the bottom of a crater made by a shell, you got yourself back to your commanding officer — who then sent you off to look after horses, without food for them or for you. For how long?

Well, I was only there for about ten days.

On your own, in this shellshocked state, and you were aged — what, 20?

That was in 1916 — 19, yeah.

They treated you hard, didn't they.

Well, the need for reinforcements was desperate, because the slaughter going on on both sides was beyond description. So every able-bodied man — if he'd still got some able in his body! — well they didn't want to send him away. They hoped he'd get better, as many of them did. Up to a degree I think that maybe I was being kept there because the casualty rate in Signals was very heavy. Every 24 hours there was another casualty. I suppose they thought that I'd recover, just looking after a few horses. It didn't work and I think they must have decided that I'd had it anyhow. The big military hospital just near Albert confirmed that I was a write-off. And away I went to England. I was hospitalised there for a while and they confirmed the general diagnosis. And so they decided to send me back to Australia.

When Jack Hazlitt arrived back in Australia the reunion with his mother brought another shock. She had moved back to Melbourne from Western Australia and was dramatically altered. The experience of losing two sons during the war years had had a devastating effect. The mother who had struggled so bravely and effectively to take care of her boys was now in a distressed and unstable state, and her behaviour and personality were affected for the rest of her life. Richard had been her favourite, and the loss of her eldest son as well had been too much for her. Jack himself was still suffering from what we would now call post-traumatic stress syndrome. He was regularly wakened from sleep by appalling nightmares which continued for some considerable time after his return. Characteristically, he was reluctant to engage in detailed conversation about his mother or about this stressful time in his life in which he attempted to come to terms with his personal legacy of war. It was a matter that still produced strong but well-concealed emotion in him.

I think my mother was pretty well bonkers by then. She lived for a number of years after this, but she was never the same.

Really seriously disturbed, or just distressed about the death of her boys?

Oh well, you know — I think it was a bit of each.

Did you stay with her when you came back?

Yes, she had become very dependent, and possessive of me. She had a little house down at Hampton, a suburb of Melbourne, and returned soldiers didn't count for much at that time. The Repatriation Department was still a struggling government thing trying to get going. And the first thing they tried to do was establish soldiers on blocks of land, which was a grave error because a lot of them weren't farming material — never been on the land in their lives and ended up stuck there with a few hundred acres, a horse and a cow — and of course a lot of them went broke. What saved my day was the old headmaster at Haileybury. He used to get together any of the former students and get little tea parties going at the College, and they proved useful to me on more than one occasion.

At one of these tea parties I met an electric scientist who'd been brought out to Australia from England to establish the first radio masts around the Australian coast — J. Graham Balsillie, I remember his name. In his spare time he was experimenting, trying to produce rainfall which was badly needed in Australia. Now, I've lived in the bush — day after day there's a clear sky, but now and again you get a lovely-looking black nimbus cloud drifting along and you think, this is going to break the drought! Well, in most cases it doesn't. It drifts on and the next day there's the same brazen sky. That's what he was experimenting with. He found that those big clouds, when they do come over, have got plenty of rain in them but it takes electrical action in the cloud to make the tiny particles group together, where they form a raindrop. When they get together enough, gravity takes them down and that's rain. That's how rain comes. I learned all that, because he gave me a job to run the station in the northern part of what was then desert country near the South Australian border. That was my first job.

And how long did that last?

Well, I was about 20 miles from the nearest town. I had a horse and a bell tent, just like the Army, and I was on top of a sandhill. A horsedrawn wagon used to bring out tinned stuff and water because there were absolutely no rivers running. It was particularly chosen to be a real testing spot for Balsillie's invention. But it didn't succeed, or I wouldn't be here now. I think if that had been successful I might have finished up a millionaire.

It was a good idea but it didn't work.

It worked in the laboratory. He had the idea right, but not the equipment to make it work. I think I was out there on my own for about six months. I used to go into the nearest town occasionally on a horse. The station had been established with all the instruments that I had to look after. I had to keep a complete record of wind direction, wind strength, barometers — all that sort of thing. It was extremely barren country, but it was the home of brown snakes. Big fellas they were too, where I had my tent. They took a bit of getting used to! I found that with snakes if you leave them alone they'll leave you alone.

I hope you had something better to eat than a hard biscuit and tinned beef.

No, only tinned food. I used to get it brought out from Hopetoun which was the nearest town there. I used to be very fond of tinned sheep's tongues.

And tinned asparagus?

No! Never! I ate so much asparagus in that tent over on the Somme that the very smell of asparagus made me almost — well, you know.

It was at another of his old headmaster's tea parties that Jack met the man who was to become his next employer. He was a British airforce officer, Harry Turner Shaw. He was just starting up a small aviation company in Melbourne and he took a liking to Jack, who was still trying to establish himself. Shaw and his partner, a man named Ross, had started a company called Shawross Engineering and Aviation. They were trying to get a small staff together and were looking for somebody with an interest in mechanical things. Jack was taken on to be trained. In those days licences weren't required and he learned to fly very rapidly. After two hours of instruction he went solo. But in this new job it was not always smooth flying and Jack's career of risk-taking and endurance continued in his peacetime work.

The aeroplanes themselves were crudely made and unreliable. They mostly had rotary engines which had a nasty habit of sounding fine when you swung the propeller, would take off all right, get up flying speed and all of a sudden start to conk out. So having nasty crashes was quite frequent in those days. Naturally, because they didn't fly at the speeds of the modern jets, the damage was mostly to the plane itself and the pilot and passenger would survive.

Were you ever involved in a crash?

Over 12 of them, dotted around Victoria. The worst one was when this little company that I was working for had got a very lucrative contract from a big insurance company, APA as it was in those days. It had booked to take the plane from Melbourne, landing at various places on the way. We went to Mildura, and then up the Darling River, landing at a lot of the big station homesteads — some of them are still there. And we carried with us a very colourful man who specialised in writing probate insurances for huge fees. We used to land at anything that looked like a landing near each of these homesteads, and of course, almost invariably, nobody there had ever seen a plane, let alone gone up in one. We used to entice the owner of the property to go up. In those days some of them were still owned by English people and had a manager. Owner or manager, we'd take him up for a quarter of an hour and let him have a look at his property. This was always very popular. Afterwards, of course, this insurance representative used to go back to the homestead and start talking and asking questions about the man's life, and then sell him probate insurance. He was a master at this, and it cost an enormous sum in those days. This insurance agent used to get the whole of the first year's premium as his commission. When we finally got to Broken Hill we were given a mayoral reception there because they'd never seen a plane before. I landed on the football ground and we were there a couple of days. Flying back to Melbourne all went well, until we had to land for fuel at a little town in Victoria. I wasn't flying the plane. Jack Fullerton was the pilot that day. All I remember is he was coming in to land at this little town and all of a sudden it put its nose down into a spin which wouldn't have mattered if we'd been high enough up, any pilot can pull a plane out of a spin, but we were too low and we hit the ground in this little town. That finished me off for a year in hospital. The pilot lost most of his nose and upper lip, I think, because of the little windscreen in front of him. He wasn't killed but he took a long time to recover.

What happened to you?

Well, you see, my whole left leg was shattered from a piece of the metal undercarriage which came up through the floor when we hit the ground. And they had a terrible time getting it all together again. I couldn't walk for a long time.

Did it mend completely?

Mostly, but I was warned that when I got older, it'd probably get arthritis in it — they always do, these wounds — but so far it hasn't.

So that leg is still fine for you but it might come against you when you get old.

It still carries me around, but half a mile along a beach is about as much as I can do and I want to go home. Well that was the worst one, but it is so hard these days to realise the difference in aviation because they very rarely have any trouble with their engines. The jet engines have made the thing so reliable. It was risky then, and I had a few more spills, but that was the worst.

Why did you leave the Shawross company?

After I'd been there a year or two the partner got killed. He got into a spin and couldn't get out of it, and he killed himself and the two passengers. Shaw wasn't mentally the same material as the partner had been, and I'd heard about Qantas just starting with an airmail contract. I got in touch with them and, even though I was not very experienced, apparently I was good enough. So they offered me a job and I went off up to Longreach.

How long were you with Qantas?

Just on three years. I could have stayed with them — but I've got to bring my mother back into this now. She was down in Melbourne and quite miserable. I found a miserable letter had arrived and so I sent her the money and she came up by train. We rented a little house in Longreach and she was able to rent a piano and that kept her happy for a while. But she became upset and unsettled and I thought, well, it's going to be rather miserable for her — and for me too, because at Qantas in those days it was long hours, very poor pay and it was hard to think what the prospects were, so I resigned. I'd heard there was another aircraft company starting in New South Wales and I thought it would be a much more civilised life. The firm was called Larkin Aircraft Supply Company and they got the contract from Sydney to Narrandera, Hay, Mildura, Adelaide. I was with them about a couple of years.

Was your mother happier?

Oh yes, I think it was a good move. But I do sometimes think about Qantas. The staff then was eight people and I might've got somewhere in Qantas if I'd stayed there.

Jack Hazlitt's new job was based at Hay in the Riverina. During his time there he boarded at the only decent hotel in town, where a young French teacher at the War Memorial High School was also living. Her name was Beatrice and they decided to marry. Jack was on the verge of settling down; he needed a more stable and reliable type of employment. He had refused to sign airworthiness certificates for defective aircraft and in consequence fell out with his employer. He decided to leave aviation. He was given an introduction to a firm that had just been set up to handle the Chrysler dealership in Sydney. It was called Larke, Neave and Carter (later to become LNC Industries). Jack became its Service Manager. He joined the company in 1926 and stayed there for 40 years, until his retirement in 1966. Peace and security had become very precious to him and he wanted to raise his children in a settled environment.

I take it your job with Larke, Neave and Carter saw you through the Depression.

Yeah, right through. But we nearly folded and we only survived by an arrangement that I don't think the unions would stand for now. We used to put everybody off for one week, no pay, and they could fiddle around. Nobody could get jobs anyhow. And then we'd put them on for another week and they'd get paid. That went on for months and months and months. It kept the doors of the company open when we were almost ready to fold up — that was in the depth of the Depression. And then, just when that was recovering, we went into the Second World War.

When the Second World War broke out, did you want to go?

I was tempted, because they badly needed people with the experience that I had, particularly with aircraft. The only thing that stopped me was that I had four young kids by then. They were all very young and, of course, the wife. I'd been in my job for a long time and I didn't want to lose it, so I resisted the temptation.

Were you influenced at all by your experiences in the First World War?

I didn't feel any great eagerness to go and get into it. If it hadn't been for the kids I think I'd have probably gone out of a sense of duty, but I felt my duty was now to them.

When did you get married — and what sort of person was your wife?

We got married in 1926, three months after I got this job. She was about three years younger than me. I can't really describe her. She was good looking and well educated. We got married in June at a little church in Manly. There was nothing wonderful about the wedding because in those days she was a Catholic — and I wasn't. And there was always a fuss made over that. So we weren't even married in the little church; we were married in the *porch* of the church. That's as far as I was allowed to go!

But the fact that she was a Catholic didn't bother you?

No. When two people get pretty keen on each other, I don't think anything bothers them. Of course I had to yield to the demands of that day — which have been buried for years now. Any issue of the marriage had to be baptised as Catholics. So all my four kids were baptised into the Catholic religion.

Were you happy with that?

Oh yes. All the lurid stories I'd heard about being married to a Catholic — the house is full of nuns, and priests call in — I found that didn't happen. In fact, during the whole married period we never even had a decent row.

It was always a happy marriage?

Yes, even when there was a problem with my mother. I had a house at Lane Cove, a big house. I rented it. My mother was living in a little bit of a flat down near Dee Why and I got her back and gave her a big bedroom there to live in, in the same house as my wife and two kids. They never got on. I'm certain it was a deep-seated possessiveness on the part of my poor old mother. She wanted just me to be around, as long as she lived.

How did you manage the situation between your wife and your mother?

Well, it was never bad but there were squabbles. In the end I got my mother another little house near Curl Curl, down on the coast, and transported her down there. She was still able to get around but she wasn't teaching music any more. She was just living a very quiet life. And from there her health failed and she finished up in a little nursing home down near Narrabeen.

What was the secret of the happiness of your marriage?

[He laughs.] I almost want to ask for time to think that one out! We did a lot of travelling around in holiday time. Of course we saw that the four kids all got good educations. She was very keen on that and so was I. We never got bored with each other. We were always good mates. We could have a conversation together without getting into an argument. I never once thumped her [he laughs again] — never wanted to. She finished up as a French teacher at North Sydney Girls' High School. That's where she died. On her birthday she'd gone off to teach at the school from where we lived at Hunters Hill, and I was phoned up at midday to say that she'd fallen on the floor and was dead. And I didn't suspect that there was anything wrong with her. I wonder why I'm telling you all this.

Because I'm asking you.

Well, you'd better just see that I don't go into too much detail!

You remarried when you were in your seventies. How did you meet your second wife, and what has that marriage meant to you?

As a matter of fact, I met her up here in this neighbourhood [McMasters Beach on the New South Wales central coast]. She had this property up here and I had been spending holiday time down the hill, about half a mile away. I had two blocks of land down there. When my first wife was alive, the kids and I used to go there for school holidays and that sort of thing. When my first wife died, suddenly, I was left very lonely and my kids were scattered by then, all over the place. And when I met Lesley at a local party she provided the remedy for loneliness. I think it's a terribly hard thing for anybody to grow old on their own. Most of the old chaps, Gallipoli veterans that are still alive, their wives aren't — and they're either in a nursing home or living on their own. I don't think they're exactly happy about it. Whereas, if their wife hadn't predeceased them, they'd have been much better off. We've been married now 20 years and — I'm not going to make this statement as a dramatic one — but I'm quite certain that if I hadn't met Lesley in my seventies I don't think I'd have gone on too long. She tells me I'm looking better than when she first met me. And I think she means it! She's been a tremendous factor in the last few years I've been alive.

She's quite a lot younger than you?

Yes, well, I know she won't hit me over the head if I say she was born in 1924. And I was born in 1897, so there *is* a bit of difference!

Did you hesitate to marry someone so much younger than you?

Very much so, and her children were a bit perplexed over it too. I wondered very much about it because I knew of so many cases where it didn't work — people who remarry after years of being on their own. Whoever they marry at that age, they think differently and they don't get on. Anyhow, it's been a terrific experience for me being married to Lesley. I don't say I hope it'll last a long time, because you only say that when you're in your younger years.

You married a Catholic; your only son is a priest. What about your own religious views? Are you a religious man?

Well, I believe in the Christian faith. The older I get the more that belief is very strong. I saw samples of that, actually, on the frontline. We had all sorts of fellas, real scallywags many of them, language worse than a bullocky. And they seemed to have no beliefs. But I've seen them hit and obviously not going to make it, hit with a shellcase or machine-gun bullets, and so often you'd hear them appealing to the Deity, just before they expired. That made me think, more than once — even those hardbitten blokes who professed no beliefs!

What does it mean to you, your religious belief in your daily life?

My present wife has a very very strong belief — she's a regular churchgoer. When we decided to leave Sydney to come and live up here, I know she wouldn't have been happy here if we hadn't found Avoca Beach's St David's — just the right kind of people in it; they share their beliefs and she's very happy over it. So that's been her attitude right through, she is a very strongly motivated Christian. If I had any doubts about it at all, they've been dealt with by marrying her.

Do you think there is going to be life for you after death?

Oh, that's a curly one! I know it's very strong in the teachings but I'd best say that my strongest belief is that, if people grow up and try their best to practise the teachings of Christ and the Christian religion, there's nothing better — or as good — to help them through life and not get in some way torn apart. What happens afterwards is so mysterious. For instance, I think of my brother who's in that cemetery in Cambridge, in England. If I was absolutely sure, nothing would make me happier than perhaps to meet up with him some day in some mystery. But I can't make myself believe that that's 100 per cent sure.

You've faced death many times, haven't you?

Oh yes.

Many more times than most people. Have you thought about it a lot?

No. Take me at the present moment — I'm hanging on but, without sounding dramatic, I know that I can't expect to go much longer.

You read about some of these people up in the Himalayas. They're supposed to live to 130 and 140, but I don't think I'll ever be one of them. It doesn't impose on me. It doesn't make me feel miserable. The main thing is that I hope when it happens to me it's quick, not like some of these poor old fellas I know that are hanging on, very unwell, everything wrong with them. They can't see or they can't hear or they can't sleep and life's just . . . they're better off to go. But it doesn't frighten me, not a bit.

Your story of your life, particularly your experiences in the war, is an extraordinary story of endurance. What's been the legacy of that for you?

There is only one word that would really cover it. I think it is sadly lacking in the population today, in its proper sense, and that's the word 'discipline'. I think that my life in the services taught me discipline.

What do you mean by discipline?

Well, if you're working for yourself, running a little business or a shop, the only discipline that's needed is to discipline yourself. You have to discipline yourself to get up in the morning and to do what you must during the day. When you work for an employer, *they* have to run the business and *they* have to have discipline in the way it's run. What you do, what instructions you get, is up to them, and at times you may feel that an instruction is wrong, a mistake. But rather than say that to your boss, you just do what you've been told to do — that's discipline.

You experienced the 'Great War'. What do you feel now, looking back with the wisdom of old age, about the whole business of war?

The idea of overwhelming another country is a bad one. The original idea was that you take possession of what you've captured, enlarge your own country. I think that was the primitive approach to it, fighting battles. Neither of World War I or World War II ever proved any sense in that thinking. I went over to Germany after World War II on behalf of the company, on business. Germany had taken a dreadful battering from our bombing during World War II. But when I went over there — about three years after the war finished — I noticed, in a lot of the factories I inspected, the most modern machinery, spanking new, humming away. And back in England they still had old machines driven by belts with the shaft overhead. They were way behind the Germans — and yet it was the British that had 'won' the war. War solves nothing. It's just a lot of misery and loss of life.

Jack Hazlitt died in 1993, fairly much in the way he had hoped for. His widow, Lesley, buried his ashes under a tree where he liked to sit peacefully, at their home at McMasters Beach.

FILM AUSTRALIA

NATIONAL INTEREST PROGRAM

Film Australia's *Australian Biography* series as seen on SBS TV
is available for purchase on video from Film Australia.
This growing collection of programs is an invaluable resource
for schools, universities, libraries and the home.
In addition to the seven people featured in **Australian Lives**,
there are another 21 programs available on video.
The full range of *Australian Biography* videos features
the following eminent Australians:

SERIES ONE

Sir Marcus Oliphant — Nuclear Physicist
Donald Horne — Writer and Academic
Nancy Bird Walton — Pioneer Aviator
Dame Joan Hammond — Opera Singer
Dr H C 'Nugget' Coombs — Economist
Neville Bonner — Former Senator
Jack Hazlitt — First World War Veteran (1897–1993)

SERIES TWO

Phillip Law — Scientist
Faith Bandler — Civil Rights Activist
Elizabeth Riddell — Journalist and Poet
Franco Belgiorno-Nettis — Industrialist
Frank Hardy — Author (1917–94)
Dame Roma Mitchell — Lawyer and Former Governor
of South Australia
Nancy Cato — Author

SERIES THREE

Hayes Gordon — Actor and Director
Sister Veronica Brady — Nun and Academic
Smoky Dawson — Entertainer
Flo Bjelke-Petersen — Former Senator
Albert Tucker — Artist
Lois O'Donoghue — Indigenous Leader
Malcolm Fraser — Former Prime Minister

SERIES FOUR

Freda Brown — Communist and Activist
Shirley Strickland de la Hunty — Athlete and Conservationist
Graeme Bell — Musician
Professor Helen Hughes — Economist
Lily Ah Toy — Northern Territory Pioneer
Rosalie Kunoth-Monks — Actor and Aboriginal Activist
James McClelland — Lawyer and Politician

Executive Producers: Ron Saunders and Sharon Connolly
Producer, Researcher, Director and Editor: Frank Heimans
Duration: approximately 26 minutes each
Production years: 1992–95 inclusive

A Film Australia National Interest Program
Special prices and discounts are available for home video,
education, business, government organisations
and other institutions.

Please contact Film Australia National Sales Office
for details on:

Tel. (02) 9413 8777
Fax (02) 9416 9401
e-mail: sales@filmaust.com.au
http: //www.filmaust.com.au
or write to:
National Sales Office
Film Australia Ltd
Freepost 25
PO Box 46
Lindfield NSW 2070